Rearview Mirror

Rearview Mirror

B.L. Clark

SAPPHIRE BOOKS

SALINAS, CALIFORNIA

Rearview Mirror
Copyright © 2019 by BL Clark. All rights reserved.

ISBN - 978-1-948232-75-3

This is a work of fiction - names, characters, places, and incidents are the product of the author's imagination or are used fictitiously. Any resemblance to actual persons living or dead, business, events or locales is entirely coincidental.

All rights reserved. No part of this publication may be reproduced, distributed, or transmitted in any form or by any means, including photocopying, recording, or other electronic or mechanical methods, without written permission of the publisher.

Editor - Tara Young
Book Design - LJ Reynolds
Cover Design - Fineline Cover Design

Sapphire Books Publishing, LLC
P.O. Box 8142
Salinas, CA 93912
www.sapphirebooks.com

Printed in the United States of America
First Edition – August 2019

This and other Sapphire Books titles can be found at
www.sapphirebooks.com

Dedication

To my family for their love and support.

Acknowledgments

Sapphire Books – Chris and Schileen, thank you for taking another chance on me and allowing me to yet again make a dream come true.

Carter Steele – Thank you for being a fantastic beta reader. Your input helped make this a stronger story.

Tara Wentz – Thank you for always being a great friend and supporter. I truly appreciate you beta reading for me and all your suggestions to make this a better story.

Tara Young – Thank you for your edits and suggestions. You helped make this a stronger story.

Chris Slipper – Thank you for the years of friendship and support. You have no idea what it has meant to me.

Mom & Dad – Thank you for loving me and always standing behind my decisions (even when you didn't fully agree with them). I love you both!

Prologue

David and Jeffrey Knight didn't care much for women. No, they thought women should be in the background of life. David Knight was going to make sure his daughter knew her place if it killed her.

"You best respect your brother and me. Unless you like the pain," David yelled at his eighteen-year-old daughter lying sprawled out on the kitchen floor bleeding. Her brown hair matted to her head with blood. He raised his large fist and swung it down, connecting with her left forearm as she raised it to try to hold off the blow. She heard the bone break from the force of his movement.

"David, stop," cried Karen Knight, his wife. "She's just a young girl."

"No, she isn't. She's a woman and old enough to know her place."

"Yeah," Jeffrey Knight yelled. "Don't forget about those losers she hangs out with, Dad. Make her pay for them, especially her 'friendship' with that Nicole chick. Something isn't right between them."

"Jeffrey, you stay out of this." Karen glared at her twenty-two-year-old son.

"Woman, you will not speak to him that way." David reached back and slapped his wife with an open hand. "I run this house, and you will do as I say."

"M-mama, please, stay out of this," Amber pleaded from the floor. "I'll b-be okay. I can't handle you being hurt because of me."

Oh, baby girl, you are so brave. "David, please stop this now. She's paid enough." Karen again tried to put herself between her husband and her daughter but was shoved aside.

"I'll say when she's paid enough. Jeffrey, go get the belt."

"Yes, sir!" Jeffrey left the room almost skipping he was so happy that his little sister was getting the beating she deserved. He'd prefer to be the one giving it, but if she was getting one, he was pacified.

David and Jeffrey took turns swinging and hitting Amber with the belt. David enjoyed the sound of the leather hitting her skin, while Jeffrey loved to make the buckle hit her instead. He hated Amber and loved it when his father gave him the opportunity to beat on her. Jeffrey was ruthless in his hits and kicks.

"E-enough," whispered Amber, hoping for the pain and beating to stop.

"You think you've had enough?" David asked as he took the belt from Jeffrey. "Where is your place, girl?"

"N-nowhere, sir. I'm not to be seen or heard." Amber spit out blood as she coughed out the words.

"Clean yourself up, then clean up this mess you left on the floor." With that, David roughly grabbed Jeffrey by the collar and dragged him out of the room, leaving Amber and Karen alone.

"Baby girl, why do you push him? You know how they are."

"I w-wasn't pushing. I was late by accident. I was with Nicole..."

"You need to leave here. You need to run away and never return."

"Mama? Y-you, don't want me here?"

"Baby, I love you and there's nothing more than I want for you to be safe. Here isn't safe. You need to pack a bag and run away. Run far away. I can't save you if this keeps up."

"I d-don't want to leave you here. You know he's going to take it out on you."

"Yes, but it's better than me watching him and Jeffrey take it out on you. Now go clean yourself up, pack a bag, and get ready to sneak out tonight after they fall asleep."

Amber nodded her understanding and made her way into her room. Where would she go? Where would she be safe? What damage did they do to her tonight that she was going to have to live with? So many questions, so few answers.

※ ※ ※ ※

Amber boarded the train, one bag on her shoulder, the other in her good hand. Because it was late, there weren't many people getting on, for which she was grateful. Amber found a seat in the back row and rested her head on the window.

Chapter One

Ten Years Later

"Zach, your stroke is all wrong for this painting," Amber said as she tried to help her fellow painter and best friend.

"It's an original work. How can the stroke be wrong?"

"The aesthetics are off. Here, let me show you." Amber took the brush he was using and with a few strokes changed the whole scope of the painting. "There, how's that?"

"How is it that you aren't a famous painter yet? How is it you're still a grunt painter like me? I can't create anything original like you can."

"Lucky for you, I guess," Amber said, laughing.

The pair were still laughing when the gallery curator came by. "Amber, I'd like to see you in my office when you're done today."

"Yes, Ms. Baer."

Amber looked at Zach, trying to gauge if he had any idea.

"Do you want me to wait for you after work?"

"Please! I feel like I'm being called to the principal's office, and I have no clue what I did wrong."

"Well, you kinda are," Zach said, amused. "Seriously, though, I'm sure it's nothing bad. You and Lucinda have a good relationship. She probably just wants to talk about your art or the job you're doing here in the gallery."

"I hope so. I just don't know what I'd do if I lost this job."

"You aren't losing your job. They'll get rid of me long before they get rid of you."

"Well, I'm done with my painting. I'm going to go check with the supervisor and see if I can clean up and head to Lucinda's office."

"Good luck! I'll be waiting out back for you," Zach said as Amber walked away.

※ ※ ※ ※

Amber cleaned up her paint station, grabbed a clean coat, and headed upstairs to the management offices to speak with Lucinda. Amber took the stairs to give herself a few minutes to compose herself. Once she reached the office, she knocked on the door and heard a muffled "come in" from the other side of the door.

Amber opened the door and started to walk in. "Y-you wanted to see me, Ms. Baer?"

"Yes, Amber, please, have a seat." Lucinda motioned to the chairs in front of her desk. Amber grabbed one and sat, placing her hands in her lap. "You've been working here for what—ten years now?" Amber nodded her agreement. "And we've talked about your portfolio before, and your artwork is really coming along. The work you've done in the past couple of months has been some of the best I've ever seen out of you. I'd like to put you into our next 'Up and Coming Artists' show."

"Wow," Amber replied, stunned. "I don't know

what to say. It means a lot that you've even looked at my work."

"Well, you're one of the few female artists we have, and that alone made me keep a close eye on you. But your work has really been improving. Your portfolio is well rounded between paintings and photographs. I've seen some of the freelance work you've been doing."

"Thank you, Ms. Baer. I've been working hard on my portfolio."

"Well, I've chosen four photographs and four paintings that I'd like to use in your show. There's just one problem."

"What's that?" Amber asked, her heart sinking a little.

"We need to get release forms signed by the people in the pictures. Now, two of the four are older, but I still need you to get the forms signed. I know this could pose an issue, but I have faith that you'll make it happen."

"Which pictures?"

Lucinda pulled out a contact sheet and showed the pictures to Amber. What she thankfully didn't hear was the internal groan that Amber let out seeing that two of the pictures were more than ten years earlier.

"I'm going to need to take some time off to get these signed. Two of the pictures are from my high school years, and I'll have to go out of town for those."

"Do what you need to, just make it happen," Lucinda said, not realizing the hardship she was putting Amber in.

"Thank you. Was there anything else?"

"Nope. Oh, here's a copy of the contact sheet for you. I'm certain you'll want to show Zach which pieces of your portfolio I've chosen."

"Thank you again. I really appreciate the opportunity." Amber grabbed the contact sheet and made her way out of the office and back down to the painting area. It was after hours now, so there was nobody around. Amber placed her coat at her station, then made her way to the employee exit to meet Zach.

As Amber walked out, she could see Zach pacing.

"Well?" Zach asked eagerly.

"She wants to put me in the next 'Up and Coming Artists' show." The disbelief in her voice was evident, but so was the excitement.

"Oh, my god, that's amazing," Zach gushed as he picked her up and swung her around. "Why aren't you happier?"

"Part of it is because I'm in shock. Part of it is because she chose two photos from my youth, and I have to get release forms signed."

"Oh, are these people you've kept in touch with?"

"Not in the past ten years. I don't even know if they still live in the area I grew up in."

"We'll figure it out. Come on, let's get a cab and go to your place and see if we can track any of the people down. Then, you'll at least have a starting point."

"Thank you for being the voice of reason." Amber wasn't sure what to do. She couldn't go back to her old town, could she? It'd been ten years since she up and disappeared one night. Were her parents still around? What about Jeffrey? Could she risk seeing them? Risk being seen *by* them?

※※※※※

Zach and Amber took a cab to the brownstone

she was renting an apartment in. They ordered a pizza and camped out on the couch in Amber's living room.

"Okay, who's the first person we need to look up?" Zach took Amber's laptop from her.

Amber let out a loud sigh before responding. "Heather Woods."

"Okay, so, let's see here." Zach started surfing the internet. "And Google says…we have a winner. There is a Heather Woods in Eagle Peak. Next…"

"Erik Harrison."

"Google says…we don't have anyone with that name there. Maybe he's listed under his wife's name. Or maybe one of the others knows where to find him. Who's the last one we need to find?"

Amber took a deep breath as she looked at the contact sheet in her hand and at the picture of the third and final person. "Nicole Brooks."

"Is this *the* Nicole?"

"Yes, that Nicole."

"We have another winner. So, now what do you need to do? Do you call them, or do you have to go there?"

"I have to go there to get the forms signed."

"Should you call and warn them that you're on your way?"

"I don't even know what I'd say. 'Hey, remember me? Yeah, ten years ago, we used to be friends until I left' or…"

"Or you just show up on their doorstep and hope the element of surprise works to your advantage."

"Let's just schedule the flight and call it a night," Amber suggested. The fear of going back to that place overwhelmed her.

Amber pulled into Eagle Peak and headed down Main Street. The smell of the old tire factory made her sick to her stomach. She could remember her father and Jeffrey coming home smelling like rubber. Amber gave a full-body shiver at the thought. She had reserved a room at the one hotel in town. As she drove along, she was reminded of her time here and the fear she felt.

Amber parked her car in front of the hotel, grabbed her bags, and went to check in.

"Welcome to the Woods Retreat. My name is Sidney. How can I help you?" the front desk clerk said.

"I have a room reserved. Amber Pellot."

Sidney played around with the computer and got the room and the keycards settled. "You're in our Bonsai Suite on the fourth floor."

"I didn't reserve a suite…"

"No, but it's available, and I hate to see it just sitting there, so I upgraded your room for you, but the cost is still the same. Plus, you have the most unique eye color I've ever seen. It's captivating."

"Thank you, but I don't want to get you in trouble."

"The manager and I go way back from school, don't worry about it. Enjoy your stay."

"Thank you again." Amber smiled and walked toward the glass elevator. Once she reached the fourth floor, she turned left out of the elevator, and straight ahead was the Bonsai Suite. Amber smiled as she opened the door. The suite did its name justice. It was decorated in an Asian flair, right down to the platform bed and bonsai tree decorations.

Well, at least it's a nice room. Amber set her bags

on the bed.

After settling in, Amber decided to go for a walk. After being cooped up on the plane and then in the car, the last thing she wanted was to just sit in the hotel room. Amber grabbed the keycard and put it in her back pocket and headed out the door. When she got to the lobby, she saw Sidney talking to a tall slender brunette. As the elevator dinged and announced its arrival, both women looked toward Amber.

"Amber?" the brunette asked. "Amber Knight?" The woman walked toward her, and as she got closer, Amber thought she looked familiar, but she didn't know how she was recognized. She'd changed her hair color, her hairstyle was different, she now wore glasses, even her body shape was different.

"Do I know you?" Amber asked hesitantly.

"Oh, my god, it is you." The woman raced over and engulfed Amber in a hug.

Amber felt very awkward and just patted the woman on the back. She had no clue who this was, but apparently, she knew her. "Do I know you?" she asked again.

"I suppose it has been a while and everything. It's me, Heather Woods."

"Heather? Wow, you grew up," Amber said, laughing at the stupidity of her statement. "I don't know what to say. How did you recognize me?"

"You never forget the first crush you ever had…"

"I was your first crush? Wow."

"What are you doing back here? Where've you been for the last ten years? Hasn't Nicole been through enough?"

"I'm only back to get some release forms signed, then I'm out of here again. I'm not here to cause any trouble. I wouldn't be here if this wasn't important."

"What kind of release forms?"

"I'm going to be in an art show in a couple of months at the gallery I work with, and in order to use the photographs in my portfolio, I need to get permission from the people in the pictures. Two of the pictures include people from here."

"Who are you here to see?" Heather's tone became serious. "Wait, let's go into my office." Heather led them to the manager's office. "Now who exactly are you here to see?"

"Well, you, actually. And Nicole Brooks and Erik Harrison. Although when I was looking up people, I couldn't find Erik."

"He's still around. He lives mostly at the firehouse now."

"The firehouse?"

"Erik is an EMT."

"Oh, okay, I understand."

"Do you know anything that has gone on here since you left?" Heather asked.

"No, I haven't had any contact with anyone."

"Not even your family?"

"Especially not my family."

"Well, a lot has gone on…" Heather started before the door to her office was ripped open and in stormed a redheaded woman. "Shit."

"Well, look what the cat dragged in," she spat, looking directly at Amber.

"Nicole, relax. You know it isn't good for you to get upset." Heather started to get up from her desk but stopped before moving from behind it.

"Oh, I'm far from upset." Nicole looked from Heather to Amber and glared. "What gives you the right to come back here? After all this time."

"Nicole, I'm just here to get some signatures and then I'm gone again. I'm not here to cause any trouble. I wouldn't be here if it wasn't important. I just need signatures from you, Heather, and Erik."

"Like hell are you getting anything from me."

"Nicole, how did you know Amber was here?"

"Sidney told me you were meeting in your office with someone named Amber who had the most gorgeous turquoise blue eyes she'd ever seen." With that, Nicole turned and stormed out of the office and out of the hotel.

"I'm going to kill Sidney." Heather pinched the bridge of her nose. "Well, that went better than I expected."

༄༄༄༄

Nicole burst out of the hotel, her anger overtaking her. She needed to get as far away from there as she could and quick.

She has no right to be back here. She left, she abandoned us and never looked back. No, she cannot have a stupid signature from me. Like I will do anything for her. Who the fuck does she think she is? What gives her the right to come back here? Nicole rushed through the streets toward her home, her sanctuary.

Nicole opened the door to her house and closed and locked it. There were three locks on the door, three locks that daily reminded her of Amber, of the fallout of her leaving. Staggering, her mind so jumbled, Nicole made her way to the recliner and sat, burying her face in her hands, trying to fend off the memories.

"Open this door now," David Knight screamed. "I want in, and I want my wife back."

"David, it's over. You signed the papers, please just go away," Karen cried.

"I'll break down this door if you don't open it this minute!"

"I'm calling the police." Nicole had positioned herself between Karen and the door where on the other side was Karen's ex-husband. He had beaten Karen almost to death after Amber left, beaten her because she hadn't tried to stop Amber, beaten her because he felt he had the right to do so. Nicole was sick to her stomach. She could still hear Erik's voice on the phone when he called and said they had responded to a disturbance at the Knight house and that he was in the ambulance heading to the hospital with Amber's mom in critical condition, and it didn't look good.

Nicole had helped Karen heal. She had taken care of her, made sure she was never lonely, made sure she knew she was loved and needed and wanted somewhere. After Karen was well enough to go home, she moved in with Nicole and had filed for a restraining order and for divorce. The divorce would take three years to get finalized, but it had finally happened. Now here was the maniac pounding on Nicole's door, trying to get to Karen.

"911, what is your emergency?" the male voice on the other end of the phone asked.

"Yes, there's an angry and violent man pounding on my door and trying to break into my house," Nicole said.

"What is your address?"

"Eleven eighteen seventy-second street," Nicole said.

"Police are on the way. Please stay on the line with me until they arrive."

Then it happened. The lock gave way on the door, and in came David Knight. He made his way toward Nicole, grabbing the phone out of her hand. He screamed, "Time to pay, bitch," and tossed the phone aside.

Karen was cowering in the corner. She knew what he was capable of, knew she was the one who could stop him from hurting Nicole, but she couldn't move. Fear paralyzed her.

"The police are on their way," Nicole said as David reached for her.

"Like I care. You'll be dead long before they get here," he said with a sneer. He reached out and grabbed her forearm and pulled her toward him just as the police arrived.

"Let her go, sir," one of the officers said.

"Fuck you," David said as he made a fist with his other hand and pulled back, readying to hit Nicole.

"Sir, let…her…go." The other officer drew his weapon and aimed it at David.

"I don't think so," he said as his fist moved toward Nicole's face but never connected.

Nicole heard the loud noise, felt a warm liquid on her face, felt herself being pulled to the ground, and then she heard Karen scream. It was a piercing scream, one of complete and utter terror. Nicole tried to twist herself so she could see Karen, but she couldn't. She hit the ground hard, hitting her head and was knocked unconscious.

After being checked out and cleared by the paramedics, Karen took Nicole and helped her get cleaned up, and they held on to each other that night and several nights after.

The memory felt like it happened yesterday, though it had been almost seven years earlier. Seeing Amber had brought it all back. Nicole didn't feel safe, she didn't know where to go or what to do. She sat in the recliner rocking anxiously.

❧❧❧❧

"Heather, why is she so upset?" Amber was confused about why Nicole had such a strong reaction to her being there. It had been ten years since they'd last had any contact.

"Gee, part of it may be because she was your girlfriend for two years and you walked out on her ten years ago without so much as a word or a letter. Anything further is her story to tell."

"I had my reasons for going. It isn't something I want to talk about."

"Well, I'll call Erik and have him stop by the hotel if you'd like. I don't know if he'll be willing to sign, but you can talk to him."

"That'd be great. Are you willing to sign?"

"I want to see what photographs we're talking about. You took a lot of pictures when we were in school."

"I have a contact sheet up in my room. It shows all the artwork that's going in the show. You're welcome to come and see it, or I can bring it down later…I was going to go for a walk, but after that visit from Nicole, I think I'm going to go lay down for a while."

"Okay, I'll bring Erik up when he gets here."

"Thanks again." Amber rose and left the office and headed toward the elevator.

"Is everything okay?" Sidney asked as Amber

passed the front desk.

"I'm honestly not sure what's going on." Amber continued her way upstairs. Once she arrived in her room, she decided to call Zach. He always made things better.

⁂

Heather waited for the door to click closed before she picked up the phone and dialed.

"Heather, what's up?" the voice on the other end said.

"Hey, Erik, we have a problem," Heather said.

"Okay, that sounds serious."

"Amber is back in town, staying here at the hotel, and to top it off, Nicole knows."

"That's a big problem! How did Nicole find out?"

"She stopped by to see me, and Sid told her I was meeting with someone named Amber, then described her. Nicole came bursting into my office. She snapped at Amber and left."

"Have you called her yet?"

"Not yet," Heather said.

"I'll swing by her house in a few minutes, then I'll come by the hotel. I'd like to have a few choice words with Amber."

"She needs to talk to you, as well. She needs you to sign a release form for some photographs she's going to be putting in an art show."

"Okay, I'll see you in about fifteen or twenty minutes." Erik hung up the phone, grabbed his keys, and headed to Nicole's house.

⁂

"Hey, beautiful," Zach said when he answered Amber's call.

"Hey," Amber replied, her voice distant.

"So, how's it going?"

"Not well. I'm seriously not sure that using those pictures are worth this."

"What happened?"

Amber told Zach about what had transpired since she arrived in Eagle Peak.

"Sounds horrible. What would you say if I told you I was on my way there?"

"I'd say you had better not be lying to me." Amber felt hopeful for the first time since she arrived in Eagle Peak.

"I would never lie about that."

"How are you on your way?"

"I figured this was going to be hard on you, and I decided to catch the next plane out. I'll text you when I get there."

"I love you, you know that."

"Yeah, I'm a pretty great guy." They both laughed, then Zach told her to get some rest and hopefully he'd be there soon.

What could have happened to Nicole for Heather to be so cautious and for her to freak out the way she did? How am I going to convince her to sign the form? That photo of her is one of the most important pictures I've ever taken. Amber sat in her room after she hung up with Zach.

⁂

Nicole was pacing the room when she heard the

doorbell ring. She froze until she heard Erik call her through the door. She quickly made her way over and opened the door.

"Hey, Nic."

"Hi," Nicole said softly.

"I heard you had a little shock today. I wanted to see how you were doing." Erik moved into the living room and sat.

"Amber's in town," Nicole whispered, staring at the ground.

"I heard. That doesn't tell me how you're doing, though."

"I had an episode after I got home." Nicole started to cry.

"Come here." Erik wrapped his arms around her, pulling her close.

"I…she…" Nicole stammered.

"Shh, Heather said she just wants us to sign some stupid form and then she'll be gone."

"I don't want her gone, I want to know why!" Nicole cried harder.

"Well, you can ask her that if you want. You just need to calm down and talk to her."

"Yeah, that goes so well." Nicole pulled back and wiped the tears from her face. "I burst into the office and yelled and told her I wasn't giving her the damn signature."

"You were in shock, it was an understandable reaction. Now you need to figure out if you can handle finding out why and being in the same room as her."

"Will you and Heather be there with me?" Nicole asked timidly.

"If you want us there, we'll do what you want and need."

"I need you guys there." Her tone was desperate. "I don't think I can be alone with her."

"Do you need time, or would you like to come with me now? I'm heading over there to meet with Heather and Amber, but I wanted to check on you first. You take priority in my book."

"I don't know. Do you think it'd be okay?"

"I don't care if it's okay or not. If you want to come with, then you're coming with." Erik smiled.

"And you won't leave me alone with her?"

"Nope. Not unless you tell me to."

"Then I want to go with," Nicole said.

"Great, you go wash your face and get ready, then we'll leave. I'm going to text Heather to let her know you're coming with me."

Nicole smiled at him and then hurried upstairs to freshen up and prepare herself to see Amber again.

Erik sent a text to Heather letting her know that Nicole was coming along and they may want to move the meeting to a different place. Heather said she would move it to Amber's room. She told him to come up to the Bonsai Suite when they got there.

Nicole came back downstairs, smiled at Erik as he stood, and they made their way to the hotel.

Chapter Two

And So It Begins

Amber heard a knock at her door. She took a deep breath and let it out slowly as she made her way to answer it.

"Sorry to be early, but I thought I should warn you that Nicole is coming with Erik to talk to you. She can't do it alone, so she wants him and me to be here. Are you okay with this?"

"I guess I have to be. I don't want to upset anyone. I didn't come back for that."

"I know, but you left and should have suspected that seeing you again might upset people."

A knock at the door a few minutes later startled Amber and Heather, who were lost in thought. Amber answered the door, allowing Erik and Nicole to enter. They joined Heather in the pseudo-living room. Erik and Nicole sat next to each other on the couch, and Heather and Amber sat in the chairs. They were all looking at one another wondering who was going to speak first.

"Well, we all know that Amber is here to get release forms signed. Amber, can you explain why?" Heather got the conversation going.

"I've been offered a spot in an art show coming up at the gallery I work with. The selections they've made consist of four paintings and four photographs.

Because you three are in those photographs, I need to get a release form signed for them to be shown. I have a copy of the proof if you want to see what will be displayed." Amber looked each person in the eye.

"I want to see for certain." Heather took the proof that Amber was holding. After looking through it, she handed it to Erik, who then passed it to Nicole.

Amber sat quietly while each person looked at the proof, and she tried to read what they were thinking.

"These are really good," Nicole said as Erik and Heather nodded in agreement.

"Thank you."

"You said you work with a gallery. What do you do there?" Erik asked.

"I work as a replicator. We take paintings that are popular and replicate them for sale in the gift shop. I'm also a freelance artist and photographer."

"So, you forge paintings?" Heather asked.

"No, we have permission from the owners or painters to replicate them for sale."

"So, you re-create the paintings?" Erik asked.

"Yes, and that's what has helped me improve my painting skills to create a better-rounded portfolio."

"So, if we don't sign the release, you can't use the photographs?" Nicole asked.

"Correct." Amber didn't like how this was going.

"Why'd you leave?" Erik blurted out, receiving looks from all three women. "What? We all want to know, why shouldn't we just ask?"

"After being my dad and Jeffrey's punching bag that night, I couldn't stay there anymore. They had gotten carried away and hit me where the bruises were going to show. Would any of you have let it go had you seen them?" Amber looked at the three. "Nicole, realistically, what would you have done had you seen them or seen me flinch or grimace while we were kissing?" The room was eerily silent. "You all would have acted in a way that would have resulted in my getting beaten to death." Amber heard a scoffing noise from Nicole's direction. "I couldn't continue to be a punching bag for them. Plus, my mother told me to leave for my own safety. So, I packed my bags, waited until everyone was asleep, and left. I didn't honestly expect to make it out of the house, but I did without anyone hearing me."

"Why didn't you tell anyone?" Heather said.

"I was scared of what my dad or Jeffrey would do to anyone who helped me. I knew if I stayed here, they would find me, and I'm certain they would have killed me."

"We could have helped you," Nicole said barely above a whisper.

"I couldn't risk him hurting any of you because of me. Especially you, Nic. If that happened, I would never have been able to live with myself."

"It's been ten years, Amber. Do you ever wonder what happened after you left? Did you ever think about those of us you abandoned and left behind?" Nicole's anger took over again.

"Not a day has gone by that I haven't thought about you, Nicole," Amber whispered.

"You wouldn't know that from here. From here, it looks like you only thought about yourself. Why didn't you ever try to contact us? In ten years, you couldn't pick up a fucking phone? Send a fucking letter?" Nicole nearly yelled.

"I thought about it. I wrote tons of letters to you, Jill, and Heather. I was too afraid to send them. I did pick up the phone on several occasions and call, but I chickened out before saying anything. I wanted to, I tried to speak, but no words or sounds would come out."

"Those are excuses, bullshit answers," Heather said, causing Amber to wince.

"They may be, but they're the truth." Amber tried to contain her defensiveness.

"Well, I hope you're enjoying your new life," Heather said.

"I know you can't still be this angry at me for leaving. What happened after I left? Why are you all still so mad?"

"Do you really want to know? Will it really matter?" Nicole asked, full of anger now.

"Nicole, you need to calm down," Erik placed a hand on Nicole's arm. "You had an episode already today. Getting worked up is just going to make it worse."

"You had an episode? Nicole, are you okay? Was it a bad one?" Heather asked in rapid fire as she moved quickly from her chair to kneel in front of Nicole.

Amber was confused and very concerned. She had no idea what they were talking about, but it seemed serious and it involved Nicole. She had never stopped loving the woman, but she didn't want to put her in harm's way, either. Amber had convinced herself that staying away was best.

"It was after I got home. It was powerful, but I answered the door when Erik knocked." Nicole wiped a tear from Heather's cheek. "I'm okay, I promise. You worry too much."

"I worry just the right amount. You're my best friend, Nic," Heather said. "We don't have to go through things today, we can wait and do it tomorrow."

"I'm okay, I promise. Dr. Scott said it might help me to talk about it and especially to Amber. If I ever got the chance."

"I don't know if it's the best idea with emotions so high, but all right. The moment you start to regress, we end it, though."

"Fine, we'll play it by your rules," Nicole conceded.

"Nicole?" Amber asked, concern coming through in her face and her voice.

"I think we should all take bathroom breaks and get some food and drinks," Erik said.

"I'll get Keyser to send us up an assortment." Heather went over to the phone and dialed room service.

Nicole went to the bathroom, Erik walked over to the window and stared out. Amber pulled out her phone and sent a message to Zach asking if he was close. He said he was just getting to the hotel.

"Heather, I have a friend who just arrived at the hotel who's coming upstairs. I need to go talk to him quickly," Amber said quietly.

"Did you move on to boys? I noticed you weren't checked in under your own last name. Is this your husband?"

"It's his last name, but no, I still only date women. Zach is my best friend. He's here to help me."

"Fine, I'll stall them, but he better not interfere," Heather warned as she looked at Nicole and Erik. "I'll tell them someone else is joining us. You can explain the rest."

"Thank you." Amber made her way out the door and into the hallway to meet Zach.

"Where'd Amber go?" Nicole asked.

"She's meeting someone, who I guess is here to help her. I told her she had to explain."

"I can't do this if it's her girlfriend or boyfriend."

"I already clarified that it isn't."

⁂

Amber leaned against the wall by the elevator waiting for it to arrive. She heard the bell ding, and relief filled her as the doors opened and Zach was standing there with his arms open, ready to pull her into a hug.

"Come here, sweetie," Zach said as Amber practically ran into his arms. He wrapped her into a hug and felt her arms go around him and squeezed him tightly. "Amber, are you okay?"

"That has to be one of the stupidest questions you have ever asked me." Amber pulled back from the hug.

"What's going on?"

"Well, I've got Erik, Heather, and Nicole in my room at the moment."

"*The* Nicole?"

"*The* Nicole, there's only one. Something happened after I left, and Nicole is going to tell me what it is," Amber said. "I'm scared about what she's going to say. Just before I sent you that text, they were talking about Nicole having an episode and how it wasn't as bad and that she was still able to open the door when Erik arrived."

"Wow, I'm glad I told Lucinda that I needed to be here for you." Zach offered her a soft smile and wrapped an arm around her shoulders. "Should we get you back in there?"

"Yeah," Amber said as they walked to the door,

and she slid the keycard in the slot.

Opening the door caused everyone to turn and look at Amber and the man with her as they entered. They made their way to where the others were, Zach grabbing the desk chair so he could sit next to Amber.

"Everyone, this is Zach, my best friend. Zach, this is Heather, Erik, and Nicole."

"Wow, it's nice to meet you all and nice to put faces with names. Amber has told me a lot about all of you," Zach said in a soft but sincere voice.

Heather and Erik shook his hand. Nicole looked at him, trying to figure out if there was more to him or his and Amber's relationship.

"Nicole, are you okay?" Amber asked.

"How long have you known him?" Nicole asked.

"I met him my second week in New York City. He kinda helped me get the job as a replicator."

"And you talked to him about us?"

"I told you earlier, not a day has gone by that I haven't thought about you. Zach will tell you I mean it. He's the one I talk about you all to," Amber said as all eyes went from her to Zach, who nodded that she was telling the truth.

"I know you don't know me, but I promise if you give me a chance, you'll see I'm here strictly to support Amber and help any of you in any way I can. I feel as though I know you all," Zach said.

Nicole was just about to ask Zach a question when there was a knock at the door.

"That has to be Keyser with the food and drinks." Heather made her way to the door and let the man in the chef's coat in. He placed the cart near where they were sitting and quickly left.

"Let's eat and then Nicole can tell you what she

has to say," Heather said.

Amber and Zach let the others get their food before they grabbed some fruit and water.

"So, do you do showings like Amber?" Heather asked.

"No, she's far more talented than I am. I can replicate pictures, but I can't create something on my own," Zach said. "At least nothing sale-worthy like Amber."

✦ ✦ ✦ ✦

Silence filled the room as everyone ate and took in what Zach had said. Erik, Heather, and especially Nicole had thought that Amber had never thought twice about them after she left, and now, they knew that she had, and she had talked about them with Zach.

Amber and Zach sat there wondering what it was that Nicole was going to tell them. Zach was hoping he would be able to support Amber in the way she needed. Amber was hoping she could emotionally handle what Nicole was going to tell her. She knew from everyone's reaction that it was serious.

Heather finished eating and put her plate back on the tray. She offered to take Erik and Nicole's plates, as well. Nicole sat there with a vacant look on her face.

"Nic," Heather said as she looked at her. When she received no response, she knelt and softly said Nicole's name again, and still got no response. Heather quickly glanced over at Erik before placing her hand on Nicole's arm and saying her name a third time. This time, Nicole looked at her.

"Where'd you go?" Heather said softly.

"I'm sorry," Nicole said as a tear rolled down her face.

"Nic, don't be sorry. You have nothing to be sorry for. I was just wondering where you went in your head."

Glancing over at Amber, whose face was etched in concern, and Zach, who was holding her hand, Nicole said, "I went back to just days before Amber left when we went swimming at Old Miller's Pond."

"I remember that day," Amber said with a smirk and turned a slight shade of red.

"It's one of the happy memories that has kept me grounded and helped me survive the past ten years." Nicole looked at her hands that were now in her lap as Heather had taken her plate from her.

Amber got up and knelt in front of Nicole. This was the closest they had been since Amber's arrival. She was slow and cautious. She reached out her hand and tentatively touched Nicole's hand, causing her to flinch slightly but also look up.

"Hi." Amber offered Nicole a lopsided smile.

"Hi." Nicole stared into Amber's eyes before raising her hand to Amber's hair and running her fingertips through it. "How long have you been blond?"

"About ten years."

"I like it."

"What can I do to make this easier for you?" Amber asked.

"I-I really need to tell you this stuff, but I'm scared."

"Why are you scared?"

"Because I know how painful it is, and I don't want to..." Nicole started as her emotions built up inside her.

Amber saw the anxiety and distress Nicole was in and took a hold of Nicole's hand. When she didn't pull away, Amber moved slowly and brought Nicole into a hug. As her arms wrapped around Nicole, she felt Nicole grab her and hold on for dear life. Amber just held her and started to cry, as well.

Zach watched the interaction among the four and realized that as close as he and Amber had gotten over the years, she had still held a significant part of herself from him.

Erik stood and motioned for Heather and Zach to follow him and give Nicole and Amber a moment together.

Nicole realized that Amber was holding her, that she was clinging to life because of this woman. The woman who had abandoned her, her mother, her friends, everyone. But in Amber's arms, she felt safe.

Amber pulled back from the hug a little and placed a soft kiss on top of Nicole's head. It wasn't done as a romantic gesture but as a comforting one.

"Amber," Nicole said in a small, almost childish voice.

"Yeah?" Amber said, her gaze meeting Nicole's.

"Can we sit on the couch together while I tell you everything?"

"Sure. Are you okay to do this now?"

"Yeah, I just have some tough moments," Nicole said. "What I have to tell you will be hard for you to hear…"

"I know, but I want to know." Amber brushed a strand of Nicole's hair behind her ear.

Nicole and Amber moved to the couch, and Nicole called the others back. She asked Zach to sit next to Amber, stating that she would probably need his support, as well. Heather and Erik sat across from the trio, trying to imagine how this was going to go.

Chapter Three

Disclosure

"Nic, just take your time, and if we need to stop, we can." Amber saw the stress and anxiety on Nicole's face and felt the tension coming from Erik and Heather.

"So, um, starting with the morning after you left." Nicole swallowed hard and looked down at her hands. "Your dad decided that it was your mom's fault you were gone. He, um, he beat her, bad, he almost killed her." Nicole heard Amber gasp, and Zach wrapped an arm around her. "Erik called me and told me while they were on the way to the hospital. He was doing a ride-along that day to make sure being a paramedic was what he wanted to do."

"It was what made me want to be one more than ever," Erik interjected.

"Oh, Mama," Amber whispered, tears filling her eyes.

Nicole continued to tell Amber about her mother's hospital stay, about her recovery, and how close they became within that time. Nicole then told Amber about her mom getting the strength and filing for divorce before moving in with Nicole.

"Part of why she moved in with me was obviously because we had become so close, but it was also to help me. My parents were both killed in a small plane crash around the same time she was getting out of the hospital." Nicole continued to look down at her hands. She couldn't meet Amber's gaze. She couldn't see the hurt in her eyes.

"I'm so sorry, Nic." Amber reached out toward Nicole but then pulled back.

"Your mom and I took care of each other. It-it helped us both a lot. I think it was also a way for us both to hold on to you." Nicole slid back on the couch a little farther, knowing that what she was about to tell Amber was going to hurt, but what came after it was going to be even more painful. "Then things went bad. This part is also the 'episode' I had today. I, um, have flashbacks, some are crippling. This one used to be one of the harder ones. Well, until today, it was. It took three years for the divorce to become final. Once it did, we thought—no, hoped—that we were rid of your father. We weren't..." Nicole let her gaze drift off as she recounted her episode from earlier in the day; she couldn't watch Amber's reaction. As she told her, she could hear Amber whimpering and Zach trying to comfort her. "After the police left, your mom helped me wipe his blood off my face and body. That was when I had the first mental breakdown. I couldn't leave my room for days fearing that he would be in the living room waiting for me."

"Nic," Amber whispered. Zach was holding her back so she couldn't engulf Nicole in her arms. He could tell it wouldn't help either of them. Nicole needed to get this out.

Heather and Erik shared a look knowing that as devastated and guilty as Amber felt now, it was about to get a whole lot worse.

"It took me about four months before I was able to be in the house alone. Karen made sure that if she wasn't there that someone else was. I had to go to court to testify against your dad. That sent me into a backward spiral, but Karen stood by me." Tears rolled down Nicole's face thinking about the woman who was more of a mother to her than her own mother had been. "Not long after the trial, just as things started to take on some semblance of normal, Karen started feeling sick. We went to the doctor and found out she had stage three liver cancer."

Tears streamed down Amber's face. Erik and Heather felt bad for her. Zach wasn't sure how much more his friend could take; she was shaking and having a hard time breathing. He wasn't sure if it was from crying or from the shock of what she was being told.

"Do you need a minute?" Nicole asked, seeing the anguish in Amber's eyes.

"No, a minute isn't going to help, but thank you." Amber tried to control the tears streaming down her face.

"We tried to fight the cancer aggressively, but there was nothing we could do. She made it two years before she passed away. She asked me to give you a letter she wrote if you should ever come back here."

"I don't deserve it," Amber cried as Zach held her and Nicole moved forward and took her hand.

"Amber, she loved you. You were her daughter," Nicole said softly.

"I know that's supposed to help, but I'm…I should have been here…I should have helped her."

"I'm going to give you two a minute together," Zach said, feeling Amber calming down. He got up, kissed the side of Amber's head, and walked out of the room. Heather and Erik followed. They had been silently taking in everything that was going on, the interaction between Amber and Nicole and especially Amber and Zach.

※※※※

"So, what's your deal? What do you get out of being here with Amber?" Erik asked bluntly.

"I'm sorry, I don't know what you mean by either question," Zach said.

"Well, you and Amber are pretty chummy, and I'm just wondering why. And what's in it for you to come here to 'support' her?"

"Amber is my best friend. She was there for me when my wife walked out on me and my two-year-old son. She was there to help me pick up the pieces of my life. When my son Travis was sick, she was there with me, in the hospital, in the doctor's office. Then when he died, she helped me not join him because of the grief and guilt I felt for not being able to do more to help him. He was just a little kid. So, what's in it for me? I get to help someone who cares about me no matter what."

"Nice she could be there for you but not for anyone here," Heather mumbled bitterly.

"I can't speak for why she stayed away so long or why she didn't write or call. I can only say that she talks about you all daily. She told me stories about growing up with you, Erik, about dating and falling in love with Nicole. She even told me about you and your sister, Jill."

"Shit, we never called Jill," Heather said.

"I think we should ask Nicole if she wants us to call her or not," Erik said.

"You wuss, you just don't want Jill to yell in your

ear," Heather said.

"I'm not stupid," Erik said, causing all three to giggle.

※※※※

"He seems really nice," Nicole said, watching Zach and the others leave.

"He is. We've been through a lot together. His wife walked out on him and his son, then his son got really sick and passed away."

"That's horrible. Kids shouldn't die."

"I agree. Travis was only three. He was so smart and funny. Zach took it hard. Although I think that's to be expected from a true parent."

"Wow, I can't imagine." Nicole reached in her pocket and pulled out the letter from Amber's mom. "Um, here's the letter your mom wanted me to give you."

Amber stared at the envelope in Nicole's hand. She was afraid to touch it, afraid of what it was going to say. She was even afraid of what it wouldn't say.

"You don't have to read it now, but please, she wanted you to have it. If you want, er…um…if it would help, I'll…um…I can be there when you read it."

"I'd like that a lot. I think having you there, knowing you were with her at the end, will help me be able to read it. Thank you. Do you know what it says? Did she let you read it?"

"No, I just know she wrote it about a day before she died." Nicole handed the letter to Amber, and their hands brushed together. "Should we let them come back in yet?"

"Not yet, if it's okay with you. I'd like another

couple of minutes with just you. I know you don't believe me, but I have missed you a lot."

"I missed you, too."

❧❧❧❧

"Hey, Nic." Heather peeked around the corner.

"Yeah?" Nicole turned her gaze toward Heather.

"We realized that we haven't told Jill about Amber being back, and we were wondering if you thought we should."

"That's Amber's call, not mine," Nicole said. "Amber?"

"What type of a comeback would it be without having Jill here?" Amber forced a smile.

"It's okay if you don't want us to call her." Nicole noticed Amber was uncomfortable.

"No, I'm okay with it. She isn't going to beat me up, is she?"

"She may intimidate you, but no, she won't hurt you." Nicole smiled.

Heather ducked back around the corner, leaving Nicole and Amber to their moment. She pulled out her cellphone and dialed Jill's number.

"Hey, Squirt!"

"Jill, you know I hate it when you call me that," Heather said.

"Yep, and that's why I do it."

"Fine, be an ass. Can you come by the hotel?"

"Sure, official or personal business?"

"Personal. When you get here, come up to the fourth floor, Bonsai Suite."

"Okay, I'll be there in about five minutes or so."

When everyone came back into the room, Amber excused herself to go to the bathroom to wash her face.

"So, did you reach Jill?" Nicole asked.

"Yeah, she said she'd be over in about five minutes," Heather said, then there was a knock at the door. Erik answered it and ushered Jill in to join the others. Jill gave Zach an inquisitive look.

Amber came out of the bathroom and stopped as she entered the room. There was Jill wearing what looked like a sheriff's or deputy's uniform. Amber took a deep breath and slowly moved to join the group. Nicole's gaze flashed over to her, and Jill turned to see what Nicole was looking at.

Jill stood there staring at the blonde who had just entered the room. She looked familiar, but Jill couldn't place why. As she continued to look at the woman, their gazes met, then Jill's eyes went wide. She knew in that instant *who* this was. Everyone had been silent, watching as realization dawned for Jill.

Amber swallowed hard as Jill studied her. She looked past Jill to Nicole and then Zach. Nicole got up and moved toward Amber at the same time Jill did. Jill reached her first. The room was stunned when they heard the slap and saw Amber's head jerk to one side. Zach was the first to get to Amber. He knew he needed to protect his friend. He moved between Jill and Amber, his back to Jill. He pulled Amber into his arms and held her. Nicole was right there by Amber's side, and she glared at Jill.

"What the hell was that for?" Nicole asked, her anger coming through in her voice.

"That? That was for the hell she put us all

through. That was for the pain she caused you. She's lucky to have only gotten a slap," Jill spat out.

"You were out of line, Jill," Heather snapped.

"Am I the only one that remembers what the last ten years have been like? What Nicole went through?"

"No, but it wasn't your place," Nicole said as Zach pulled back from Amber and allowed Nicole an opportunity to see her.

"Who the hell is this anyway?" Jill pointed at Zach.

"He's my friend and support," Amber said.

"Are you okay?" Nicole asked.

"I'll be fine. I endured worse living in my house for years. It just surprised me." Amber looked hard and cold at Jill before softening and moving to Nicole.

"Well, that went well." Erik let out an exasperated sigh as he sat in one of the chairs.

"So, you're back? For how long?" Jill asked, glaring at Amber.

"I'm here for a few days and then I have to get back to New York," Amber said flatly.

"Well, in my opinion, it can't be soon enough."

"Amber, who the hell is this?" Zach asked.

"This is Jill, my sister," Heather said coldly.

"Jill, you don't know what's been going on here," Nicole said, concerned that Jill was going to ruin her chance to talk with or at least spend time with Amber.

"I don't care to know, either. She hurt you. No, she crushed you. There's no excuse for that," Jill snapped. "So, Amber, enlighten me as to why you left, why you couldn't say goodbye or even make contact."

"Jill, stop," Nicole said. Erik noticed a quiver in Nicole's voice and rushed over to stabilize her.

"Jill, she's already had an episode today, back

off," Heather said through gritted teeth.

"I'm guessing it was no thanks to blondie over there."

"Jill, hate me, whatever, but stop upsetting Nicole." Amber moved over to stand next to Nicole.

"What do you honestly care? You abandoned her. You just up and disappeared for ten years."

"Yes, I left after getting beaten by my brother and father. I left because there was no way I could take another beating, and there was no way I could hide what they had done to me that night." Amber moved within inches of Jill, her voice cold as steel. "Do you want to know the full extent of what happened? Every detail? Will that make *you* happy?"

"Yes, it will help," Jill said coldly.

"Fine, but, Zach, Nicole, will you both please leave? Heather, Erik, I'd prefer you to leave, too, but it's your choice." Amber's gaze was still locked on Jill's.

"I'm not leaving," Nicole said directly.

"I'm sorry, Amber, but I'm with Nicole. I'm not going anywhere," Zach said.

Amber turned to face them both. "Please, I don't know that I can handle either of you hearing this. Knowing these details," Amber pleaded, her eyes filling with tears.

"Please, let us stay. Nicole and I just want to be here for you." Zach took Amber's hand, and Nicole nodded her agreement. "And frankly, I don't trust Jill."

"Fine," Amber said in defeat, turning back to face Jill.

"So, please, tell me what happened. Enlighten me as to why you had to leave as you did. Why was it acceptable to crush the woman you supposedly loved?"

"I can't be here for this. Not after knowing what

happened to your mom," Erik said as he headed for the door. "Nicole, call me later."

"Heather?" Jill asked.

"I'm staying," she said, glaring at Jill.

"Usually, my dad and brother hit me where the bruises wouldn't be seen or noticed," Amber started. "That night, something snapped in them both. They were ruthless in their punches. Jeffrey aimed for my legs, my dad liked to hit in the middle area. That night, though, they didn't seem to care where the punches and belt landed."

"Belt," Nicole whispered. Zach moved over and tentatively put his arm around her, helping her to a chair. He sat next to Nicole, and she took his hand in hers.

Amber couldn't look at either of them. She kept her gaze locked on Jill. Pulling up her shirt, she showed Jill four puncture wounds on her left side. "Those marks, the belt buckles they were using, went in, and two of the four almost punctured part of my left kidney. I had four broken ribs. One was so bad that had I moved wrong, I would have punctured my lung. My right kidney was severely bruised. My left forearm was fractured, I have scars on my legs from Jeffrey beating me with the belt. I was knocked down the stairs, you remember the steep ones going to the lower level. I have a three-inch scar on the back of my head from hitting the wall, and last but certainly not least, I had a severe concussion."

Jill was looking at Amber, her eyes filling with tears, she couldn't breathe. Nicole and Heather were crying. Zach was trying to remain strong, but he couldn't help but cry, as well. He knew that when he met Amber something had happened, but she had played it off as a car accident.

"Do you want to feel the scars? Do you want to feel where the ribs were broken, and not for the first time and therefore didn't heal properly? What do you want, Jill? Please, now you enlighten me. Tell me what it'll take to make you understand. I have pictures. Do you want me to send you the pictures?" Amber asked coldly.

Jill opened and closed her mouth. She had no words, no idea what to say, what to do. She looked past Amber and saw Nicole being comforted by Zach and Heather. She then looked back at Amber.

"Zach thought I was in a car accident. He helped me as I healed. The nightmares I had because of that night, he helped me through. When I couldn't leave the house because I was afraid my father or brother would find me, he sneaked me out to work. He barely left my side when I needed someone for the first several months we knew each other. Without him, I would probably not still be here because of the depression. So, you wanted to know why I left the way I did and haven't had any contact for ten years. Does that give you some enlightenment?"

"You could have come to us," Jill whispered, unable to find her full voice.

"No, because my father and Jeffrey both knew all about everyone I hung out with, and they threatened to hurt you if I said a word. They weren't really known for lying about those types of threats." Amber pulled her shirt back down and stared at the ground.

"Amber," Nicole said, her voice raspy and shaking. This caused Amber to turn around and walk over and sit on the table in front of Nicole. "Why did you lie earlier? Why didn't you tell us how bad it was?"

"Because I knew you had been hurt enough. I didn't want you to know the truth," Amber said, softly wiping away the tears streaming down Nicole's face.

"Amber, why didn't you ever tell me?" Zach said.

"Because I didn't want you to think less of me or to be my friend out of pity." She looked down, unable to meet his or Nicole's gaze.

"Seriously?" Nicole lifted Amber's chin. "We all love you...well, I don't know about Jill, but Heather, Erik, Zach, and I, we love you and would never pity you."

"I'm so sorry, Amber," Jill finally said. "I don't know how you survived all that."

"I didn't have a choice. I got used to it. I had been beaten by them since I was four," Amber admitted, and then groaned at what she had just revealed and the gasps that had echoed through the room.

Chapter Four

Processing

The room was eerily silent as the group processed Amber's revelation. Amber spent her time in the awkward silence staring at the ground, unable to meet anyone's gaze. She was ashamed of what she had just revealed. Ashamed of what had happened to her. She could feel their gazes on her. After several minutes of silence, Amber abruptly stood and announced that she needed to get some air. When Nicole and Zach offered to go with her, she told them she needed to be alone, she needed time to process things, as well. She promised to be back before it was dark, and she grabbed her cellphone and headed out the door.

After Amber left the room, everyone looked at one another. Zach felt the most awkward since he had no clue who these people were outside of what Amber had told him. The others were simply in shock.

"Did any of you have any idea or suspect anything about Amber's past?" Heather looked between Jill and Nicole.

"In the ten years I've known her, she has told me about you all and that she was in a car accident. I don't even know what to say after what she revealed today," Zach said, his mind spinning.

"Jill, we've known Amber since kindergarten.

How could we have not known that they were hurting her?" Nicole tried to hold back the tears, her heart breaking for the woman she loved so much.

"As she said, they hit her where the bruises wouldn't show." Jill replayed their childhood to see if there were signs they missed.

"She always claimed to be clumsy," Heather said quietly as another tear slid down her cheek.

"Um, Jill, not to add to this upsetting situation, but are any of Amber's family members around? Or people that could see and hurt her while she's out there alone and distracted?" Zach asked.

"Her dad is in prison for life, and her brother, damn it, I think he got out a week or two ago," Jill said. "I think I should follow her and make sure she isn't alone and that she's safe."

"Why do you have to do it?" Heather said.

"Hello, the little badge with the title sheriff." Jill pointed to the badge on her shirt.

"I'm going with you." Nicole stood.

"No, you're staying put. All we need is for Jeffrey Knight to see either you or Amber and it'll be all over."

"May I come with you?" Zach asked.

"No, you three please stay here and wait for us. I think I owe Amber some privacy and apologies."

"Fine," the three said as they sat in defeat as they were all lost in their own thoughts.

Jill grabbed her coat and headed downstairs. When she reached the lobby, she saw Sidney at the desk.

"Hey, Sid." Jill walked up to the desk.

"Hi, Jill. How are you today?"

"I've had better days. Did you happen to see Amber leave?"

"Yeah, she seemed really out of it. I tried to talk to her, but it was like she was in a fog. She didn't even acknowledge that I was talking to her."

"She's had a rough day, and I made it harder on her. I really want to talk to her and apologize. Do you know which way she went?"

"Um, she looked to be headed to the town square," Sidney said, concern etched in her voice.

"Great, thank you." Jill rushed out of the building and headed toward the town square.

※※※※

Amber took the elevator to the lobby and walked out, not noticing that Sidney was talking to her. She needed to get out of there, get some air, to be able to breathe.

Nice job there, Amber. You revealed all your well-kept secrets. Now every time they look at you, it will be with pity for what you endured. Pity for what your father and brother put you through. Why did Nicole and Zach have to stay? That makes this whole thing even worse. What are you going to do? How are you ever going to face them again? And why does Nicole still have to look so damn amazing? You have all these scars, and she's still a flawless beauty. She'll never want you. Why would she? What could you offer her? You screwed up with her by trying to protect her. I bet now that you're here, she'll have closure and will never want to see you again.

Amber's mind had become a bit unstable since that night all those years ago that she left home. The night she left everyone she loved and everyone she hated behind. The doctors and therapists she had seen over the years had told her it was post-traumatic stress disorder from what she endured. This was one of the reasons she had never dated after leaving Nicole. That and she loved the woman to this day, and it wouldn't be fair to lead someone to believe she could have her heart. Amber knew she would never subject Nicole to whatever was wrong inside her mind.

Amber neared the town square. She was in awe of its beauty. There were four small white gazebos placed at each corner and one large white one in the center. The pathways connecting the gazebos were lined with flowers and outdoor lights. It was nice to see that the town cared about its appearance.

Moving into the square, Amber spotted a bench that was empty and out of the way, hidden by some trees. She made her way over to the bench and sat. She was able to see the full square from there. As she scanned the square, she saw two familiar faces, one she wasn't surprised to see. Jill had followed her. In the back of her mind, she had expected someone to follow her, to come talk to her. The second face, that one disturbed her, and sent an ice-cold chill down her spine. Standing not forty feet from her was her tormentor, the star of her nightmares—her brother, Jeffrey. Amber watched him, saw him scanning the area and the people. She suspected it was to find someone to rob; he had that look about him. As she watched him, Jill came and sat next to her.

"You know, if you keep staring at him, he's going to notice you," Jill said nonchalantly.

"I can't help but stare. His face has haunted me for so many years. Years growing up, years as an adult. He and my father robbed me of so much."

"I wish we would have known. I know they

threatened our safety, but I still wish we would have known."

"How did you know where to find me? Or did you follow me out the door?" Amber still watched Jeffrey out of the corner of her eye.

"Zach asked if Jeffrey or your father were out and if you would run the risk of running into them. He's a pretty smart guy. I realized Jeffrey was let out of jail a couple of weeks ago, so I decided I would follow you or just walk next to you as protection, and I wanted to talk with you alone. When I got downstairs, Sidney told me what direction you went in. I guessed that you were in Zombieland, and you would probably end up here."

"I think Sidney was trying to talk to me as I left," Amber said with a small laugh.

"She seems to have taken an interest in you. And yes, she was trying to talk to you. She better watch it, though. I don't believe she's the *only* person that has taken an interest in you," Jill said with a smile.

"Zach and I are just friends. He dates women, so do I. It wouldn't work between us."

"He wasn't who I was referring to, but yeah, I can see he cares very deeply for you."

"Then who were you talking about?"

"Duh, Nicole."

"That wasn't interest you saw from her, that was pity. I hurt her so badly, I don't deserve the time of day from her."

"And yet here you are. What made you come back here anyway?"

"I've been given the opportunity to have several pieces of artwork and photographs shown in an art show, but for me to show the photographs, I need to get release forms signed by Heather, Erik, and Nicole. I knew if I mailed them that they would just toss them, so I came here to beg and plead with them in person. I wasn't sure I was going to find anyone still here, but I knew I had to try."

"Congratulations," Jill said. "How many pieces are you showing?"

"I have four paintings and four photographs. The photograph of Nicole is Lucinda's favorite."

"Who's Lucinda?" Jill raised an eyebrow.

"Sorry, she's the curator of the gallery Zach and I work with, and she's the one sponsoring me in the showing."

"Wow, a gallery curator sponsoring you, not too shabby." Jill laughed. "Listen, I want to say I'm sorry about earlier. I shouldn't have slapped you."

"I deserved it. I didn't expect it from you, but I deserved it." Amber could still feel a slight burn on her cheek.

"No, you didn't. I appreciate you trying to make me feel better, though."

"So, how long have you been the sheriff?"

"About three years. After what went on with your mom and Nicole, I wanted to make a difference and keep scum from hurting innocent people."

"That's awesome. I'm certain you'll help a lot of people."

Jeffrey moved closer to where Jill and Amber were sitting. Jill noticed and hoped he would see her uniform and leave. Amber was looking at the ground when Jeffrey looked over and saw Jill watching him. He knew if he got caught again, he was facing the three-strikes law and he was going to jail for life. He wasn't willing to let that happen over some petty theft. Jeffrey quickly left the square.

"She never stopped loving you," Jill said, turning to face Amber.

"I never stopped loving her," Amber admitted, looking at her hands in her lap.

"Here's an idea. Feel free to say no, but how about we go back to the hotel because everyone is probably freaking out worrying about you. I thought I was going to have to fight Nicole and Zach when I told them I was coming alone to talk to you. Once we get back, I'll call Erik and we can all go out to eat. Or if you would rather stay in, we can do what we did as teens and order pizza and have a slumber party in my living room."

"Really? You want to have a slumber party?"

"Why not? Are you too good to do that now?"

"No, not at all. Let's go see what the others have to say. I think after how the day has gone, I would prefer to stay in," Amber said as they got up from the bench and headed back to the hotel.

Once they made it back, Jill called the station to have someone find Jeffrey Knight and keep tabs on him. She said he was acting suspiciously. What she didn't say was that she wanted him watched in case he found out Amber was in town. She wanted to be sure Amber was safe.

While Jill was on the phone, Sidney came over to flirt with Amber. Jill noticed and sent a text to Heather to send Nicole down.

"You seem to have caused quite a stir here." Sidney moved closer to Amber.

"It wasn't intentional." Amber looked toward Jill and saw she was still on the phone.

"I'm sure it's all very overwhelming! Would you

like to go out for a drink later? I'm a great listener. I get done here around eight. There are some nice bars in the area. Or we could go back to my place." Sidney reached for Amber's hand.

Amber felt very uncomfortable and was trying to come up with a way to say no when she felt arms wrapping around her waist from behind. Amber knew instantly who it was from the feel of the arms and the breath on her neck. Amber leaned into the embrace; she had missed being held. Most of all, though, she had missed being held by Nicole.

"Hey, gorgeous." Nicole held Amber close and rested her chin on Amber's shoulder. "I was starting to worry about you. Do you feel better now that you got some air?"

Amber couldn't answer, she was afraid she would cry if she tried. She nodded her reply. The feeling of Nicole's breath on her neck was overwhelming.

Sidney looked between the two women before making her way back to the front desk.

Jill strolled over and leaned in, smiling toward Sidney. "They go *way* back. Just some friendly advice; you might not want to hit on Amber. Nicole is the jealous type."

"I didn't know. Plus, everyone has always said Nicole was single," Sidney said softly.

"She was or is, but that's because Amber left." A smile grew on Jill's face as she watched the two enjoying the closeness.

"I didn't know." Sidney said again, watching Jill walk back over to the other two women.

"Jealous much there, Nic?" Jill said, quietly giggling at them.

"Shush." Nicole tried to scowl and not laugh at

Jill.

Jill glanced over and saw a smile on Sidney's face as she shook her head and watched them. This was a side of Nicole that Sidney had never seen, but Nicole seemed very natural with Amber.

"I've missed you so much," Nicole whispered into Amber's ear.

"I've missed you, too," Amber said, feeling Nicole pull her even closer.

"All right, enough sappy stuff. Let's go back upstairs." Jill interrupted the moment between Nicole and Amber.

The two women pulled apart but stayed close.

They walked back into the room, and Amber saw Zach physically let out a breath as soon as he saw her.

"Feel better?" Heather asked, relieved to have Amber back at the hotel.

"Much," Amber said, a smile growing across her face. "Although I think Nicole may have broken Sidney."

"What did you do? I just got her broken in," Heather whined, looking at Nicole, who was wearing a sheepish grin.

"Sidney was hitting on Amber, which is why I had you send Nicole down. Well, Nicole came in and got all cuddly with Amber, squashing Sid's dreams of ever getting a date." Jill giggled, causing Nicole and Amber to blush a deep shade of red while Heather and Zach had to laugh.

"Gee, Nic, I never knew you were so territorial," Heather teased.

"Hey, technically, Amber and I never broke up, so really, she's still mine, and Sid needed to be shown that." Nicole stuck her tongue out at Heather, which caused Amber to blush an even deeper shade of red.

"Gee, Amber, I don't think I've ever seen you turn *that* shade of red before." Zach laughed as he snapped a picture of her with his phone.

"Delete that picture, Pellot," Amber said sternly, looking at Zach, who was shaking his head.

"Never, and I emailed it to work, so if you delete it from my phone, I still have a copy."

"Ass," Amber mumbled, causing Nicole to laugh.

"What are you laughing at?" Amber asked Nicole, cocking an eyebrow.

"I'm sorry, but the last time I saw you that shade of red wa—" Amber put her hand over Nicole's mouth before she could continue.

"I know when, and you will *not* mention that." Amber knew Nicole was thinking about the time they went skinny dipping at Old Miller's Pond and were making out in the middle of the pond when Old Man Miller came up and talked to them.

"Nicole, I'd be happy to protect you if you want to divulge the story," Heather said, and Zach nodded his agreement.

Looking deep into Amber's eyes, Nicole felt her heart race. "Sorry, guys, I have to respect Amber's wishes and keep this just between her and me." Nicole winked at Amber, causing Amber to give her the patented lopsided smile.

"Okay, now that we're done embarrassing Nicole and Amber... While Amber and I were out, I suggested that we call Erik and all of us go over to my house and have one of our slumber parties. Pizza, movies, pool..."

"Are you sure?" Nicole looked at Jill.

"Yep, now, Amber and Zach, grab what you're going to need for tonight and let's go," Jill said. "Nic, I still have your spare bag at the house unless you want to stop by your place."

"Nah, I'll just use what I have there." Nicole watched as Amber and Zach grabbed a couple of things. Nicole saw Amber pack the letter she had given her earlier. After they had their stuff together, the group headed out for Jill's house.

Chapter Five

Two Steps Forward, One Step Back

Once the group arrived at Jill's house, Jill called Erik, who said he'd be right over. He was never one to pass up free pizza. While Jill was calling Erik and ordering the pizzas, the rest of the group adjusted in the living room, so they were all going to have a spot for everyone.

"Hey, Amber…um…are you sure you'll be okay sitting and/or laying on the floor? What about your back and ribs?" Zach asked quietly, but not quiet enough, and Nicole overheard him.

"What does he mean about your back and ribs?" Nicole asked, concern etched on her face.

"I'll be fine," Amber said to Zach, then turned to Nicole and took her hand. "I sometimes have a problem with hard floors, beds, and chairs. It's from the way my ribs healed and my back starts to hurt from compensating at times. I'll be fine, though. Please, trust me. Both of you."

Nicole's eyes filled with tears, but she fought to keep them from spilling over. What this woman had overcome, and still, she was reminded of the bad.

"Nic, this is why I wanted you and Zach to leave before I told Jill anything. I didn't want you guys looking at me with pity. I don't want you to treat me differently." Amber looked at Nicole and Zach. She was fighting the tears. She knew this would happen if they found out the truth. Why hadn't she been more insistent on them leaving?

"Hey, there's no pity here. I've known you since we were five. I still remember in school Erik stealing and breaking my new blue crayon and you giving me yours to use. We go back too far for there to be pity," Nicole said.

"I agree with Nicole. Honestly, Amber. Why would I pity you if you don't pity me for what I've been through in the ten years you've known me? Or for what I wanted to do when Travis died? I love you. You're my best friend, and I just don't like to see you hurting. I will never pity you or think less of you for what you've gone through because you had no control over it," Zach said.

"Fine. How about this? I'll let you both know if it gets to be too much. How is that? Fair?"

"Fair," Nicole and Zach said in unison. They each were planning to be extra attentive to Amber to make sure she didn't put herself in pain.

"All right, dinner will be here in thirty minutes or less. Well, that's what they said at least." Jill entered the room followed by Erik. "Everyone, find a seat."

Nicole grabbed two large floor pillows and a comforter. "Wanna share?" Nicole asked Amber.

"Are you sure? I don't want to make things harder for you or cause you to have another episode."

"Telling you about things earlier actually helped me like Dr. Scott said it would. I'm hoping that maybe this will help me some more." Nicole offered a hesitant smile.

"Then who am I to say *no* to sharing with you?" Amber gave Nicole another lopsided smile.

Nicole placed the pillows and took a seat on Amber's left. Zach took a seat on the right. Amber felt safe, secure. Seeing Jeffrey earlier had caused her anxiety to spike and her fear and panic to become more pronounced. This, though, was nice and would help.

Just as everyone got situated, the doorbell rang, and Jill jumped up to get the pizzas. Heather went with her to help. Once they returned, Nicole put in the movie. They had decided on *Fantastic Beasts and Where to Find Them* for the first movie while they ate. Once the movie started, they passed the pizzas around, and everybody chose what they wanted.

"All right, now someone is going to have to explain this movie to me," Jill said, even though the movie was two minutes in.

"None of us has seen it," Nicole said. "Unless, Amber, have you two seen it?"

"Zach and I rented it twice, and we both fell asleep about fifteen minutes in," Amber said.

"I blame you for that." Zach chuckled.

"Me? What the hell did I do?"

"I seem to recall you had spiked the drinks both times."

"Oh, yeah, oops." Amber giggled and gave him a sheepish look as the others laughed.

"Where did you learn to mix drinks anyway?" Zach asked.

"Jill." Amber pointed at the woman seated across the room from them.

"Hey! We learned together." Jill stuck her tongue out at Amber.

Nicole was watching the interaction between Amber and Zach, and it pulled at something deep inside her. She missed that connection with Amber, she missed feeling the closeness. She had been back in her life for less than four hours, and Nicole could feel her insides craving more time and closeness with this amazing woman. *If she leaves in a couple of days, I don't know what I'll do. She's still my everything.*

As the movie progressed, Nicole and Amber had stretched out on the floor pillows. Shortly after lying down, they found themselves under the comforter that Nicole had snagged before anyone else could get it. What they didn't seem to notice were the quick glances that the others were giving them. Especially the looks from Zach.

Zach couldn't help but notice how relaxed Amber was when Nicole was close to her. He was seeing a side of her he had never seen before but always hoped to see. Amber was relaxed, happy, and in love. It was something that made him truly happy for her and angry at her father and brother for robbing Nicole and Amber of their serenity.

Jill, Erik, and Heather were also watching the two women, hoping that Amber could help Nicole begin to heal. And from what they learned about Amber and her past, they were hopeful that Nicole could help Amber heal, as well.

As the movie ended, Nicole called for a bathroom break. She bounced over the bodies littering the floor. Amber was right behind her followed by Erik and Heather. Jill and Zach took the opportunity to clean up the living room from dinner.

"Jill, I want to thank you for including me," Zach said while they were in the kitchen.

"Even though I didn't show it initially, Amber is very important to me and, well, us. And since you are important to Amber, we want to get to know you.

Amber was never one to choose her friends lightly or at least not without serious thought. Even when we were in grade school, she was very particular about *who* she was friends with."

"Well, I appreciate it. And you're right, Amber is very important to me. I'm wondering one thing, though."

"What's that?"

"When Nicole is around, Amber seems…"

"More at ease? More serene?" Jill finished.

"Yeah, exactly."

"They've always been like that. We all noticed it even before they were a couple. They always managed to calm each other down."

"I thought maybe I was just reading into things."

"No, you weren't."

With the cleanup completed and the bathroom breaks done, they settled back into their spots. Heather had turned the lights down, and they were ready for the next movie.

"All right, Amber's choice," Erik said. *"The Avengers* or *Justice League?"*

"There's no contest. They're both awesome, but it has to be *The Avengers.*"

"You just want to gawk over the redhead," Zach teased.

"What can I say? I have a weakness for hot redheads." Amber involuntarily glanced at Nicole and caused the room to erupt into laughter. Nicole was glad the lights were turned down so nobody could see her deep blush.

"There are so many comments that come to mind." Erik laughed.

"Shut it," Nicole said, mock glaring at Erik.

"Movie time." Amber was still blushing as her mind quickly came up with some of those comments that Erik was holding back.

As the movie started, Nicole and Amber got comfortable. They subconsciously moved closer to each other. Amber could smell the faint scent of strawberries coming from Nicole. She had missed that smell over the years.

"You okay?" Nicole whispered, noticing that Amber wasn't watching the movie.

"Yeah, I just never thought I'd be here with any of you. Most of all, I never thought I'd be near you again."

"I never thought I'd see or be near you again, either." A tear rolled down Nicole's face, and she quickly wiped it away.

"Let's watch the movie, but maybe tomorrow we can spend some time together," Amber said.

"Just us?"

"I'd like that a lot."

They went back to watching the movie, both smiling inside. When the movie ended, Erik announced he was exhausted and went to sleep on the couch in the den. Zach was shown to one of the guest bedrooms upstairs. Heather took the other guestroom.

"We're going to watch another movie. We'll crash down here." Nicole received a nod from Amber.

"Fine, but you at least have to use the air mattress," Jill said.

"I don't want to be any trouble. Really, it isn't necessary," Amber said.

"You aren't. Now shush and let me do this. Please?"

Jill went downstairs and got the air mattress and

pump, then she blew the mattress up in the living room and put some sheets and blankets on it for Amber while Nicole made a bed on the couch.

"All right, good night, you two," Jill said, smiling to herself as she started up the stairs.

"Night, Jill," they responded.

✦✦✦✦

"Hey, Nicole, would you still sit by me until we're ready to sleep? I really think it helps me," Amber said.

"I think it helps me, too." Nicole smiled.

They were sitting on the air mattress watching the movie, but as it got later and their eyes started to droop, they lay down and continued to try to watch the movie. Neither noticed that the other was falling asleep. As they slept, out of instinct, their bodies were drawn together, and Nicole ended up behind Amber, her body pressed against Amber's. One arm draped over Amber's waist, holding her close.

✦✦✦✦

"Girl, where the hell have you been?" David asked, anger oozing from his voice.

"I was out with my friends," seven-year-old Amber said as she cautiously entered the house.

"Did you get your chores done?"

"No, sir. I came home to do them now."

"Well, now is too late. I'm already home, and you know that chores are always to be done before I get home," he said, his voice rising.

"I'm sorry, sir, it won't happen again," Amber cried, fearing her father's anger.

"You're right, it won't happen again. We're going to have to punish you for this. After you complete your chores."

"Yes, sir," Amber said.

"Well, go get your chores done. And be quick about it," her father yelled.

Amber ran off and cleaned the bathroom. She scrubbed the toilet, the tub, the sink, the floors. She polished the mirror, making sure every smudge was removed. After that, she moved to the laundry and started her father and brother's clothes as they were not allowed to be washed with hers and her mother's. While the laundry was washing, she ironed her father's shirts and hung them with the proper spacing. Two of her fingers in between each hanger. She remembered the one time she didn't space them properly and her father told her he would use the belt to make sure she would never forget and be more careful going forward. Dread set in as she feared he would use the belt again today. The belt marks were always the hardest to hide. Amber heard the washer finish and moved the clothes to the dryer. She knew her mother would fold them after she got home. Then she remembered that she wasn't going to be home tonight, and Amber was going to have to fold them herself. She would have to remember the exact steps her mother had taught her in folding.

"Sir, I've finished my set chores and will complete Mama's folding once the clothes in the dryer are done. Is there anything else you want me to take care of?" Amber asked timidly, hoping for more to prolong her punishment.

"No, now it's time for your punishment. Afterward, you will still complete the folding," he said with a smile. "Jeffrey, come in here."

"Yes, Father?" Jeffrey said innocently. He loved it when his father yelled at his sister.

"Your sister needs to be punished for not doing her chores before I got home. I want you to watch and learn the proper way to punish her. It'll be both of our responsibility to make sure that Amber and your mother stay in line and know their place in this household."

"Yes, sir," Jeffrey said, eager to learn from his father to have the control and power.

David took out two wooden paddles and handed one to Jeffrey. Amber felt fear well up inside her. She barely survived her father hitting her with the paddle the last time. Now her brother and her father were going to use it on her. She was sure she was going to die from the pain.

"Amber, you know what you're supposed to do."

"Yes, sir." Amber moved over to the chair that had been placed in the middle of the room and leaned over the arm so that her butt was in the air and the back of her legs exposed.

"Now, son, you can't use all your strength, that will leave marks that we don't want to have to explain. Watch me, then I'm going to have you practice on the pillow I set up on the couch. The next time we have to punish your sister, you'll be prepared."

"Yes, sir," Jeffrey said, eagerly trying to contain his excitement.

Amber gritted her teeth and waited for the pain to start. Her father pulled back and swung and the paddle made contact. Amber felt an explosion of pain through her upper thighs and butt, but she didn't cry out. She had learned that by crying out she was made to endure more pain.

"Like this?" Jeffrey asked as he swung and hit the

pillow with all his might.

"No, like this," *her father said as he swung and hit her again.*

≈≈≈≈≈

Amber was whimpering in her sleep and twitching enough that she woke Nicole. As Nicole tried to figure out what it was that woke her, she heard Amber cry out softly once and then again.

Nicole reached over to touch Amber, to wake her from the nightmare she was having. Her hand connected with Amber's hip, and Amber cried out a loud *no* before she bolted from the bed and into the corner of the room. She was crouching in a ball, trying to make herself as small as she could. She kept repeating "no more, please no more" over and over, the shaking becoming greater with each second that passed.

Zach had heard Amber cry out and was out of bed and headed down the stairs in a heartbeat. When he got to the bottom of the stairs, he saw Amber cowering in the corner and Nicole moving toward her slowly, talking to her as she moved closer.

"Please, no more…please…oh, please no more." Amber was repeating her pleas as tears streamed down her face, and she looked frantically around the room, never seeing where she really was.

"Amber, it's me, Nicole. You're okay. You're safe in Jill's house." Nicole moved closer.

"What happened?" Zach asked, startling Nicole.

"I think she had a nightmare. When I woke up, she was twitching and whimpering in her sleep, and then I put my hand on her hip to wake her. That was when she cried out and ran and cowered in the corner."

"Crap, she hasn't had one of these in a while. And not one this bad," Zach said. "Keep talking to her. If your voice wasn't soothing, the whole house would know by now."

Nicole nodded and turned her attention back to Amber. "Amber? Look at me, sweetheart. It's me, Nicole," she started. Amber continued to cower, tears flowing faster and her breathing becoming more labored.

"Amber, honey, it's me, Zach. I know you're scared, I know you don't know what's real and what isn't. Please, come back to me. Nicole is here, and you're scaring her. Come back to us."

"No, Nicole has to be protected. If my father finds out about us, he'll kill her. He told me he would kill her slowly and painfully. He'll let Jeffrey help in her torture. I have to protect Nicole no matter what," Amber muttered, her gaze frantically shifting from side to side.

"Amber, it's me, Zach."

"Zach, you have to protect Nicole. Please, don't let them get her. I can't live in a world without her in it."

"Amber, honey. Look at me." Zach now stood next to Nicole about four feet from Amber.

What Nicole and Zach hadn't noticed was that the others had heard them and were standing at the edge of the room watching the events unfold. Heather's heart was breaking seeing Amber looking so frail and vulnerable. Erik was at a loss at what he was seeing and hearing. Jill's fists clenched as anger, and hatred rose within her.

"Amber, I'm right here. Zach is here with me," Nicole said softly.

"Nicole, no, you can't be here. You have to hide. If they see you here, they'll use the paddles again. It hurts so much when Daddy lets Jeffrey do the punishment. Please, don't let them catch you here." Amber started to move down the wall toward the stairs, crawling on her hands and knees, looking around frantically. Amber bolted across the room, hurdling the coffee table and air mattress to cower in another corner.

Everyone in the room felt their breath catch as she moved so feral like.

"Amber, baby, where's your mom?" Nicole asked, panic rising within her and starting to impact her voice.

"She had to go to Florida to sell Grandma and Grandpa's house. She's going to be gone for four whole days. Please don't tell her I was naughty and forgot to do my chores. I don't want her mad at me, too."

"Her mom went to Florida when we were about seven or eight to sell her parents' house," Nicole turned and told Zach.

They advanced another couple of steps and were now within a foot of the trembling woman. Nicole reached out and took Amber's hand. She held it tight as Amber tried to pull away. Her breathing got more labored. Erik was afraid she was going to pass out since she was borderline hyperventilating and hysterical.

"Amber, my love. Look at me. See me. Really see who I am. Come back to me, baby," Nicole cried as she pulled Amber's hand to her face and let her feel her cheek. Then Nicole kissed Amber's hand. Amber pulled away again and was trying to find a way to escape from where she was now trapped with the wall behind her and Zach and Nicole directly in front of her.

"Come on, Amber. Listen to my voice," Nicole

cried.

"Amber, come on...you've beaten this before, you can beat it again. Don't let them win. Don't let them take you away from us." Zach tried to keep his voice under control. "I'm right here with Nicole. She's safe, honey, but she needs you to come back to us. Please..."

"Nicole?" Amber asked in a timid childlike voice.

"Yeah, baby. I'm right here." Nicole took Amber's hand and pulled her forward into her arms and held her close as Amber started to cry again.

Zach finally noticed the others and motioned for them to leave the room so as not to frighten or embarrass Amber more. He then sat in the corner that Amber had been crouched in and pulled both women into his arms. He wanted them both to feel safe and secure.

"Zach," Amber whispered, looking up at him.

"Hey, pretty lady. Welcome back."

"Was it bad?"

"Yes, but we've dealt with much worse. We have Nicole to thank really. Had Nicole not been so close, this one had the potential of getting really bad."

"Nicole," Amber cried. "Oh, god. You weren't supposed to see that. You aren't supposed to know how damaged I am."

Nicole cupped Amber's face in her hands. "Oh, my sweet. We're all damaged in some way."

"No, not like this, not like me. I don't know how to fix me," Amber said, sniffling. She tried to pull away, but Nicole wouldn't let her. "They've tried and they can't. I'm so broken."

"Nicole is right, Amber, you aren't any more damaged than the rest of us. We still love you." Zach hugged her close.

"He's right, we love you no matter what." Nicole pulled Amber into a hug and held her tight.

"You came back to us. That right there shows that you aren't so broken that there isn't hope. You haven't had one of these in a couple of years. Do you remember the dream?" Zach said.

Amber nodded. She felt the pain from the dream radiate through her body.

"You were trying to protect me," Nicole said.

"I always try to protect you. I can't live in a world without you." Amber looked Nicole in the eyes.

"Are you ready for some water?" Zach asked, receiving a small nod from Amber.

Nicole helped Amber stand and move back to the air mattress as Zach went into the kitchen. Zach quickly returned with a large glass of water.

"Drink it all, please," he said to her in a soft and soothing tone before turning to Nicole. "We found that her nerves calm down quicker when she drinks a full glass of water. She gets dehydrated during those things."

"Do you have these often?" Nicole asked.

"When I first left, I had them almost nightly. I don't know how many times Zach found me cowering in a corner or hiding under a desk. Over the years, I've gotten better at controlling them. I would say now I get one every few months depending on my stress level."

"I'm sure being here with us and seeing Jeffrey was enough stress to trigger it. Did you ever try seeing someone about the trauma and nightmares?"

"Yeah, I've been seeing someone for a while. She told me the PTSD would be with me for the rest of my life. There will be periods where it isn't bad, but it'll only take one stressful day or situation to cause it to come back."

"Baby, I'm so sorry." Nicole wrapped her arms around Amber again, almost knocking the glass of water out of her hand.

"Amber, honey, finish the water," Zach said. Amber looked down and brought the glass back up to her lips and finished the remainder before handing the glass back to Zach. "Do you want some more?"

"No. Thank you both. I'm sorry for waking you and being such a burden," Amber said, casting her gaze down as she pulled away from them slightly. She was so ashamed at what had happened and that Nicole of all people had seen it.

"You are never a burden. We love you," Zach said.

"You can go back to bed, I'm okay now," Amber told Zach.

"I'll be here to look after her, and I know if I need you that you're just up the stairs." Nicole again wrapped her arms protectively around Amber and held her tight as she tried to pull away.

"All right, but only if you promise that you aren't trying to just get rid of me. Promise that you're really okay now." Zach saw Amber smile as she reached out and squeezed his hand.

"Good night." He leaned over and kissed the top of Amber's head and squeezed Nicole's hand.

Once he had gone to bed, Nicole coaxed Amber into lying back down on the air mattress with her, and Nicole pulled Amber into her arms and held her.

"You sleep, my sweet. You're safe in my arms. I won't let anything happen to you." Nicole kissed Amber's forehead and rubbed her back.

"Nicole, are you sure you want me laying close? What if I have another nightmare?"

"You won't. I told you I'm going to be right here holding you. I won't let anything happen to you."

"You need sleep, too," Amber said.

"I'll meet you in our dreams. Say at Old Miller's Pond for some secret skinny dipping?" Nicole caused Amber to smile and move even closer. After a while, Amber drifted to sleep. Silent tears fell down Nicole's face as she watched Amber sleep and before sleep overtook her, as well.

Chapter Six

Familiar Places

The next morning, Jill awoke early and quietly walked down the stairs. She found Nicole and Amber cuddled together on the air mattress, and she had a flashback of seeing them like that before Amber had left. She was amazed at how they always seemed to calm each other. Heather and Zach had heard her pass their room and came down quietly behind her. They stopped and smiled when they saw Nicole and Amber together. Jill motioned for them to follow her into the kitchen, so they didn't wake the two.

"Were they always that cute together?" Zach motioned back toward the living room.

"Yes," Heather and Jill said in unison as they smiled.

"I love what Amber has brought to my life, but I would give it all away for the opportunity to throttle her father and brother for what they did to her and for causing those two to separate. I've watched her sleep for the past ten years, and she has *never* looked so content. Especially after having a nightmare like she had last night."

"I have to say that Nicole hasn't looked that relaxed in years, either," Heather said, sitting at the island.

"Are we discussing coffee? Or could we be

discussing coffee?" Erik asked as he entered the kitchen.

"No, we were discussing how cute and relaxed Nicole and Amber look holding each other," Jill said.

"Oh, yeah. That was adorable when I walked past. So, coffee?"

"Erik, you know the moment that Nicole smells the coffee, she'll be up and in here, right?" Heather said.

※※※※

Slowly, Nicole started to wake up. As she became aware of her surroundings, she felt someone's breath on her neck, the pressure of an arm draped across her body, and the warmth of someone pressed against her. Her mind fluttered back to the events of the previous day. The hurt and excitement of seeing Amber. The anger of finding out why she left and her nightmare. Looking toward her, Nicole couldn't help but smile.

Amber started to stir, and when she opened her eyes, she saw Nicole's sparkling green eyes smiling at her. She had to think for a moment to make sure this wasn't a dream.

"Good morning," Nicole said softly.

"Good morning," Amber said shyly as she started to pull away from the embrace only to have her movement halted as Nicole held her tighter.

"Please, don't move yet," Nicole whispered. "I've spent so many years dreaming of holding you again that I selfishly don't want this to end."

"I've dreamt of waking up in your arms so often that I wasn't sure if I was still dreaming or not." Amber's cheeks turned pink.

"How are you doing after last night?"

"Physically or mentally?"

"Both." Nicole smiled at her.

"Physically, I'm still a little shaken. And mentally, I'm embarrassed, annoyed, and unsure about what was and wasn't real," Amber answered honestly. "Reality and fantasy mesh, and it takes a while for me to sort it all out in my head."

"Are the nightmares always like that? That intense. Or did I make it worse because I touched you before you were fully awake?" Nicole looked down.

"Last night, I think was worse because of seeing Jeffrey, reliving the events that caused me to leave, and the guilt of what happened to you because of me. I don't know if you touching me before I was fully awake had an impact on it. You can't blame yourself, you had no clue what was going on." Amber lifted Nicole's head to look in her eyes.

"Amber, you have nothing to feel guilty about." Nicole held eye contact.

"I feel as though I do. My mother was hurt because of my leaving. You were traumatized because of me. Not to mention just hurting you in general by leaving." Tears streamed out of Amber's eyes.

Pulling Amber into an embrace, Nicole placed a kiss on top of Amber's head. "You couldn't control what they did or the choices your father and brother made. I'll admit I was livid with you for leaving, but after hearing why you left…baby, I'm so amazed by your strength."

"Are you sure it wasn't just me being a coward?"

"I'm positive. Are you ready to get up and face everyone? I can hear people in the kitchen."

"Yes, to getting up. Does everyone know what happened last night?"

"Yeah, they all came downstairs, but Zach shooed them away before you could notice them."

"Well, now I'm scared to face them."

"You have nothing to be scared of. And even if you do, I'm going to be there with you."

"Why are you being so nice to me?"

"Because I now understand more of what happened and the fact that you couldn't control things. I don't agree with you not contacting us for ten years, but I do understand more." Nicole offered a smile.

"I don't deserve you being this nice." Amber shook her head.

"Yeah, you do," Nicole said sternly. "Now I smell coffee, and the one thing you should know hasn't changed is my intense need for coffee in the morning."

"It was never just in the morning that you felt the 'intense need' for coffee. That was sort of an all day, every day kind of thing." Amber laughed as Nicole stuck her tongue out at her.

"Brat," Nicole said.

They got up and folded the blankets, then headed into the kitchen.

§§§§§

Jill started the coffee brewing and then hunted through the cupboards to find something to make for breakfast.

"Morning," Nicole said as she and Amber entered the kitchen.

"I think that's a record." Erik laughed. "That took you all of two minutes from the time she hit the start button to get in here."

"Very funny," Nicole said as everyone else started to laugh.

"Morning, Amber." Zach went over and hugged her. "How are you doing?"

"I'm okay." Amber tried to hide behind her hair as he pulled away. "I'm sorry for waking everyone last night."

"Are you really okay?" Heather put a hand on Amber's shoulder.

"I'm still parsing out what was real and what was generated by my mind. I'm mostly embarrassed that you all had to see that."

"You have nothing to be embarrassed about. Hell, you've seen me scream like a little schoolgirl…hundreds…of…well, never mind that," Erik said as everyone chuckled.

"Well, now that Erik has embarrassed himself for the morning, let's talk breakfast. I was trying to figure out what to make, and I have no ideas." Jill looked at everyone gathered at the island.

"I have an idea if that's okay," Amber said.

"Hey, if you want to cook for us, I won't be the one stopping you," Jill said.

"Okay." Amber looked in a couple of spots and found the ingredients she needed. "You all can go sit in the living room and I'll make breakfast."

"I'll stay and help," Nicole said.

"I'm grabbing a coffee then. The hell if I'm leaving a full pot of coffee in here with Nicole," Heather said, and the others nodded and lined up to get their coffee.

"I'm not that bad." Nicole pretended to be offended.

"Well, I wouldn't trust Amber with a full coffeepot, either." Zach received a raised eyebrow from Amber. "What? You're the one that has your own coffeemaker at your painting station. And might I add, you rarely share."

"Get out of here before I decide not to share

breakfast with you, either, smartass." Amber pushed Zach toward the door. "Nic, you can go sit with the others, it shouldn't take too long."

"I've missed cooking with you. The last time we cooked together was for your birthday."

"I don't recall us getting a lot of cooking done that morning." Amber blushed.

"Well, eventually, we did…after we celebrated the morning of your birth. I've missed you, and I want to spend some time with you before you leave," Nicole admitted.

"Well then, my little helper, I need a bowl and a frying pan."

"Really? Little helper?"

"Well, I didn't think you'd appreciate being called my little fairy or pixie." Amber laughed, receiving a friendly glare from Nicole.

"I'll get you back at some point, Knight. You just wait! I promise you that." Nicole gestured with the frying pan.

"Sure, you will," Amber mocked as she took the pan.

The two went about making pancakes, eggs, and toast for the group. Once they had the breakfast made, Amber and Nicole set the table, and then called the others to eat.

"Jackpot," Zach said, smiling at Amber and Nicole.

"Wait, Amber pancakes…right?" Heather said.

"Yep," Amber said.

"Score!"

"I'm going to agree with both of them," Jill said.

Erik had just sat and started to fill his plate when he realized it was extremely quiet. He looked up and saw everyone staring at him.

"What? I do remember what Amber's food tastes like. I'm not going to waste time asking questions or talking when I can be putting the goodness into my belly," Erik said.

"You're a very smart man." Zach sat and started to fill his plate, as well, then passed the food to Heather.

"Nic, sit down and eat," Amber said.

"Aren't you going to eat?" Nicole asked, sitting at the table.

"I, er, um," Amber stammered.

"You, er, um, what?"

"I'm going to get the rest of the pancakes." Amber bolted out of the room.

"I'll be right back." Nicole rose and followed Amber into the kitchen.

When Amber got into the kitchen, she went over by the sink and turned the water on to wash the dishes. She hadn't heard Nicole come in and was surprised when she wrapped her arms around her waist from behind and rested her chin on Amber's shoulder.

"Wanna tell me what's going on inside that pretty head of yours?" Nicole asked.

"It's nothing, really. Just my messed-up mind." Amber didn't turn to face her.

"Are you too upset to eat?"

Amber shook her head.

"Are you still upset about the nightmare?"

Again, she received a head shake.

"Talk to me, Amber. Let me help."

"I'm nervous about my mom's letter." Amber looked down at the dishes in the sink.

"Hey, how about just you and I go to Old Miller's Pond? The tree we used to cuddle under is still there. We can go there, and you can read it and I'll be there for support."

"You'd do that for me?"

"Of course," Nicole said. "Now please, come eat something."

"Just a little, though," Amber said.

The two exited the kitchen and joined the others. Amber ate a couple of pieces of toast, hoping to calm her stomach. After they ate, Amber pulled Zach aside and told him about her plans with Nicole. She felt bad leaving him after he came all the way there to help her. He assured her it was fine and that Heather and Jill had offered to let him hang out with them. He also said she looked happy when she was with Nicole, and it was nice to see. That helped ease some of Amber's tensions.

Amber showered and got dressed. Nicole did the same, and they headed off to the pond.

≈≈≈≈

Zach finished getting ready. He decided he was going to spend the day with Heather since she had some interesting insight into Amber and seemed more willing to share. Jill wasn't as forthcoming. He wanted to know more about his best friend.

"Ready to head back to the hotel for a while?" Heather asked.

"I'm all set." Zach grabbed his and Amber's things.

They took Heather's car back to the hotel, and when they got there, Sidney was working at the front desk. She smiled at the two as they walked past her.

"Hey, Sid! How has the morning been so far?" Heather asked.

"Slow, honestly."

"Well, Sidney, this is Amber's friend from New York, Zach. Zach, this is my assistant manager, Sidney."

"It's nice to meet you," Zach said.

"You too."

"I hear you were hitting on Amber last night." Heather giggled.

"You could have clued me in about her and Nicole." Sidney smiled.

"I had no idea that Nicole was still going to be so territorial. I mean, it's been years since they've seen each other."

"I can understand the attraction, though." Zach laughed.

"Hey, I'm not the one that had a crush on her first." Sidney laughed as she pointed toward Heather.

"You weren't supposed to hear that." Heather blushed.

"Seriously? You?" Zach asked.

"Well, have you seen her? Hello!"

"Oh, I know. I've had to fend people off her for years. Men and women going after her."

"I believe that. I think we're going to have to save those stories for when I can watch Amber blush," Heather said.

They finished their conversation with Sidney and went back into Heather's office.

※ ※ ※ ※

After a short walk, Nicole and Amber arrived at the pond and sat under their favorite tree.

"It's still so pretty here," Amber said.

"Yeah, it's like time stood still."

"Do you come out here often?"

"After you first left, I did. It was a place that made me feel like I was closer to you. Over the years, it started to frustrate me and make me miss you more, so

I haven't been here in a couple of years."

"I'm so sorry I hurt you," Amber said, looking into Nicole's eyes.

"I understand why you did what you did." Nicole put her hand on Amber's, feeling their fingers thread together as they always had before.

"It doesn't excuse what I did."

"I know, but we don't have to talk about that stuff now. I would rather enjoy the time together." Nicole smiled at her.

"I'd like that."

Nicole and Amber walked out onto the pier and sat at the end of it, and Amber gazed over the water remembering earlier times.

"Last one in has to buy the pizza tonight," Jill called as they changed into their swimsuits.

As Amber ripped her T-shirt and shorts off, she ran down the pier and dove into the pond as Nicole gawked at the sleek black one-piece Amber was wearing.

"Nic, you keep drooling, and you're going to be the last one in," Jill said as she ran past.

Nicole quickly disrobed and ran past Erik, who was trying to get his pants off without his shorts coming down.

Nicole dove into the water and came up next to Amber.

"Hey, sexy," Amber said as she pulled her closer.

"Hey, yourself." Nicole leaned in and kissed her softly.

"Woohoo, girl-on-girl action," Erik called as he finally made it to the end of the pier.

"Erik, don't be a pig," Jill said.

"Fine, but you need to stop taunting me." He

pouted.

"Erik, we're seventeen and in love, cut us some slack." Amber kissed Nicole again before releasing her.

The group played Marco Polo for a while and swam before they got tired of it and decided to lay out in the sun to dry off. Nicole and Amber put their towels next to each other while Jill and Erik put theirs across from them.

"So, what do you guys want to do tonight?" Amber asked.

"Well, it's the Fourth of July, so we could go up on top of the hill and watch the fireworks," Nicole suggested.

"I see fireworks every time you kiss me." Amber leaned over and kissed Nicole quickly.

"That was really cheesy, Amber. I expect something like that from Erik, not you."

"Hey," Erik said.

"Sorry. I know one thing for tonight, Erik is going to provide dinner." Jill laughed.

"I think you all cheated since two out of the three of you are in bikinis!"

"We did not." Nicole smiled at how good Amber looked in her suit.

Later that night, the group went to the top of the nearby hill, ate pizza, and watched the fireworks. Nicole and Amber were cuddled together and felt as though they didn't have a care in the world.

"What are you thinking about?" Nicole noticed a distant smile on Amber's face.

"That last Fourth of July when we were all here together and then we went up the hill to watch the fireworks. We were so happy. How can things go from so right to so wrong so quickly?"

"I don't know, they just do."

"It wasn't fair." Amber got up from the edge of the pier and walked toward the tree, their tree.

"Do you want to talk for a while or read your mom's letter?" Nicole asked, following Amber.

"Will you stay close while I read it?" Amber asked nervously.

"Of course I will." Nicole leaned against the tree and then motioned for Amber to sit between her legs. Once Amber was comfortable, Nicole wrapped her arms around Amber's waist and rested her head on Amber's shoulder. "Is this okay?"

"Perfect," Amber said. "You can read along if you want."

"No, this is your letter to read. If you want to share it afterward, then I'll be honored to read it."

Amber sat back, opened the envelope, took a deep breath, and read.

To my beautiful precious daughter,

I want you to know that I have loved you since the day I first felt I was pregnant with you. I wish I could have protected you better and saved you from all the pain you had to endure. I wasn't strong enough. It took me losing you to really see how bad things were. To admit honestly how bad things were. I have missed you so much over the years, baby girl. I have some things I want to say. I wish I could have done this in person, but I respect you and the reasoning for distancing yourself from us and this place.

Most important, and first and foremost, I love you! I always have, and I always will. I knew for weeks before I got it confirmed from the doctor that I was pregnant with you. I knew you were a girl, and I was so excited.

You have to know that you were, are, and will always be the best thing that came out of my life with that man. You have grown into such a beautiful woman. I know this is true because of the beautiful woman you were when you left.

Since you're reading this, that means you came back. I'm hoping that Nicole is with you while you're reading this. She has been such an amazing help to me over the past few years. She helped me survive after you left, and she has helped me while I've been sick. Oh, my darling, you were right when you told me that she was an angel put on earth. I wish for you both to find happiness, and I'm secretly hoping that you will somehow find your way back to each other and find the happiness together.

Amber, I love you so much and I will be watching over you always. Please know that loving someone doesn't have to be a bad experience, you just have to make sure you don't compromise yourself. I'm getting really tired. I don't have the strength and stamina to do a lot now. I think what I really want you to know is that I love you and admire you for being able to leave and not come back.

I love you with all my heart and soul.
Mama

As Amber finished the letter, tears were streaming down her face. Nicole had pulled her tighter to her body.

"Oh, Mama, I love you, too," Amber cried. "I've missed you so much!"

They sat there while Amber grieved for the loss of her mother, for the loss of so much.

"She talked about you often." Nicole placed a kiss on the side of Amber's head. "When she was going through the cancer treatments, she would hallucinate and apologize to you over and over. It broke my heart to hear her. I don't know what she said in the letter, but you have to believe that you were the most precious piece of her life."

"Thank you for taking care of her and for loving her."

"It was my pleasure. It allowed me to hold on to you for a while longer. I never stopped loving you or missing you," Nicole admitted.

"I love you, too." Amber turned her head and pressed her lips to Nicole's. She had caught Nicole by surprise, but it only took a heartbeat for Nicole to respond to the kiss.

The kiss was slow, passion-filled, and quickly took their breath away. Amber turned her body slightly and threaded her hand into the back of Nicole's hair. A groan from Nicole told Amber that Nicole was feeling this just as deeply as she was. As they broke the kiss, Nicole leaned her forehead against Amber's.

"Wow, that was...amazing," Nicole said.

"I agree." Amber smiled at Nicole and then leaned forward and kissed her again.

They sat there, Nicole holding Amber, gently placing kisses into her hair. They were enjoying the feeling of being close, of being someplace that had so many memories for them. Amber was still processing all that her mother's letter had to say.

"Nic," Amber said, breaking the silence.

"Mm-hmm?"

"Do you want to read the letter?"

"That's your letter. Your mom wrote that for you."

"I know, and now I'm asking if you, someone

deeply important to both of us, would like to read it." Amber turned in Nicole's arms so she could look at her.

"Are you sure?"

"I've been sitting here thinking about the letter, all that you said happened. I think it's fitting that you read it. You're the only person I would feel right sharing it with."

"I...erm...I would like to if you're sure."

"Okay, but you have to switch spots with me, so I can hold you while you read it. I know it's going to have as much and maybe more meaning at times for you than it did for me."

Nicole nodded, and they traded spots. Amber leaned against the tree, and Nicole leaned against Amber. Nicole felt Amber wrap her arms around her waist and pull her close. When they were finally situated, Nicole opened the letter and read the words of the woman she loved as her own mother. A woman who had brought into the world the most important and cherished person Nicole could ever know. Tears rolled down her face as she neared the end. When she finished, she folded the letter and handed it to Amber. Nicole curled into a ball in Amber's arms, and they cried together.

As the sun had moved in the sky, they knew it was now well after noon, and they needed to get back to the hotel. Nicole stood and reached down to help Amber up. Amber wrapped her arms around Nicole's waist and felt Nicole wrap her arms around Amber's neck. Amber leaned forward and kissed her. The kiss was gentle, conveying love, but not demanding.

"We should get back," Amber said as they broke the kiss.

"Thank you for coming here today with me and for sharing your letter with me. I know it's deeply personal."

"Thank you for sitting with me, holding me, and just being here for support."

Nicole took Amber's hand, and the two left Old Miller's Pond to go back to the hotel. They walked in silence, both processing the letter, the kisses, just being together, and what they wanted for the future.

※ ※ ※ ※

Heather and Zach were sitting in her office. Heather was going through some paperwork, and Zach was on his tablet looking at various items from work.

"So, you've known Amber since she moved to New York?" Heather broke the silence.

"Pretty much. I met her after she had been in town for a couple of weeks."

"How'd you meet her?"

"I had just started at the gallery, and she was looking at one of the paintings I had replicated and, well, how did you put it…'have you seen her?' I went over to talk to her. I asked if she liked the artist, and she said she wouldn't know because this was a fake. I started to laugh and told her I knew because I was the one that had painted it. She looked at me like I had kicked her kitten or something. She was horrified. I explained how we get permission to duplicate the art. She then told me it was a good replica. I told her it couldn't have been too good if she could tell it was a fake. She showed me where my flaw was. It was a simple brushstroke that I had done wrong. The curator, Lucinda, overheard us talking and asked Amber if she could paint as well as she could assess paintings. When

Amber said she could, Lucinda offered her a job on the spot."

"Seriously? Only Amber could be at an art gallery and get hit on and a job all in one afternoon." Heather laughed. After thinking about it for a moment, Zach joined in the laughter.

Sidney knocked on the door. Hearing the laughter, she peeked her head in.

"Okay, you two are having way too much fun in here to actually be working," she said.

"No, Zach just told me how he met Amber," Heather said.

"Does she have some special power that draws people to her?" Sidney joked.

"It's her kindness and gentleness," Zach said, smiling.

"Even after everything she's been through," Heather mumbled loud enough for only Zach to hear. "So, what's up?"

"Um, well, Lori is here…" Sidney started.

"One of these days, you're going to have to learn how to deal with her," Heather said.

"I know, but can today not be that day?"

"Fine, I'll be out in a minute."

Sidney smiled and went to tell Lori that Heather would be right out.

"Who's Lori?" Zach asked.

"Erik's ex-fiancée and a total pain in the ass when she chooses."

"So, can I come and watch a master handle someone so destructive?"

"Well, I could call Jill, but I was thinking of handling it myself," Heather joked as she headed for the front desk. Zach was right behind her.

Chapter Seven

Holding on to the Past

"Hey, Erik! What brings you by?" Jill asked as he entered the police station.

"I just wanted to talk to you about something quick if you have a moment."

"Okay, come into my office," Jill said. Once they entered, she closed the door and sat behind the desk, putting her feet up on it.

"I'm worried about Nicole," he blurted out.

"Worried? Why?" Jill sat up and intently listened to what Erik had to say.

"I'm afraid she's going to get her hopes up that Amber is going to stay or that they can have a relationship."

"Amber has only been back maybe twenty-four hours, and after hearing *why* she left, I don't think Nicole is going to read more into it."

"She can't survive another heartbreak from Amber," Erik said.

"I know that, but let's see where they stand after their time out at the pond, then we can decide what to do," Jill said.

"Were you not there this morning to see how close and cuddly they were being?"

"I was, but I don't think they're just going to jump back into things as if the past ten years have been erased."

"I just don't want Nicole being hurt anymore."

"Nobody does. I'm certain that Amber feels the same way."

"I hope you're right," Erik said. "I'm glad to have Amber back here and to get to know who she is now. I just need to look out for Nicole. She's still really fragile."

"I know, Erik. I know."

※ ※ ※ ※

"Do you want me to come to the hotel with you?" Nicole asked as she and Amber walked back from the pond holding hands.

"Of course I do." Amber offered a soft smile.

"I just don't want to crowd you."

"If you start to crowd me, I'll let you know." Amber squeezed Nicole's hand as they neared the edge of town.

"When do you go back to New York?"

"Day after tomorrow. I believe Zach goes back tomorrow. The gallery can't be down two replicators for too long."

"That must be such an amazing job," Nicole said.

"Why do you think that?"

"Hello, you're copying original masterpieces."

"I am, but it's work. Yeah, being close to a masterpiece is like nothing else. Yet when I'm replicating it, I just see the brushstrokes and what I need to get it done and accurately."

"Still, from here, it sounds amazing."

"It was very intimidating at first. Although by doing the replicating, it has really helped me improve my painting skills."

"You always had more talent than you gave yourself credit for." Nicole smiled.

"And you were always biased." Amber offered a smile that melted Nicole's heart.

"And honest," Nicole said as they neared the hotel.

≈≈≈≈

"Lori." Heather came around the corner and walked up to the desk.

"Well, it's about ti—" Lori stopped when she saw Zach come up behind Heather. "Hi, I'm Lori Jenkins. And you are?"

"He's not here for you." Heather blocked Lori's hand that was extended toward Zach.

"Well, maybe not, but there's no reason to be rude to such an amazing specimen of manly goodness."

"I'm Zach," he said, shaking Lori's hand. "I'm just visiting. The…um…person I'm with just stepped out, so I'm shadowing Heather."

"Well, that's pretty rude to ditch you and leave you with Junior Woods here." Lori scoffed.

"Hey," Heather said, wishing that Lori would stop talking.

"Oh, it wasn't meant as anything bad. Some people can be so sensitive."

"And some people can be so rude." Heather looked directly at Lori. "What brings you by the hotel today?"

"Well, we're having several big-wigs visiting from the corporate office of the tire factory, and I was hoping to get a block of suites reserved," Lori said, then turned to Zach. "I'm the director of finance for the tire factory. And what do you do?"

"Quit flirting with him." Heather growled, pulling up the reservation calendar in the computer.

"Well, I don't see a wedding ring on his finger, and we all know that I'm single, no thanks to Erik."

"Heather is right, I'll be leaving for New York tomorrow, so the flirting isn't necessary," Zach said.

"Pity! What does New York have that I can't give you?" Lori moved closer to Zach.

"When do you need the block, how many, and for how long?" Heather asked, hearing a giggle from Sidney's direction.

"Right. I'll need ten suites for eight days starting the first of next month."

"I can guarantee that we can do that. Thank you for giving us ample advanced notice this time," Heather said as she blocked off the rooms.

"Yeah, it wasn't my fault you wouldn't move those people around last time."

"I realize it wasn't, but I'm still thanking you for the advanced notice. I blocked the suites for you, so we're all set."

"Thank you," Lori said. "So, handsome, do you have plans tonight? Your last night in our little town."

"He does," Nicole said as she and Amber came in the front door.

Sidney, Heather, and Zach noticed they were holding hands but quickly dropped them when Nicole addressed Lori.

"So, you know our little friend here, Nicole?" Lori asked.

"Yes, I do."

"Oh, don't tell me the one you're with is that hot

little number standing next to Nicole."

"I am," Zach said, offering Nicole and Amber a pleading look.

"Hi, sweetie, sorry we were gone so long." Amber walked over and hugged Zach.

"It's okay. I know how time flies when you're spending time with old friends." Zach kept his arm around Amber and held her close.

"You really should get a ring on his finger before someone like me steals him away." Lori turned to look directly at Amber.

"It has been a topic of discussion hasn't it, sweetie?" Amber smiled lovingly up at Zach as he hugged her even closer. Nicole, Heather, and Sidney were trying to contain their laughter.

"Well, Heather, do you need anything else from me for that block reservation?"

"No, we're good." Heather hoped the woman would leave, she wasn't sure how much more Lori she could take.

"Fine, it was nice meeting you, handsome. If you ever get bored with blondie here, give me a call." Lori handed Zach her card before turning and leaving.

Zach just stood there in disbelief.

"Who the hell was that?" Amber asked after Lori had left as she extricated herself from Zach's tight hold.

"That's Lori…Erik's ex-fiancée." Nicole giggled.

"She's what?" Amber asked in surprise.

Nicole was about to explain the force known as Lori when Erik and Jill walked in.

"Ah, perfect timing, you two." Nicole looked directly at Erik.

"That's never a good greeting," Jill said as she and Erik slowly backed away.

"Freeze, Woods. You too, Harrison," Amber said, eager to find out more about Lori.

"What did we do?" Erik asked nervously.

"Oh, you just missed Lori." Heather giggled. At the woman's name, Erik and Jill gave a full-body shiver.

"That sounds like perfect timing if we missed her." Erik sat on a chair in the lobby area near the others.

Amber moved from her seat between Nicole and Zach to sit on the arm of Erik's chair in hopes of making it so he couldn't run away. "Yeah, but now you get to explain her to *me*!"

"Crap!" Erik exclaimed.

"So, ex-fiancée, huh?" Amber teased as she leaned back and put her head on his shoulder.

"Yeah, she moved here about two years after you left. We dated for a couple of years, I proposed, she said yes…"

"He got cold feet and wussed out on the day of the rehearsal," Jill added, picking up where Erik had trailed off.

"Seriously?" Amber asked.

"Yes, not one of my finer moments. It was still better than doing it the day of the wedding," he said, looking down. "What was she doing here?"

"She came to reserve some rooms and hit on Zach." Heather laughed as Zach glared at her and shook his head, turning a bright shade of red.

"How bad was she?" Erik asked, mortified.

"Oh, yeah, it was full-blown Lori on the prowl," Heather said.

"Man, I am *so* very sorry."

"We all are," Nicole said. "Amber and I walked in to see some of it. Then Amber became the doting and loving girlfriend to tame her a bit, and she still gave him her card and told him to call her if he ever got bored with Amber."

"Oh, god." Erik blushed. He was really wishing Amber would move so he could bolt out of there. Lori Jenkins was not a subject he wanted to discuss.

"Yeah, Erik, it wasn't cool of your ex to hit on my honey," Amber teased.

"I'm going to guess that she didn't take the breakup well," Zach said.

"Not in the slightest," Jill said. "I had to put Erik in protective custody for a few days. She was on a mission to make him pay. She wanted vengeance."

"So, what stopped her?" Amber asked.

"She found a new guy," Nicole deadpanned and held her hand out for Amber to return to sitting next to her.

Amber moved back over to sit by Nicole and Zach. Everyone noted how close Amber and Nicole were sitting.

"I have an idea." Nicole changed the subject after seeing how uncomfortable Erik was.

"What's that?" Amber asked.

"Why don't we get Chinese and all go back to my place and hang out?"

"I'm in." Amber smiled at the idea of seeing Nicole's house and what her life had become.

"If Amber's in, I'm in." Zach wanted to get to know Nicole better. Someone who could bring out so much joy in Amber was someone he needed to know more about.

"I'm in," Jill said. "Heather?"

"Yep, I just need to finish a couple of things here and then I can head over. Why don't you place the order and I'll pick it up on my way?"

"Sounds good. Um, Amber, can I talk to you for a minute?" Nicole asked nervously.

"Sure, sweetie, why don't you come up to my room with me while I put the letter away?"

"Okay." They headed to the elevator and up to Amber's room.

"I wonder what that's about," Jill said.

"I don't know, but does everyone remember that Amber's mom lived at Nicole's...the exact same house where we're going tonight, the same house that Nicole was terrorized in?" Erik looked at the group.

"What?" Zach was shocked by this fact. "I didn't realize this was the same house. Do you think that Amber can handle being there? I won't let anything upset her like yesterday."

"Down, boy." Jill put a hand on Zach's arm. "I know Amber can handle it. Part of it may be hard, but I think it'll be good for her and Nic."

"If you're sure," Zach said warily.

"If she starts to have problems, we'll come back here or go to my place," Jill reassured.

৵৵৶৶

Amber unlocked her room and entered with Nicole following nervously behind her.

"What's going on?" Amber asked as they walked over and sat on the edge of the platform bed.

"I...um...wanted to remind you that your mom lived with me at my place for the last several years of her life. Are you okay with being there? It isn't going to be too difficult, is it?"

"Oh, I hadn't thought about that. I think I'll be

okay. If not, you'll be there to help me," Amber said with a smile, hoping she was strong enough to handle this.

"Of course I'll be wherever you want me. Do you want to bring some clothes to stay over? I mean, if it gets late or something. Not that I'm pushing you or expecting anything, I just, I don't know. I had such a good time today, and I'm afraid that if the day ends, you'll be gone. And I know we have separate lives now, but I don't know…I'm babbling, and I can't stop myself."

"Nic, relax, please." Amber took Nicole's hand in her own. "I would like to bring some clothes and stay over. Not if it gets too late, but just plan that I'll stay over. I had a great time today, too. Spending time with you is incredible and not something I thought would ever happen again."

"You really want to stay?" Nicole asked.

"Yeah, I really want to stay. I want to spend as much time as I can with you. Zach goes back to New York tomorrow. I don't go back until the following night."

"Oh, can I sign that form for you now? I don't want to forget later," Nicole said.

"Sure." Amber got up, grabbed the form off the desk and a pen, and handed them to Nicole. "The photo of you is the one Lucinda likes best."

"Well, we all know that I'm incredibly photogenic." Nicole laughed, and Amber joined in.

After signing the release form, Amber put it in her bag, then packed a few items to take to Nicole's for the night. They then headed back downstairs to meet with the others.

"I hope they hurry up, I'm starving," Jill said.

"Well, we could order now, and then as soon as they get down here, leave. I'm sure Zach knows what Amber likes," Erik suggested.

"That's a great idea. I know what Nicole will want. Zach?"

"Amber likes General Tso chicken, extra spicy. I like the steamed dumplings."

"I want the same thing as Amber," Erik said.

"I'll take the beef and broccoli." Heather left them and went to her office to finish her work for the day.

"All right then, I'll call this in, and as soon as those two get down here, we can leave," Jill said. Just as she finished her sentence, she heard the elevator ding, and they saw Nicole and Amber.

"Sorry that took so long," Amber said.

"That's fine. I'm going to call in the order. Amber, Zach said you would want General Tso. Is that what you want?"

"Yep! Extra spicy."

"Nic, the usual?"

"Yeah, that would be great."

"Great, I'll call this in, and we can head out." Jill pulled out her cellphone and called in their order. Once she hung up, she told Heather they were leaving, and the order would be ready for pickup in twenty minutes.

The group left for Nicole's place. Amber walked between Nicole and Zach, unaware that Lori was watching them. Lori just wasn't sure that the blonde was what was best for that dashing man, and she could sense that there was more to the story of the mysterious woman.

The group arrived at Nicole's, and once she unlocked the door, everyone stood back to let Nicole and Amber enter first as this was going to affect them both emotionally on a deep level.

"You have a nice place," Amber said as she entered.

"Thanks," Nicole said, suddenly feeling overwhelmed by emotion and flooded with memories.

They moved farther inside, and the others entered, as well, and moved to the living room off to the left while Nicole and Amber stayed in the entry. Nicole closed the door and then locked the three locks on the door. Amber froze, and tears welled in her eyes and then streamed down her face.

"Oh, goddess," she whispered as she realized that even after all these years, Nicole was still tormented by what *her* father had done. She backed up several steps until she bumped into a wall, and then slid down the wall, covering her face with her hands and crying softly.

"Amber." Zach tried to make his way to her, but he was stopped by Jill and Erik.

"Let them process this," Erik whispered as he watched Nicole turn and see Amber sitting on the ground.

"Amber? Baby?" Nicole said with a shaky voice. When Amber didn't look up, Nicole knew she was going to need more than words. Nicole moved over and knelt in front of Amber, placing a kiss on top of her head.

"I am so sorry. I am so sorry for what he did. It was my fault, it *is* my fault that you have to live like this," Amber cried into her knees. She couldn't make herself look up into those amazing emerald eyes. She felt so ashamed.

Everyone in the living room felt their heart break when they heard Amber's words. Zach crumpled into a chair hurting for his friend, wanting to help her but knowing that Erik was right. Nicole and Amber needed to help each other through this.

"Amber, no! It is not your fault. Look at me." Nicole waited until she saw Amber look up at her. "There's my beautiful girl. Baby, you did not cause this. You weren't the one that made him do this. Your leaving set your mother free from that bastard. You saved her, and you saved yourself."

"Yes, I saved myself, but I didn't think of what would happen to the rest of you."

"You said you didn't tell us what was going on because he threatened us. You did think of us when you left. As for your mother, you saved her. She left him. She had the strength to do it because of you, baby. Don't you see that?"

"You were the one that took care of her. You were the one that gave her strength, I just left."

"Come here." Nicole pulled Amber into her arms as she slid back a couple of feet to lean against another wall. "She had the strength to leave because she saw you succeed in leaving."

"You have three locks on your door because he came here and caused one to fail…you live with that fear. I should have stayed and protected you."

"Had you stayed, you would have died," Jill finally interjected.

"Maybe, but she wouldn't be living in fear because of him." Amber looked Jill in the eyes.

"I'd rather be traumatized and have you alive

than the other way around," Nicole whispered. "This will continue to get better over time...you being gone would be a permanent empty hole in my heart and soul that wouldn't ever be able to be filled or repaired."

"I'm so sorry."

"I know you are, baby, but you have no reason to be." Nicole kissed the side of Amber's head as she squeezed her closer.

"Amber, do you want to stay here, or do you want to go back to my house?" Jill asked.

"I want to stay here, I-I need to face it."

"Would you like to see your mom's room while you're here?" Nicole received a questioning look from Amber.

"I've kept it the way she had it in hopes that you would come, and I could show you it," Nicole admitted.

"I would love to." Amber took a deep breath to calm herself and her tears. "Can we do it now?"

"Jill, you know where everything is, just help yourself to whatever. We're going to...um...go..."

"We heard. Take your time, and call if you need us," Jill said.

"Amber, are you sure about this?" Zach asked, kneeling next to the two women.

"I'll be okay. Stay here and hang with the others, but be ready to come if I can't handle it."

"You know I'm always here for you." Zach rubbed a hand on her back and offered Nicole a smile to show his support for her.

The two women rose, and while holding on to each other, they ascended the stairs and moved toward the room Nicole had kept for Amber to see.

Sidney was finishing up at the front desk and filling in Shawn, the night desk manager, on how the day had been when Heather came out of her office.

"Hey." Shawn nodded to Heather.

"Hi, Shawn, how are you doing tonight?"

"Good. Seems like it was a good day here," he said.

"Pretty slow actually," Sidney said. "You're all caught up, so if you have no questions, I'm going to head out."

"Have a great night," Shawn said as Sidney went in back to get her stuff.

"I have to get going, as well. If you have any problems, you know how to reach me," Heather said.

"I do, and I won't bother you." Shawn laughed as he waved to her and Sidney, who had just exited the back area and was now walking out with Heather.

"So, big plans tonight?" Sidney asked.

"Nah, I've had enough excitement with Lori showing up today." Heather laughed.

"She is a handful, isn't she? Heather, can I ask you something before you head off?"

"Sure, what's up?" Heather pulled them over to a nearby bench.

"What's the deal with Nicole and Amber?"

"They dated for a couple of years before Amber left. This is the first time she's been back in ten years. I don't know what's going on now, though. Why do you ask?"

"Well, the whole time I've known Nicole, she's been single and unavailable, and I just wondered if that was because of Amber. They seem perfect for each other."

"They are. I think Jill used to call them soul mates."

"That seems to describe it pretty well. They just fit together. I feel bad for hitting on Amber when she first got here now that I've seen her and Nicole together."

"Don't feel bad. You didn't know, and you wouldn't have believed their connection had you not seen it."

"True, it is intense." Sidney shook her head.

"This is nothing like it was ten years ago. This is weak compared to that."

"That's a scary thought. I should let you get going. I was just curious."

"No problem. I'll see you tomorrow." Heather got up and waved to Sidney.

Sidney sat there for a minute and then headed to her apartment above the clothing store nearby.

Heather headed to the Chinese restaurant and got their order and drove to Nicole's house.

Chapter Eight

Times Gone By

As they neared the room, Nicole could feel Amber tense. "Are you sure about this? We don't have to do this now if you aren't ready," Nicole said as they stood at the top of the stairs.

"I don't know, but I really feel like I need to see it." Amber looked toward Nicole.

Nicole stopped them outside the room, pulling Amber into a hug and holding her close. Amber wrapped her arms around Nicole, and they enjoyed the closeness for a bit. As they started to pull away, Amber smiled at Nicole.

"What's that smile for?"

"Thank you for doing this. For allowing me the opportunity to see where my mom spent the last years of her life."

"It was a pleasure having her here. She was a mother to me, too, more than my mother ever was," Nicole said honestly, moving toward the door.

They entered the room. It wasn't big, but it had an attached bathroom. There were two large windows with chairs in front of them. Amber could picture her mom sitting in them basking in the sunlight. A four-poster queen-sized bed had a nightstand on each side and a hope chest at the foot of it. The room colors were country themed, which Amber knew her mother loved, and the pictures on the wall and on the dresser were of Amber, Nicole, her mom, and some of them together. Amber picked one up, trying to figure out where and when it was taken. She recognized the location but couldn't place it.

"That was one that I took when I went to New York on business," Nicole said proudly.

"You took this?" Amber turned to face Nicole, who was leaning against the doorjamb.

"Where was this taken? I've seen it, I recognize it, but I can't place it."

"Let me see." Nicole stood next to Amber and looked at the picture. "That was taken at the Brooklyn Children's Museum."

"I've been there once. Zach, Lucinda, and I went there to help with an art program for kids. I was teaching seven- and eight-year-olds how to use painting and sculpting to express their feelings."

"That's amazing. It must have been so rewarding to work with the kids."

"Well, it was, thanks to one of the kids in the program. She came from a past resembling mine, only it was her mom who was the destructive force and her dad took her away from the abuse. We connected, and she was able to get out a lot of emotion in that short two-hour class. She smiled when she showed her dad her painting, and he came up to me afterward and told me it was the first time since they had left several months prior that she had genuinely smiled."

They arrived at the museum just before it opened and set up their display and the various art stations. Lucinda supervised mostly while Amber and Zach did the work. Once they were set up, they stood off to the side while the kids were brought into the large room.

"Hello, everyone. My name's Lucinda, and I'm a gallery curator. Today, we're here to show you how to use art as a form of expression."

"What does that mean?" one of the kids in the front row asked.

"That means we're going to teach you how to put all that stuff that you're holding inside into something artistic. Maybe you want to paint something to get out the frustration of getting a C on that last test, though you studied hard for it, or maybe you want to sculpt that monster from your dream in clay and then you can smash it so it doesn't come back into your dream. I brought two of my favorite artists from my gallery to help. Amber is a fantastic painter, and Zach is a good painter and sculptor. Each of you will get a chance to choose what you want to try, and if you get bored or don't like the station, you can move and try something different. I'll help anyone who wants to draw."

With the speech over, they allowed the kids to choose a station. Zach had several kids come over to his station and start to build with clay. Lucinda had a couple of kids who she helped with drawing, and Amber had three kids who were interested in painting.

"Hi, I'm Amber," she said, kneeling so that she was at their level. "Do any of you paint on a regular basis now?" Amber saw one hand go up. "Well, then you're going to have to be my helper if anyone needs help." The little boy smiled back at her as if she had just given him the biggest cookie ever.

"Do you do a lot of painting?" one of the girls asked.

"I do. Painting is what helps me calm down and get out all that bad stuff I've been holding inside."

"What kind of stuff?" the little boy asked.

"Like when I have a bad day at work or when someone says or does something that hurts my feelings. When I sit down to paint, I forget all that and focus on what I love and how happy it makes me. Why don't we get you something to cover your clothes, so they don't get covered in paint and then we can get started."

Amber and the kids put on their smocks and moved over to where she had placed four canvases. Each kid picked a canvas. Amber brought them each a set of paints and brushes.

"All right, why don't you each close your eyes and picture something that you want to paint, something that will make you happy and make you forget the bad stuff? Once you have that picture in your mind, move over to your canvas and try to paint it. I'll be here to help if you need it."

The kids closed their eyes and thought for a minute before they got started. Amber walked between them, looking at their pictures and asking questions.

"What are you painting?" Amber asked one of the two girls.

"I'm painting my mommy in her flower garden. She's always smiling and happy when she's out there, and she looks so pretty. I just don't know how to paint her."

"Well, would you like some help?"

"Yes, please," the brown-haired girl said.

Amber took a brush, and after finding out the mother's hair and eye color, she painted her into the girl's picture for her.

"Wow, that looks like her." The girl giggled and went on painting more flowers.

"What are you painting?" Amber asked the only

boy in the group.

"I'm painting my soccer game where I scored the winning goal." He smiled. "Do you know how to make a soccer ball?"

Amber nodded and painted one for him and then moved on to the littlest girl.

"Hi, what are you painting?" Amber knelt next to the redhead who reminded her of a young Nicole.

The girl just looked at Amber; the fear in her eyes broke Amber's heart. She knew how this girl felt, and she was going to do whatever she could to help her.

"When I was little, my daddy wasn't very happy with me, and he used to yell a lot. I would always feel so sad for upsetting him. I would go to my room and paint pictures of what he looked like yelling at me to get it out of my mind. Do you have someone who does stuff that makes you unhappy?" she asked, receiving a slight nod. "Well, what if we painted something together? Would that be okay?"

The little girl thought about it for a moment and then handed Amber one of the brushes. They spent the next hour painting together, and Amber started to see hints of a smile as they continued. Amber checked on the others briefly. When the time was up, the kids' parents came in to get them. The girl who Amber had been working with ran over and grabbed the hand of a thin man with bright red hair and pulled him over and showed him her picture. She was smiling as she told him about it. Amber left them to enjoy it together; she could see the love the girl and her father had for each other.

"Um, excuse me," the father said as Amber was cleaning up some of the other stations.

"Hi. Your daughter is an amazing artist." Amber smiled at the little girl.

"Thank you. She told me what you said about your dad and what you two were doing. Her mother was the destructive force in her life. When I couldn't stand to see it happen anymore, she and I picked up and left. This is the first time in months that I've seen a genuine smile on her face."

"Well, I'm glad I could help. If you're interested, I can write down what you would need to set up something like this at home for her." Amber smiled over at the redheaded girl who was still beaming at the picture they had painted together.

"That would be great."

Amber wrote down the information, and the girl hugged her tightly and thanked her for giving her back her smile. Amber did her best to hold back the tears, but she couldn't help her heart from wishing someone would have taken her away from her destructive force.

After everyone was gone, Amber told Zach and Lucinda what happened, and they were amazed and proud at the way Amber was able to connect with the girl and help her.

"That's amazing. You are amazing," Nicole said. Amber smiled and put the picture back on the dresser.

"I can still smell her here," Amber whispered as she looked around the room and then moved to sit on the edge of the bed.

"I can, too," Nicole said. "She kept some journals filled with her thoughts. They're in the chest. I never read them, but I thought you might like those, as well, to be able to read what she was thinking and feeling. She wrote in the journals several times a day."

"Thank you for this." Amber motioned around the room as Nicole came and sat next to her on the bed.

"You have nothing to thank me for. I did it to hold on to a piece of you for as long as I could."

"That may be how you started it, but that isn't why you continued it."

"True, but I'm no saint in my reasons," Nicole said. "Do you want some time alone up here? I can go downstairs or to my room."

"Not right now. I don't think I could handle it. Being alone in here right now would be more overwhelming than I can handle. Maybe after everyone leaves, you and I can come back, and you can show me the photo album and the journals."

"I'd like that." Nicole took Amber's hand in her own and played with her fingers. "We should probably get back down there."

"Yeah, I know. Being here alone with you is nice, though."

"We'll kick them out early." Nicole winked at Amber, causing her to laugh.

When Heather arrived at the house, Jill let her in, and they took the food into the kitchen.

"Where are Amber and Nicole?" Heather asked.

"They're up in Amber's mom's room."

"Are you sure it's a good idea for them to be up there alone?"

"Well, if you ask Zach, no, but I think they'll let us know if they need help. After the breakdown that Amber had when we got here, I think they're okay."

"What do you mean breakdown?"

Jill explained what happened when they arrived and the reaction Amber had toward seeing the locks.

Jill and Heather felt bad for them, but they knew that they weren't going to get past this if they didn't face it. After unpacking dinner and getting everything set, Jill called upstairs for Nicole and Amber to come and eat.

They received no response from upstairs, so Jill and Zach decided they would go check on the two women. They both went in case the women needed support.

❦❦❦❦

Nicole loved the feel of Amber's hand in hers. Her mind kept drifting back to when they had kissed at the pond. How amazing she felt when Amber pressed her lips to hers.

"I can see what you're thinking about," Amber said softly, giving Nicole a coy smile.

"And what do you think I'm thinking about?" Nicole had a slight blush.

"You're thinking about kissing me," Amber said with that lopsided smile that melted every defense Nicole had.

"No, I was thinking about when *you* kissed me." Nicole blushed even more at the admission.

"And what were you thinking about that kiss?"

"I was thinking about how amazing it felt to have your lips on mine again. How much I had missed that feeling over the years."

Without thinking or questioning herself, Amber leaned forward and kissed Nicole again. This time, Nicole brought the hand that wasn't holding on to Amber's up and put it on the back of Amber's neck, pulling her in closer. They both moaned at the touch. Amber ran her tongue along Nicole's bottom lip, and Nicole opened her mouth, allowing her access to deepen the kiss. Amber pulled Nicole closer, their lips moving together, their tongues dueling for dominance.

"I love kissing you. I've missed it so much over the years," Amber said between kisses, pulling Nicole onto her lap.

"Mmm, then don't stop." Nicole pulled Amber into a deep kiss.

"Hey Nic, Amb—" Jill opened the door, and she and Zach started to walk in.

"Um...er," Zach stammered.

Nicole and Amber broke apart, and Nicole casually slid off Amber's lap and back onto the side of the bed.

"We'll...um...just be leaving," Jill said as she and Zach started to turn around.

"Y-you don't have to leave," Amber said, completely embarrassed to have been found making out on her late mother's bed.

"We were just getting ready to head back downstairs," Nicole said.

"I don't think that's what you were getting ready to do." Zach turned the same shade of red as Nicole and Amber.

"Zach Pellot, if you want to live, you will not repeat or think about what you just saw." Amber tried to sound stern.

"Yeah, sure," he said unconvincingly.

"Same goes for you, Jill," Nicole threatened.

"Right," Jill said with a smile as she leaned out of the room. "They're fine. They were just making out," she yelled down to the others.

"I'm going to stay up here now. You all have a great night," Amber said, mortified.

"Oh, no. If we have to go down, you have to go down." Zach walked over and took Amber's hand.

"You will pay, Woods. You will pay," Amber said, glaring as she let Zach drag her past Jill, who was giggling uncontrollably.

"I'm the sheriff. I don't think I will pay," she said smugly.

"You will. Trust me, you will," Nicole promised as she followed Zach and Amber downstairs, Jill bringing up the rear.

❧❧❧❧

"Hello." Erik and Heather smirked as Amber and the others entered the room.

"Hello." Amber turned a couple of shades darker as she moved to sit on the couch. Zach and Nicole sat on either side of her. Jill went into the kitchen, got the food, and brought it out on a tray.

"Heather, can you grab the drinks?" Jill asked.

"Sure." Heather went into the kitchen and came back with the drinks.

"Thanks for picking up the food, Heather," Nicole said.

"No problem."

"So, Amber, Zach was telling me earlier about how you two met," Heather said with a smile.

"Oh, he did?" Amber giggled.

"I've apologized for ten years, will you let it go?" Zach said.

"Oh, come on, it was cute," Heather said.

"I wanna hear this," Nicole said.

"I want to hear Amber's side," Heather said.

"I hadn't been in New York that long when I

started to go visit the galleries. They were usually empty, and it got me out of the place where I was staying and wouldn't allow me to dwell on my injuries. One day, I was looking at a painting, and Zach came over and asked if I liked the artist. I told him the painting was a fake. I asked him how I could know if I liked the artist if they ripped off someone else and couldn't take the time to do something original. He laughed and told me he knew the painting was a fake and that he was the one who painted it. I remember thinking he was quite obnoxious and pompous thinking that he had painted it or that it would impress me to know that he had ripped off another painter. Then he explained that they had permission. I felt a bit guilty for judging him so quickly, and I told him it was a good replica. Again, he laughed at me, which annoyed the hell out of me, and then he said it couldn't have been too good if I could tell that it was a fake almost immediately. So, I showed him where his flaws were. It was a few simple brushstrokes that he had done completely wrong."

"I wouldn't say completely wrong. You're just too anal about that stuff," Zach joked.

"You wish!"

"Amber, you know he was coming over to hit on you, don't you?" Heather asked.

"Yeah, he asked me out just before the curator came over to offer me a job. And then he asked me out after she left and as we got to know each other for the next couple of weeks."

"Yeah, and then she finally told me that she already had a true love and she missed *her* like crazy." Zach looked at Nicole. "When I asked why she left, she said it had to do with the car accident she was in, and we left it at that."

"I didn't completely lie," Amber said.

"No, you neglected to tell me that the car was your father," Zach said flatly.

"True." Amber looked down.

"Amber, I don't blame you. You didn't know me then. You could have told me over the years." Zach set his and Amber's plates on the table in front of them and then wrapped his arms around her, holding her close.

"I was afraid you wouldn't understand or you would just pity me," she whispered.

"Honey, there's nothing you could tell me that I wouldn't understand," he said. "You're my best friend and my sanity most days, so there's no room for pity."

"I'm sorry. I don't know what I did to deserve you, but thank you," Amber said as she hugged Zach.

"Don't be sorry, just know that I'm always here for you no matter what you have to tell me or need."

"Amber, can I keep him?" Jill asked.

"No, he's mine. You can have Erik." Amber giggled, holding on to Zach.

"Yeah, Zach seems like the bigger win," Jill said, smiling at Erik.

"Gee, thanks," Erik said.

"Sorry, but when was the last time you said something that sweet and meant it?"

"Way to make me look bad, man," Erik said to Zach, who laughed.

"I go home tomorrow, man. You'll be the sole stud in this group then," Zach said.

"I like how you think. I feel better now."

"Amber, I have a question, and I'm not asking to upset you or anything, but…" Jill started.

"Just ask," Amber said.

"Well, the injuries that you sustained that night. They would have required medical attention, and there's no way it would have gone unreported. Every hospital and clinic is required to report something of that caliber."

"I did get medical attention that night. Dr. Conlan lived two farms down. I made it to his house, and he helped me. He'd helped me in the past."

"Wait, you mean Kaleb Conlan?" Erik asked.

"Yeah, he had his office on the farm grounds there, and he was able to do X-rays and stitch me up. He gave me some antibiotics. I didn't want to stay there too long in case they came looking for me. His wife drove me out of town so I could catch a train and get the hell out of here."

"He's the one that called the ambulance for your mom," Erik said.

"He must have gone over there after they dropped me off. I know if he had gone before, he would have told me she was hurt, and I never would have left."

"They moved away not long after that," Jill said.

"What do you say we clean up and watch a movie?" Heather suggested, noticing how quiet and uncomfortable Nicole was getting.

"That sounds good," Nicole said, not making eye contact with anyone.

Nicole grabbed one of the trays and put the empty containers on it and then she headed into the kitchen. Amber followed her, waving at the others to stay.

"You okay?"

"Me? Yeah, I'm fine." Nicole avoided looking at Amber.

"Sweetie, this is me. Ten years apart or not, I know you well enough to know you aren't okay or fine."

"You could have died. At least with you living elsewhere, I knew you were around, somewhere. Had you died, I don't know how I would have gone on," Nicole said, a tear rolling down her face as Amber pulled her into a hug.

"Oh, sweetie. I didn't die, and I'm here with you now," Amber said in a hushed voice.

They held each other for a couple of minutes and then after composing themselves, they joined the others. Heather had already put in *Wreck-It Ralph* by the time Nicole and Amber got back.

They sat on the couch; Amber curled up against Nicole, who put her arm around Amber. As the movie continued, Amber dozed off. After the movie ended, they decided to just let her sleep, and Nicole would bring her by the hotel in the morning so they could all have breakfast together before Zach left.

Chapter Nine

Blindsided

"Hi...um...Sidney." Sidney was sitting at the bar nursing a gin and tonic when she heard a voice from behind.

"L-Lori," Sidney choked.

"I thought that was you. Are you here with anyone? Or meeting someone?" Lori looked around as she took the empty seat next to Sidney.

"No, I just needed to get out and have a drink to wind down after work."

"Do you mind if I join you for a moment? I have a couple of questions, and I'm hoping you can answer them."

"I'll answer what I can." Sidney nodded uncomfortably as Lori moved her seat closer.

"Great." Lori got the bartender's attention and ordered them each another drink.

"So, what do you want to know?"

"Well, let's start by you telling me what you know about Zach. That man is just way too hot for his own good."

"I'll take your word on that." Sidney laughed uncomfortably.

"Oh, that's right, I forgot. You probably have the hots for that blonde he was with."

"Amber? Oh, yes! She's much too hot for her

own good, as well."

"You know she isn't a real blonde, right? Sorry, I digress. So, tell me what you know about them."

"I know she isn't, but those eyes will entrance you. As for what I know about them...not much honestly," Sidney said. "Amber lived here a long time ago. They were all really close before she left, and this is the first time she's been back in years."

"Interesting. I've known all of them for a long time, and I don't recall them ever mentioning her. Do you know how long she and Zach have been together?"

"No, I only know they've known each other a long time, though. Sorry, I don't know much else. The only other thing I know is that Amber and Nicole used to be really close."

"Hmm, I'm going to have to do some checking on them. Is he really leaving tomorrow or was that just a line?"

"I overheard them say that Zach goes back to wherever they're from tomorrow and Amber the following day."

"Well, poop! Why can't it be the other way around?" Lori laughed.

"I'm perfectly okay with that order. I get another day to drool over the blond bombshell." Sidney laughed, as well, feeling some of the alcohol in the drinks.

"How about you take her, and I'll take him and we'll both be happy!"

"Deal," Sidney said and ordered another round of drinks.

Sitting nearby was a light brown-haired man with a scruffy beard who was listening in on their conversation. *So, that was Amber in the park with Sheriff Woods. I may need to find a way to pay my little sister a warm visit and remind her what family is all about, Jeffrey Knight thought.*

≈≈≈≈

Nicole closed the door behind her friends, then returned and stood in the doorway of the living room watching Amber, the love of her life, sleeping on the couch. She couldn't believe she was here, in her house. She had spent years dreaming of this, and now it was just the two of them.

"Hey, sleeping beauty," Nicole whispered in Amber's ear as she knelt next to the couch.

"Hmm." Amber's eyes slowly fluttered open.

"There are those beautiful eyes I love so much," Nicole said, causing Amber to blush.

"Where is everyone?" Amber asked, looking around the empty room.

"They left a few minutes ago. You fell asleep during the movie, and they couldn't bring themselves to wake you."

"I see, but you could?" Amber teased while trying to stifle a yawn.

"Only because it means I get to take you up to my bed." Nicole instantly turned red as what she said registered in her mind. "That sounded better and less presumptuous in my head."

"It didn't sound too bad coming out of your mouth, either," Amber said, flirting with Nicole and then leaning forward and placing a kiss on Nicole's now speechless lips.

"What do you say we move upstairs, get comfortable, and maybe try this kissing thing again?"

"Yes, please," Amber said as they got up and

headed upstairs. Nicole followed behind, making sure everything was locked up tight and shutting off the lights.

"I put your bag in my bedroom if you want to get ready for bed," Nicole said, suddenly very nervous.

"Thanks," Amber said, nervous, as well. She watched as Nicole went into the bathroom quickly.

What the hell is wrong with you, Brooks? It isn't like you haven't seen her naked or slept with her before. She's still Amber. Yeah, her body is different, but definitely not in a bad way, but so is yours. Stop being a chicken-shit! She was flirting with you.

Amber changed into a pair of short boxers and a thin midriff T-shirt. She was folding her clothes and placing them in her bag when Nicole came back into the room.

"Oh, wow, you are…um…wow." Nicole stared at Amber with hungry eyes.

"Thanks." Amber smiled seductively as she grabbed her toiletries and went into the bathroom.

Oh, hell, I'm not going to be able to keep my hands off her looking like that, Nicole thought.

She still finds me attractive. That's a bonus, Amber thought. *She hasn't changed in the past ten years. Well, she has gotten more beautiful, but that isn't a bad thing. I wonder if her skin still tastes as good.*

Nicole changed into an old T-shirt and her underwear, then pulled the covers back and crawled into bed while waiting for Amber to return. When Amber came back, she put her toiletries on top of her bag and slowly, nervously crawled into bed next to Nicole.

"Hi," Amber said softly.

"Hey there, beautiful. You come here often?"

Nicole said. "Okay, again, sounded way better in my head."

They both laughed, and some of the tension and nerves subsided.

"I'm not sure what's worse, the cheesy pickup line or what you were implying since we *are* in bed together."

"All of them…" Nicole buried her face in a pillow.

Amber removed the pillow and softly kissed Nicole. They slid down, so they were lying on their sides facing each other and continued to kiss. At times, they would deepen the kiss, other times, it was soft and sensual. Amber ran her hand down Nicole's side, and when she felt the shirt and only Nicole's underwear, her mind went to a naughty place. She used all her self-control to *not* cross any boundaries at this time. She steeled her mind back to enjoying the kissing.

Nicole felt Amber's hand on the bare skin of her upper thigh, and she could feel the internal conflict Amber was having. Nicole could tell they were having the same debate in their heads.

Do we take this further or stop here until we've discussed where this is going in the future, Nicole thought.

They kissed for an hour before exhaustion overtook them, and they found themselves spooning. Amber held Nicole close.

Amber woke the next morning pinned by Nicole lying half on top of her. It felt so good to have Nicole there that Amber couldn't bring herself to adjust for fear that Nicole would move and she would lose contact. Amber wrapped her arms around the sleeping woman and carefully pulled her more on top and held her as close as she could. After a while, Nicole woke and saw blue eyes watching her.

"Good morning." Nicole started to move off Amber, but Amber stopped her movement.

"Good morning," Amber said, leaning up and stealing a kiss.

"I like waking up like this."

"Mmm, me too!"

"Have you been awake long?" Nicole said.

"Just about ten minutes."

"Why didn't you wake me?"

"Because you were looking mighty sexy laying there on top of me, and well, it just felt *so* nice feeling your body on top of mine," Amber said, blushing.

"It's been a long time since I've had someone next to me in bed. I spent part of the night hoping I wouldn't cross a line and make you want to leave," Nicole admitted.

"I had the same fear," Amber said.

"You don't have to answer this, but have there been others, or is there someone special?"

"No others and only you for the someone special."

"Same here. Well, I mean you. That would be rather egotistical of me to say that I'm someone special to myself. I don't know why I'm suddenly nervous. I think it might have to do with your incredibly sexy body being below me. I can feel the heat emanating from you, and it just turns me on so much. Please kiss me so I stop babbling and making a fo—" Nicole babbled until Amber pressed their lips together and slid her tongue into her mouth to further help. Amber remembered when Nicole told her years ago that whenever their tongues touched her mind would go blank. She was banking on that still being the case.

"Mmm, Nicole," Amber whispered.

"I love how you say my name," Nicole said, sucking on Amber's lower lip.

"We better stop. I don't know that I'm ready mentally for this to go much further, although my body seems to think that it's more than ready."

"I agree," Nicole said as Amber allowed her to move off her this time. "We should get ready to meet the others for breakfast. You can have the shower first. You don't need to worry about saving hot water for me. After that session, I need a very cold shower."

"It looks like your water heater gets a break—I need a cold shower, too." Amber laughed.

The women showered, got dressed, and headed over to the hotel to meet up with the others. They were so lost in each other that they didn't see the old blue sedan following them.

When Nicole and Amber arrived at the hotel, Zach was talking with Heather and Erik in the lobby.

"Good morning, ladies," Zach said as he went to hug the two women.

"Good morning." Nicole returned the hug, then moved toward Heather.

"Great morning," Amber said softly.

Just as they were pulling apart, a slender man with dirty clothes walked into the lobby.

"So, my little sister returns home." He sneered as he walked toward Amber, grabbing her by the hair and pulling her away from the group. As he did that, Amber noticed the gun Jeffrey was holding.

"J-Jeffrey," Amber said, trying to keep her body in front of him and between everyone else behind her.

"Did you honestly think you could just stroll in here and not have me find out? Nobody moves, or you and my little sister here will pay," Jeffrey said as he motioned with his gun for the group to get together. Everyone moved closer as Amber was still caught in Jeffrey's grasp. Zach went to move in front of her, and she painfully moved and pushed him back.

"Zach, please, stay back." Amber winced as Jeffrey moved his hand from her hair to the back of her neck.

"So, who do we have here? Who is your knight in shining armor, Amber? Someone you care a great deal about, I see," Jeffrey said.

"Nobody you need to be concerned about." Amber felt the gun pressed painfully into her ribcage.

"How did you know she was here?" Nicole hissed, her voice shaking with fear and rage.

"Now, now, if everyone behaves, you won't have to worry about my sister's safety. Your little desk girl and that annoying woman from the tire factory were talking at the bar last night," Jeffrey said with an evil smile.

"Sidney," Heather grumbled.

"Lori," Erik grumbled.

"Yeah, those were their names." Jeffrey smirked. "I've waited a long time for you to come back, sis…I knew you would. Dad thought you were smarter than to come back here, but I knew you weren't."

"Just let them all go, Jeffrey. Your beef is with me, not with them," Amber said as Jeffrey took a step away from her but kept the gun aimed at her head.

"Oh, my beef is with you and the redheaded bitch. I'm very curious who pretty boy is, though. I thought you didn't like guys, huh, Amber? Did you finally wise up in your years away? I always knew it was all your fault," Jeffrey said, glaring at Nicole.

"Jeffrey, please, just let everyone else leave, or you and I can leave, but I don't want anyone else getting hurt." Amber moved toward him and stepped in front of the gun he had aimed at Nicole.

"I don't think I care what you want. Now *who* is the guy? Or should I shoot him and see how much he truly means to you?" Jeffrey now pointed the gun toward Zach's head.

"He's just a friend," Amber snapped, fear and panic coming through in her voice.

"Well, you seem a little too close for just being friends." Jeffrey looked between Amber and Zach.

"We're just friends. Now will you please stop pointing the gun at them? Point it at me if you have to point it at someone."

"No, I don't believe it's like that." Jeffrey aimed the gun back at Amber. Heather had started to move toward Jeffrey while his attention was focused elsewhere. Unfortunately, he saw her and backhanded her, knocking her back into the group. Nicole caught her before she hit the floor.

"I fucking said nobody moves. I mean it when I say I have no issues with shooting or killing Amber here and now. Does *anyone* else want to try to move forward and see if I mean what I say?"

They only shook their heads in response.

Amber took the opportunity while Jeffrey was distracted and moved forward, reaching out toward Jeffrey. When he saw this, he swung the butt of the gun and caught Amber's shoulder, causing her to cry out in pain as she was knocked to the ground. Nicole and Zach instinctively lunged toward her but stopped short when Jeffrey pointed the gun at them, and Amber put her other hand up to stop them.

"Nicole, Zach, please, no heroes. I'm okay," Amber said, not wanting to risk anyone else being hurt. She tried to get up but was unable to move her left arm.

"You know, sis, this is boring me. I think maybe I should just shoot you and get it over with." Jeffrey lifted Amber up by her injured shoulder and shoved her in the direction of the others.

Jeffrey pointed the gun at Amber and smiled maniacally. Amber lunged at him and knocked the gun down, but not before Jeffrey pulled the trigger, hitting Amber in the side near where the puncture wounds from the belt were. Amber fell to the ground, landing on top of Jeffrey and knocking the gun out of his hand. Within a second, Nicole was there pulling Amber off Jeffrey and holding her hand over the wound that was seeping blood. Zach had hit Jeffrey and turned him over, pinning him down. Heather called Jill and told her to get an ambulance to the hotel in a hurry.

"Nicole, sit down," Heather said as Nicole continued to pace in the hallway.

"How do you expect me to sit? Amber is in there, and we have no idea what's going on or if she's even still alive," Nicole snapped as she kept replaying the events after the shooting in her head.

Nicole could feel the warm blood seeping out of Amber's body. She made sure that Amber was still breathing. The room around her disappeared, and it was just the two of them.

"Don't leave me again," Nicole cried over and over again in her head. No sound could escape her mouth; fear had stolen her voice.

When the paramedics arrived, they gently moved Nicole out of the way and worked to stabilize Amber and to stop the bleeding.

"Is she hurt anywhere other than the gunshot wound?" one of the paramedics asked.

"Her left shoulder," Erik said, pulling Nicole into his arms. "Take extra special care of her, guys."

"We will. Do you and Nicole want to ride with us to the hospital?"

Erik and Nicole nodded and waited for them to load Amber into the ambulance before they got in.

Meanwhile, Jill arrived at the hotel.

"What the hell happened here?" Jill asked as she raced in behind the paramedics.

"Jeffrey shot Amber," Heather said.

"What the hell happened to your face?" Jill noticed Heather's swollen cheek.

"Jeffrey backhanded me," Heather said as Erik handed her an icepack before heading to the ambulance.

Jill stomped over to where Zach had Jeffrey pinned, pulling her handcuffs out of their holster.

"Zach, I got it from here," Jill said. "Jeffrey Knight, you have the right to remain silent—which I highly recommend. Anything you say can and will be used against you in a court of law. You have the right to an attorney—not that you'll need one since you're guilty as shit. If you cannot afford an attorney, one will be appointed to you. I feel sorry for that poor attorney. You have the right to consult an attorney before speaking to the police and to have an attorney present during questioning now or in the future. Again, not that you'll need one since you're guilty. If you decide to answer any questions now, without an attorney present, you will still have the right to stop answering at any time until you talk to an attorney, but I recommend keeping your mouth shut. Knowing and understanding your rights as I have explained them to you, are you willing to answer my questions without an attorney present?"

"Fuck you! I hope the bitch suffers and dies," Jeffrey spat as Jill finished handcuffing him and two of her deputies picked him up off the ground.

"I'll take that as a no. Get him out of here before I forget I'm the sheriff," Jill said.

The two officers holding Jeffrey nodded to her, and when Jeffrey didn't immediately start moving, one of the officers shoved Jeffrey hard, causing him to stumble face first into a wall.

"Heather, I want you to get that looked at when you get to the hospital. I have to go to the station to get Jeffrey processed. Zach, can you drive her?" Jill asked.

"Sure," Zach said as he took the keys from Heather.

༄ ༄ ༄ ༄

"Nicole, if she were dead, they would have come and told us," Erik said, receiving a glare from Heather and Zach. "I'm sorry."

Zach went over and wrapped his arms around Nicole, who broke down and cried. Zach murmured for her to let it out and that Amber was a fighter and she would make it through this.

"Have we heard anything?" Jill asked as she entered the surgical waiting room.

"No," Heather said, walking over to Jill. "What happened to Jeffrey?"

"He's been charged with attempted murder, assault with a deadly weapon, aggravated assault, false imprisonment, and stalking," Jill said. "He won't see the light of day until he dies."

"Good," Nicole said, pulling away from Zach.

"Heather, what did they say about your face?"

"They said I'll be tender and bruised, but there's no other damage."

"Didn't you have a flight today?" Jill looked at Zach, who was still holding Nicole.

"The second Jeffrey hit Amber with that gun, that flight went out the window," Zach said.

"I went online and got his ticket adjusted as soon as we got here," Heather said. "I needed a distraction."

Nicole started pacing again and waved off Zach, Erik, Heather, and Jill as they each went toward her to try to comfort her.

"Did they say how long she was going to be in surgery?" Jill asked.

"No, they just said it was serious, and they would update us when they could," Heather said. "Erik tried to go back and get details and was told he was banned from the area."

"Nic, Amber is going to come through this. I can feel it," Jill said.

"You didn't see her when we got here. She'd lost so much blood, and she hadn't regained consciousness."

Nicole sat in a chair away from everyone, pulled her legs up to her chest, and buried her head into her knees.

~~~

"Hello, Lucinda Baer, please," Zach said into his cellphone. "Tell her it's Zach Pellot calling."

"She's in a meeting, Zach," the receptionist said.

"It's important. Please, can you interrupt her?" The desperation came through in his voice.

"Zach, what can I do for you?" Lucinda said as she was connected with Zach.

"Hi, Lucinda. Amber and I are going to need some more time off."

"Is everything all right? You told my assistant it was important."

"Amber's in surgery right now. She was shot this morning," Zach said.

"Oh, no! What happened? She'll be all right, though, right?" Lucinda had gotten to know and care a great deal about Amber.

"Yes, or at least that's my positive thought. We won't know anything until she comes out of surgery. As for what happened, it's a long story. One better left for another time."

"Take all the time you need and keep me updated. You have my cell, right?"

"Yeah, Amber has your number in her phone," Zach said.

"All right, I'll be expecting a call from you today."

"As soon as we hear something, I'll let you know. Thanks, Lucinda."

Zach hung up and went back to join the others in their wait for news on Amber.

☙❧

"Knight family?" a man in blue scrubs called out as he came through the heavy doors.

"That's us," Jill said as everyone gathered around her and the doctor.

"Well, she's very lucky. The bullet missed her

kidney and any other vital organs. We were able to remove the bullet and stitch her up. She has a broken collarbone and a hairline fracture in the humeral head, the ball that goes into the shoulder joint. Those should take a few weeks to a couple of months to heal. What does Ms. Knight do for a living?"

"She's an artist, painter," Zach said.

"Well, as long as she takes a lot of breaks and isn't left-handed, I'll clear her to return to work in two weeks, but no sooner."

"She'll be all right, though?" Nicole asked, barely holding back the tears.

"Yes, she'll be all right physically. Mentally, that may take a lot longer."

"Thank you, Doctor. Can we see her?" Jill asked.

"She's still in recovery. I'll allow one of you to go in and sit with her," the doctor said.

"Nicole, you go." Jill received nods of agreement from the others.

"Are you sure?" Nicole asked.

"Positive," Zach said.

The doctor led Nicole back to the recovery room. Her breath caught in her throat as she saw Amber there, looking so frail and vulnerable. Wires and tubes were coming out of her, as monitors beeped with her heartbeat and tracked her vitals.

"You can sit here, hold her hand, just don't disturb the wire leads. She should wake up any time now."

"Thank you," Nicole said.

The doctor left, and Nicole sat and took Amber's hand, brought it to her lips, and kissed it.

"You know, sweetheart, this isn't how I thought the day was going to go," Nicole said. "When we woke up together this morning, it was the happiest I've been since you left. Now I'm so scared. I need you to wake up and show me those beautiful blue eyes."

Nicole sat there holding Amber's hand for at least thirty minutes before she felt Amber move and her breathing pattern change. The beeps on the monitors changed, which prompted a visit from a nurse. Amber was slowly waking up. She was groggy and disoriented, but seeing Nicole there, even with the fearful look on her face, helped her calm down.

❧❧❧❧

"I hate hospitals," Heather said. "Ever since Mom. I just can't stand this place."

"I know, Heather, I know." Jill put her arm around her.

"Why don't Zach and I go get us some coffee?" Erik suggested, wanting to give them some privacy.

"Yeah, we'll go get some coffee," Zach said, receiving a nod from Heather and Jill.

"Amber will get through this, I promise," Jill said.

❧❧❧❧

"So, you know what kind of coffee everyone likes?" Zach asked as he and Erik walked down the hallway.

"Yeah, they all choose mocha. Is Amber that predictable?"

"Yeah, although hers is always a caramel mocha coffee," Zach said with a laugh.

"So, was there ever anything between you and Amber?"

"No, not that I didn't hope. She was too hung up

on Nicole and being gay. Although after seeing them together, I get it."

"Yeah, the sad part is they were always like that. I mean before they started dating or even when we were at that age when romance was icky still. Do you think they could have a chance for something?" Erik asked.

"I wouldn't count it out, but I don't know. There are a lot of emotional scars there."

"Yeah, and some pretty intense physical ones, as well. I just want ten minutes alone with Amber's father and brother," Erik snapped.

"You and me both. I can't believe that Amber would put herself in that kind of danger to protect me," Zach said as they stopped at the coffee machine.

"Trust me, that bullet she took for us all, that was nothing compared to what she would have done. Amber cares deeply for you. I know you helped her when she first got to New York, and she's going to need that kind of help again."

"I wouldn't be anywhere else. I talked to the gallery curator and told her that Amber was in the hospital and we needed more time off. I have her covered on the New York end. Lucinda is holding her spot for the show, as well. Jeffrey isn't going to take that away from her."

"When is the show?"

"Two months from today," Zach said, grabbing two cups of coffee as Erik picked up the other two.

"Is she that good? I mean we saw the proofs, but honestly, just between us?"

"She's better than those proofs show. Amber has a lot of talent, and I agree with Lucinda that she can go far in the art world. Will she be a van Gogh or da Vinci? No, but she has talent and promise," Zach said proudly.

"I'm happy for her then," Erik said as they entered the waiting room and handed Heather and Jill their drinks.

"Any word?" Zach said.

"Knight family?" a nurse asked.

"Yes," Zach said since he was closest to the nurse.

"Amber is waking up. Once we get her into a room, you'll be able to see her. We tried to get the girl with the red hair to leave, but she was pretty adamant that she wasn't going anywhere."

"That sounds about right for Nicole," Heather said as the group laughed.

❧❧❧❧

Once settled into her private room, Amber reached out for Nicole's hand.

"Hey," Nicole said.

"Hey," Amber replied tiredly.

"I know you must feel like crap, but the others are here to see you. If you would rather wait…"

"No, I know if it were me out there, I wouldn't relax until I knew one of them was okay. First I want to hold you and talk to you about something."

"Sounds serious." Nicole sat in the chair next to the bed.

"Cuddle with me?"

Nicole's face lit up, and she adjusted the wire leads so she could lie next to Amber.

"I'm not hurting you, am I?"

"Not at all. I need to feel you close. You didn't get hurt at all, did you?" Amber asked.

"No, but I am a bit mad at you." Nicole saw the confused look on Amber's face. "You said no heroes, and then you go and get shot."

"Am I the only one that got hurt?"

"Well, Heather is going to have some bruises from Jeffrey hitting her, but the rest of us are fine. I think Jeffrey may be hurting for a while, but that's just because he 'resisted' being arrested, and one of Jill's deputies had to get physical with him."

"So, just me out of the group, though? I mean with serious injuries."

"Yes, just you, missy." Nicole saw relief in Amber's eyes.

"Nicole, I'm so sorry for what happened today."

"You have nothing to apologize for. You aren't responsible for your brother and his actions."

"He does know how to ruin a day, doesn't he?"

"Yeah, this morning and last night were perfect. Falling asleep and waking up with you was incredible," Nicole said. "It felt like—no, even better than—it used to."

"Sweetie, you know I have to go back to New York, right?" Amber held Nicole closer as she felt her tense.

"Yes, but I'm ignoring that for now."

"I don't want you to ignore it, I want you to talk to me," Amber said.

"Baby, you've been out of surgery for an hour, maybe two. Talking about you leaving can wait. Please? For me?" Nicole's voice got quieter as she spoke.

"All right, it'll wait until I get released. Then we need to talk. Fair?"

"Fair." Nicole leaned up and kissed Amber softly.

"Now go get the others, or they're going to be absolutely horrible to get rid of."

"Yes, ma'am," Nicole said as she got up.

Chapter Ten

Close

Nicole walked into the waiting room where she saw the others talking.

"Nicole." Jill noticed her first and rushed to her.

"Hi." Nicole waved at the group.

"How's Amber?" Zach asked.

"How are you?" Heather asked.

"Do you want a mocha?" Erik asked.

"Guys, let the woman talk, or she's going to go back into Amber's room, and we aren't going to get to visit Amber," Jill said.

"All right, to answer your questions…Amber is awake and alert. I'm doing okay, a bit annoyed that she brought up leaving when she had been awake for seven minutes. Yes, please, I definitely need a mocha! And I know you're all wanting to see Amber, so once I get my mocha, we can go in."

"You guys go ahead. I'll get Nicole's mocha and meet you back there. What room is she in?" Erik said.

"Room 829. Go through the doors and to the left, and it'll be on the left most of the way down the hall," Nicole said.

"Great, I'll be there soon. Anyone else need a coffee?" Erik asked, receiving a round of headshakes.

"How does she look?" Zach asked as they walked down the hall.

"She's tired and pale, but if she didn't look like that, I would be concerned." Nicole smiled back at him.

"Okay, now if you all are going in there, I need you to keep her in bed. She has gotten up twice since you left," the annoyed nurse said as she exited Amber's room.

"I was only gone for five minutes," a bewildered Nicole said.

"I know. Just tell her that she needs to stay in the damn bed. I told her if I caught her up again, I was going to put her in restraints," the nurse said sternly.

"We'll make sure of it, ma'am," Zach said.

"I'll make sure she stays put, you have my word," Nicole said.

"Thank you." The nurse gave them a curt nod before she walked away.

"Can you guys give me a minute alone with Amber?" Zach asked.

"Sure," they agreed.

☙☙☙☙

"I just want to check on your…what are you doing up?" the nurse said.

"I need to get something out of my coat," Amber said.

"Dear, your coat was covered in blood. The paramedics put it in a bag and gave it to one of your friends. Now get back in bed. Please."

Amber moved cautiously and got back in bed. The nurse left the room, and within a minute, Amber was up again. She was pacing next to the bed at least as far as the lines in the IV would allow.

"Didn't we just have this conversation? You need

to stay in bed, or we're going to have to restrain you." The nurse entered again with a shot of antibiotics and pain medication.

"I'm sorry. I don't know why I'm up. I just couldn't sit still," Amber admitted.

"Well, you need to remember that you just had surgery. You have stitches that you can't be moving, stretching, and possibly pulling out. Not to mention that there are also tubes in your body that are going to drain the fluids and keep you from getting an infection."

"I'm really sorry. I'll stay put this time." Amber climbed back into bed.

The nurse rolled her eyes and then walked over to Amber's IV. "I get how hard it is to stay put. I was in for a couple of days after surgery, and I just wanted to be out or doing my job. Please, though, don't keep getting up." The nurse then injected the antibiotics into the IV and smiled at Amber.

"I'm sorry. I really don't want to cause more damage. I have to get back to New York for work."

"Well, you're going to be in here for several days, and you aren't going to be able to fly right away, either, so get used to it. If you don't rest, you're going to be stuck in our little neck of the woods for a lot longer. When were you supposed to go back? What do you do in New York?"

"I was supposed to head back tomorrow. I guess I'll be missing that flight." Amber laughed uncomfortably. "I'm an artist, and I work at an art gallery."

"It sounds like you love what you do. You're definitely going to be missing that flight, but you seem to have some good friends with you here." The nurse smiled as she played around with the machines.

"I do." Amber smiled, too, thinking about Nicole.

"If you don't mind me asking, what happened?"

"My brother has a violent side, and he shot me," Amber said with no emotion.

"Oh, wow. I'm sorry to hear that. You seem like a nice girl, except you won't stay put and I have to babysit you."

"I promise if you leave, I'll stay in bed and not risk my stitches and drain tube again."

"You better. I meant it when I said next time I'm going to put the straps on," the nurse said in a teasing tone.

Amber smiled at her, and the nurse left the room.

≈≈≈≈

Zach walked into Amber's hospital room just after the nurse left with a look that told Amber he was not happy with her.

"Hi," Amber said sheepishly, trying to hide behind her hair.

"Hey. So, where do I start?" he asked rhetorically.

"How about with how much you love and adore me?" Amber answered, hoping to ease the tension in the room.

"You already know the answers to those. Do I want to know why you're getting up? And why you would feel the need to talk about leaving with Nicole after all that just happened? She thought she was going to lose you. Your blood was all over her hands."

"What do you mean my blood was all over her hands?" Amber asked, shocked and disturbed to learn this.

"She was the first to get to you after you were

shot. Nicole is the one who pulled you off Jeffrey." Zach paused to let this information sink in. "Amber, she put pressure on the wound to stop the bleeding. You were slowly bleeding to death in her hands."

"I-I was? She did that?"

"Yeah, she did that," Zach said. "Now I'm going to go back outside the room, send her in, and you're going to say you're sorry for being an idiot. Got it?"

"Yes, sir." Amber looked away. She was ashamed for bringing the subject up, but she didn't want to lead Nicole on, either.

"I still love you, and I'm still glad you're alive and doing well. I just don't want you to blow anything. You two are so cute together." Zach squeezed Amber's hand quickly.

"Thanks," Amber said, still ashamed.

Zach left the room and sent Nicole back in the room. He mentioned that Amber wanted to talk to her alone for a moment.

"Hey." Nicole walked into the room and quickly made her way to Amber's side.

"Hey." Amber avoided eye contact.

"Zach said you wanted to talk to me alone. Are you okay? Do you want me to go away? Did I do something wrong?"

"I'm as fine as I can be under the circumstances. And no, I don't want you to go away. I did something wrong, and I owe you an apology."

"What would you have to apologize for?" Nicole sat on the edge of Amber's bed and took her hand.

"I shouldn't have brought up my leaving. I should have thanked you. Zach told me that you were the one that pulled me off Jeffrey and then put pressure on my wound. You had my blood all over your hands.

I'm guessing you didn't even think twice about what you were doing. Thank you!"

"You don't have to thank me. I knew you didn't know about what happened after you were shot, let alone what I did. I'm just so glad that you're okay."

"I still shouldn't have done what I did. I love you, Nic, and I think I would be more freaked out if our positions were reversed." Amber brought Nicole's hand to her mouth and kissed her knuckles. "Sweetie, thank you for what you did for me."

"I love you, too. I know you're going to leave, but I don't want to think about it now. I want to concentrate on the time we do have together. The fact that we still love each other."

Amber used the hand she was holding and pulled Nicole down and kissed her deeply. Nicole leaned into the kiss as Amber slipped her tongue into Nicole's mouth. They both groaned at the surge of arousal that went through their bodies. They heard the steady beat of Amber's heart monitor speed up, but they didn't break the kiss. They were powerless over their need for each other.

"Well, I guess that's one way to keep her in that bed." The nurse laughed, causing both women to laugh and break their kiss.

"Sorry," Nicole and Amber said in unison.

"Don't be. You two look cute together. Have you been together long?" the nurse asked as she silenced and reset the monitors.

"Yes and no," Amber said.

"We were together for two years before she had to move away. Although, since we never broke up officially, you could say we've been together for twelve years," Nicole said proudly as her fingers played with

Amber's.

"Well, if you can keep her heart rate below 110, I have no problem with your method of keeping her in that bed. If you can't, you're going to have to stop," the nurse said as she left laughing, and the others came in.

"Well, she definitely left in a better mood than she came down that hall in," Jill said as she and the others entered the room and saw Nicole and Amber still a bright shade of red.

"So, what did she walk in on?" Heather waggled her eyebrows at the two. "Please, give explicit details, we can take it."

"Heather, I don't know that I personally can handle explicit details," Zach said, blushing.

"Why not? You had the hots for Amber, I have the hots for Amber, we can both live vicariously through Nicole," Heather said.

"I think not," Nicole said abruptly.

"Well, Amber sure as hell isn't going to let either of us kiss her enough to get a nurse to race in on us, is she?" Heather laughed. "And I know you two had to be kissing."

"You're right," Amber said. "You and Zach can either get over your crushes or you can just daydream about it, but you are *not* living vicariously through Nicole."

"Spoilsport." Heather pouted and sat at the end of Amber's bed. "I'm really glad you're doing better. Please don't ever scare us like that again. I thought we were going to lose you."

"We all agree with you there, Heather," Erik said, entering with Nicole's mocha.

"Hey, where's mine?" Amber asked with a pout.

"You, missy, do not get one...yet," Erik replied,

handing Nicole her mocha. "I promise to bring you one when the doctor says you're allowed."

"How's your face?" Amber asked Heather, who was sitting by her feet.

"It hurts some and is going to be bruised, but I'm fine."

The group sat around the bed. Jill explained to Amber that because everyone gave a statement and this was Jeffrey's third strike, she wouldn't have to testify or ever see him again. This was a relief to all. Mostly to Nicole and Amber, who knew there was no way Amber would be able to face Jeffrey again.

"Thank you for everything, Jill. I don't think I would survive having to relive any of my past and what a trial would put me through."

"Nobody wants you to have to go through that," Zach said.

"Um, Zach, weren't you supposed to be on a flight back home today?" Amber asked.

"Yeah, I was, but you see, my best friend got shot by her psycho brother, so my flight has been postponed," he replied. "I also called Lucinda, told her some of what was going on, and got us both more time off. She's going to hold your spot in the show."

"She is?"

"Yeah, she is. She did ask that I bring the forms back with me or that you mail them to her. She needs them by the end of next week."

"Thank you," Amber said, smiling at him.

"So, Amber, do they know how long you'll be in here?" Jill said.

"The nurse said I'll be here for about three or four days and then I can't fly back to New York for another week, so I'll be in town for another two weeks. And,

Zach, you are not staying that long. I won't have you missing that much work for me and what my dumbass brother has done."

"Not really your choice, now, is it?" Zach retorted. "Though, I will make you a deal and go back when you're out of the hospital."

"You can stay at the hotel," Heather piped in.

"And I'll pay for your room." Amber gave him a look that said "don't mess with me."

"I don't think so. You and Amber weren't paying for the rooms you were in anyway," Heather said.

"Why not?" Amber and Zach asked simultaneously.

"Family doesn't pay for rooms in my hotel." A huge smile crossed Heather's face.

"Your hotel?" Amber and Zach asked in unison again, causing the others to give them funny looks.

"Oh, did I forget to mention that I own that hotel and I'm not just the manager?"

"Yeah, you forgot to mention that," Amber said. "How? When?"

"I used my portion of the insurance money from when Mom died to buy the place. I changed the name, updated it, and now it's my baby."

"That's amazing, Heather. I'm really proud of you." Amber grinned.

"Proud enough to give me a sampling of what Nicole was hoarding all those years ago?" Heather waggled her eyebrows at Nicole and Amber. "Or is it what she's hoarding now?"

"I may not look like much, but I will kick your ass, Woods, if you move those lips anywhere near Amber's lips," Nicole warned, showing Heather her resolve face.

"Whoa, down, Nicole. I was just joking." Heather giggled. "Sheesh."

"My lips," Nicole said possessively as she leaned over and kissed Amber.

Everyone laughed as they pulled apart. Amber grabbed the collar of Nicole's shirt, looked Heather directly in the eyes, and let a mischievous smile cross her face as she said, "Yeah, her lips!" Amber then pulled Nicole into a deep kiss. When they heard the monitor start to beep faster, they broke apart and looked up to make sure they kept Amber's heart rate below 110.

"You know, you two are as mean now as you were when I was little, and you would kiss in front of me," Heather said, pouting.

"Well, back then, we didn't know you had a crush on Amber," Nicole said. "Now it's just going to be our extreme fun to make you squirm."

Amber yawned, and the others knew she needed to get some rest. They shouldn't have stayed so long, but everyone was so grateful that she was going to be okay.

"We'll let you get some rest and then we'll come back tomorrow to visit," Erik said as the others agreed.

"That'd be great," Amber said, yawning again.

Erik came over, hugged Amber, told her he was glad she was going to be okay and that he loved her and how happy she made Nicole. Jill hugged Amber, told her that she loved her, and if she needed anything to call. Heather hugged Amber, told her that she loved her, and that if she couldn't have her, she was glad it was Nicole she had chosen. She also told her she was going to have a chat with Sidney about discussing hotel guests outside of work. Amber asked her not to go too hard on her, Sidney didn't know. Zach hugged her next, told her he loved her, and he'd be back the next morning, but if she had a nightmare to call him and he'd be back sooner.

"Would you mind hanging around after everyone leaves?" Amber asked Nicole as she moved to give her a hug as the others had.

"Of course," Nicole said, smiling back at Amber.

"Do you need a ride home, Nic?" Jill asked.

"Nah, you go ahead. I'm going to stick around here for a bit."

"All right, we'll see you guys tomorrow. Get some rest," Jill said as the group left.

"Thanks for staying," Amber said as she took Nicole's hand. "I wanted some time just us…"

"I like 'just us' time." Nicole smiled and brought Amber's hand up to her mouth and kissed the back of it.

Chapter Eleven

Discovering Amber

"Zach, Heather, do you need a ride back to the hotel?" Jill asked.

"That would be great as long as I get shotgun... and Heather has to ride in the back of the cruiser." Zach looked over at Heather and smiled.

"Okay, I like that idea," Jill said with a little bounce in her step.

"You're as bad as Nicole and Amber, you know that?" Heather joked at Zach as he stuck his tongue out at her as they got in the car.

"Well, I did learn a lot from Amber. You could say I learned from the best," he said smugly.

"He's got a point, Heather. Amber was always the bigger brat when it came to those two picking on you," Jill added.

"She was?" Zach tried to imagine a different side to the Amber he knew.

"Oh, yes. When did she become a blonde anyway?" Jill asked.

"Um, you mean that isn't natural?"

"Oh, you poor delusional man. You need an Amber education before tomorrow...big-time! Heather, do you still have the albums at the hotel?" Jill looked at her in the rearview mirror.

"Yeah, I have the important ones there. I'll have

Keyser make dinner for all of us and we can enlighten Zach." Heather giggled, glancing at him.

"I can't wait." Zach rubbed his hands together. "Although I have to ask, is this going to ruin my image of Amber?"

"That depends, what is your image of Amber now?" Heather asked.

"Well, Amber is a sweet, compassionate, caring woman who has a smart-ass streak as big if not larger than the caring side of her."

"Nope, what we're going to tell you will just reinforce your image," Jill said as she parked outside the hotel.

Heather told them to go up to Zach and Amber's suite and she would be up shortly. She was going to talk with Sidney and then get Keyser working on dinner.

❧❧❦❦

"So, you wanted me to stay," Nicole said softly as she adjusted on the edge of the bed, so she could see Amber better.

"Yeah, I need snuggles, and you're the only one who can help with that…effectively." Amber gave her the lopsided smile, secretly hoping it still melted Nicole's heart.

"Vixen." Nicole giggled as she made herself comfortable on the bed, then allowed Amber to curl against her. She held Amber, kissed the top of her head, and watched her sleep. She had missed Amber more than she could describe, and feeling Amber in her arms gave Nicole a sense of being complete, something she hadn't felt since Amber left ten years earlier.

"Sidney, may I see you in my office?" Heather said as she approached the front desk. She hesitated as she walked past the spot in the lobby where Amber had lain bleeding after being shot.

"Sure." Sidney wondered if she was going to hear the full story of what had transpired earlier in the day. She had arrived at work to see Jill's team taking pictures of the lobby and then a crew had come in to clean up the damage.

"So, do you know what happened here earlier today?" Heather asked as the two women sat in her office.

"Not much. I just know that someone was shot, your sister was here when I got in, but she wouldn't say anything, then some people came in, cleaned, and left."

"This morning, Nicole and Amber arrived to meet us for breakfast with Zach before he left for New York. While we were talking in the lobby, Amber's brother, Jeffrey, came in and pulled a gun on us." Heather paused when she heard Sidney inhale. "You see, Amber was abused as a child and left here ten years ago after her father and brother almost beat her to death."

"Oh, my god." Sidney brought her hand up to cover her mouth. "H-how did her brother find her?"

"Jeffrey overheard you and Lori talking in the bar last night." Heather tried to contain the venom in her voice.

"W-what?"

"Jeffrey overheard you and Lori discussing Amber, Nicole, and Zach, and he showed up here this morning with a gun, and Amber was shot in the side."

"Is she okay?"

"She will be, but for a while, we weren't sure if she was going to make it."

"I'm so sorry to hear that."

"You need to realize that speaking about our clients is an invasion of their privacy and a breach of their trust. They come here expecting that we aren't going to be discussing who's here, why they're here, or any of that personal information. You broke that trust, and because you did, Amber is in the hospital with a gunshot wound."

"I am so sorry...Lori cornered me and started asking questions," Sidney sputtered, fighting to keep the tears in. She was certain that Heather was about to fire her, and she couldn't lose this job, not now.

"Sorry...I'm not the one you need to say you're sorry to. Amber is. You need to never let this happen again, or I will fire you without a second thought. If Lori or anyone asks you about someone who is staying here or someone they've seen here, you simply tell them that you're not at liberty to discuss anyone or anything dealing with the hotel. Is that understood?"

"Completely. I'm sorry, I should have used better judgment. It'll never happen again."

"I hope not. I see a promising future for you, Sid, don't blow it."

"I'll apologize to Amber, as well."

"You may want to be cautious about approaching her. Nicole is a bit territorial." Heather smiled.

"Oh, I remember very well. I promise I won't approach either of them without approval first."

"All right. I'm having confidentiality agreements drawn up for everyone who works here to sign so we never have something like this happen again."

"That's a good idea."

"Now go back to the desk. I need to talk to Keyser about dinner for Zach, Jill, and me."

Sidney rose from her chair and quickly exited the office. She was grateful that Heather hadn't fired her and mad as hell at herself for being dumb enough to talk about a guest. She knew better, yet the fear that Lori caused in her made her forget common sense entirely.

Heather realized that the albums were too much for her to handle alone and asked Sidney to help her carry them up to the Bonsai Suite. Heather then went to speak with Keyser to have him make the house special and to have it delivered to the suite.

Once the albums were up in the room and dinner had been delivered, Heather and Jill went about re-educating Zach on Amber.

≈≈≈≈

"So, let me get this right. Amber is a natural brunette. She was a scrawny girl with braces before she hit high school, which is when she blossomed into a brunette goddess. Tall, athletic, body to die for, popular girl I know now? Well, except I thought she was a blonde."

"Yep! Erik always called it the ugly duckling story…well, not to her face or while Nicole was around. They both would have kicked his ass." Jill smiled at Zach's reaction.

"And that's when Amber started to date Nicole? Did that go over well? What was Nicole like?"

"Nicole was always slender, a nerd with aspirations of becoming a geek." Jill pointed to a picture of a younger Nicole in the album. "Nicole was always in the advanced classes, the real brainy type. We were all friends, but it wasn't until Nicole and Amber got paired for a school project and had to spend most of their days and some nights together that they fell in love. The project was a marriage/parenting project. How they ended up paired, we never knew. Erik said the teacher had some insight since she was a lesbian. We teased them that they took the project a bit too seriously, but they were so cute together. Their relationship had a mixed reception. None of us minded, but there were some at school that had real issues with it. Amber's mom was happy for her. She saw how happy Amber was when Nicole was around. Her dad and brother wouldn't have been so happy. Thankfully, they didn't know for their two-year relationship."

"How did people at school take it? I mean, where I went to school, if a popular girl even talked to a geek or nerd, they got harassed pretty good," Zach said. "I'm guessing that Amber and Nicole were seen very differently as individuals."

"As Jill said, some people had issues, but Nicole and Amber didn't seem to care," Heather said. "They had been friends for years, so some people just let it go and lived in denial, telling themselves they were just good or close friends."

"They do look as cute together then as they do now," Zach said as he flipped through the photo albums. "Amber made a damn cute brunette, as well."

"Preaching to the choir there, buddy," Heather said.

"So, Amber never knew you had a crush on her?" Jill asked, watching Heather's sly smile appear.

"None of you did for the longest time, and well,

once anyone knew, it was about a week before she left."

"And you've held on to your love for Amber for all these years?" Zach asked.

"She was worth it. I'm not saying I haven't dated, but they've all paled when I compared them to Amber."

"I think you're going to have to finally get over that, little sister," Jill said.

"I know. Amber has and always will belong to Nicole. I wouldn't want to compete against Nicole anyway. I know I'd lose."

"Yeah, you would," Zach and Jill said in unison.

"Gee, thanks for the votes of confidence, you two. I am damn cute, you know." Heather laughed.

The nurse came in to take Amber's vitals and saw Nicole holding a very contented Amber, and she had to smile. She rarely saw patients this calm and relaxed in the hospital. Especially after everything that Amber had been through that day. The nurse thought about disturbing them and then decided that she would come back at the end of her rounds, giving them more time to rest together.

"Ow, ow, ouchie, ow," Amber said as she tried to move after just waking up.

"Baby, what's going on? Do you need me to get the nurse?" Nicole asked as she woke, hearing Amber's cries of pain.

"No, no, I'm just stiff, and it hurts to move where my incision is and maybe the muscles in that area, as well."

"I shouldn't feel sympathy for you since you were trying to get up and move around earlier, but I hate seeing you hurt. What can I do to help?"

"I need to get on my back." Amber thought that just rolling from her side to her back would be easy, but there were muscles that had been hurt, not to mention what they had done in the surgery.

Nicole got up and walked around the bed and grabbed the sheet below Amber and pulled it slowly, moving Amber's body so she was able to lean backward.

"There, baby, how's that?" Nicole asked.

Amber just nodded. She was holding her breath because of the pain.

"You know holding your breath like that is just going to make the pain worse," the nurse said as she came in.

"Is there anything she can get for the pain?" Nicole asked.

"Yeah, I was coming to see if you two were awake yet, so I could give her something," the nurse said. "My name is Jamie. I'm the night nurse."

"We slept that long?" Amber's voice was strained due to the pain.

"Well, for a good four and a half hours. That's why you're so sore and stiff. I know you're Amber, what's your name?"

"Sorry, I'm Nicole," Nicole said, shaking hands with the nurse.

"Great. I wish I had more patients that were as contented and would rest as nice as Amber did with you. It would make my job so much easier." Jamie laughed.

"Well, you just need to let them have someone

with them that they truly love," Nicole said as she watched Jamie draw a syringe of pain meds and inject it into Amber's IV.

"No, that can't be it, I've seen too many people argue with each other that way." Jamie laughed.

"Well, until two days ago, we hadn't seen each other for about ten years," Amber said.

"That definitely could be the reason," Jamie said. "Are you starting to feel some relief, Amber?"

"Yes, thank you!"

"I'll be back to check on you in about an hour. Try to move a bit to loosen up the muscles. *But* stay in bed. I'm expecting you to keep an eye on her." Jamie pointed at Nicole.

"Yes, ma'am," Nicole said as Jamie laughed and left the room. "Do you want some water or anything?"

"Nic, come here for a minute," Amber asked.

Nicole sat on the edge of the bed. Amber pulled her closer and passionately kissed her. The heart monitor beeped and then started to beep faster. Nicole tried to pull back, but Amber had threaded her hand in her hair and was keeping their lips pressed together. The meds lowered Amber's heart rate, so they didn't break the threshold.

"Mmm, that was nice," Nicole said as they finally separated. "I didn't hurt you, did I?"

"No pain. The meds are working," Amber said, smiling at Nicole.

"Good, now you need to take it easy."

"No, Nurse Jamie said I should move around."

"Yes, but you're loopy on meds, and I don't want to take advantage of you compromised like that," Nicole said.

"I don't deserve you," Amber said as a tear rolled

down her face.

"Baby, don't cry." Nicole pulled Amber close and held her.

※ ※ ※ ※

Amber started to feel better after two days and was able to leave the next day, but she wasn't going to be cleared to fly for another week or more.

"So, are you ready to leave?" Zach asked as he sat with Amber.

"I'm very ready to get out of here. Are you heading back to New York soon? And no, I'm not trying to get rid of you."

"I head back tomorrow, provided you really get out of here."

"Oh, I'm leaving, don't worry about that." Amber laughed.

"Can we talk about something?"

"Sounds serious. What's up?" Amber patted the edge of the bed for Zach to have a seat.

"I want to talk to you about Nicole." Zach saw Amber tense; he knew he was going to have to be careful with this.

"W-what about Nicole?" Amber asked defensively.

"I see how close you two are becoming and how much she makes you smile. I'm wondering what's going to happen when you get the okay to go home."

"I've tried to talk to her about it, but she avoids the subject."

"What do you want to have happen?"

"I love her, Zach, I never stopped. I know she has a job and a life here, but I can't help wanting to ask her to come to New York with me."

"You're scared to ask because you think she'll say no, aren't you?"

"Very scared, almost petrified." Amber bowed her head.

"Why would you be that scared?"

"I love her. She's the only person I've ever loved and ever want to love. That's pretty intense, then you add in all that has happened the past week."

"Okay, I can see that. She loves you, too. You two need to talk and figure out if you want a life together or not."

"What if she says she doesn't want me or a life with me? I don't know if I can handle that."

"You won't know until you talk with her."

"I know."

"Where are you going to stay when you get out of this place?"

"I was thinking that I would go back to the hotel," Amber said. "I haven't asked what the plan was, though."

"If I had a say in it, I'd send you to Nicole's." Zach smirked.

"I have a broken collarbone and shoulder and stitches in my side, I don't know that what you're hoping to happen could or would." Amber blushed, knowing he wasn't the only one hoping for more to come out of time alone with Nicole.

"I just want you two to spend time together. Heather is the one that wants to know about those other explicit details."

"Yeah, I need to talk to her about that stuff, too," Amber said.

"Why?"

"She seems to have some rather skewed views

toward me."

"Go easy on her. You were her first crush, and we all know how hard that is to get over."

"I will, I just don't want her being misled or getting false hope for anything," Amber said.

"Knock, knock," Nicole said, poking her head in the door.

"Hi, Nicole." Zach smiled.

"Hi, Zach. How is our patient?" Nicole entered and made her way over to the bed.

"I'm fine." Amber took Nicole's hand when she leaned against the bed.

"She says she's ready to leave," Zach said, smiling at the two of them.

"Very ready," Amber said.

"Well, I'm here to take you back to my place to recover." Nicole looked at Amber and saw the hesitation in her eyes. "Don't argue with me, Knight, you will not win."

Amber opened her mouth to speak and then closed it again, seeing the smirk on Zach's face.

"Do you think you'll feel up to going with us to drop Zach off tomorrow?"

"Yeah, and even if I didn't feel up to it, I would go anyway," Amber said matter-of-factly.

"The hell you would." Zach and Nicole nodded in agreement.

"I'm not an invalid..."

"No, but if you don't take care of yourself, you aren't going to be well in time for your show, and Lucinda will not be happy."

"Damn it, I have to get those forms signed."

"I already got Heather and Erik to sign theirs, but there were only two forms in the folder," Zach said.

"I signed mine already," Nicole said.

"It's in my computer bag. Will you take them back and give them to Lucinda?"

"Yep. I'm so excited to see your artwork under that bright specially designed lighting. We've been working toward this for so long." Zach and Amber shared a knowing smile.

Nicole saw the excitement in Amber's eyes and knew that this woman who had lived in New York was truly in her element and where she needed to be. She knew her heart was going to break when Amber left. Nicole knew she couldn't stand in the way of the woman she loved so much; she couldn't do anything that would take away from Amber achieving her dreams.

Zach sensed a mood change in Nicole and excused himself, saying he had to grab that form and finish packing.

Chapter Twelve

Leaving the Hospital

After Zach left, Nicole sat on the bed next to Amber. Nicole was staring at the sheet lost in thought when she felt a kiss on her neck.

"Where are you?" Amber asked softly.

"I'm here. I just realized how much of your life I know nothing about and how much of your life you hid from us before you left," Nicole said.

"We'll talk, I promise. I love you, Nicole, you have to know that." Amber took Nicole's hand and made sure they were looking into each other's eyes.

"I do, and you know I love you, too. Sometimes, that just doesn't feel like enough, though."

"Yeah, I know. At least we still have some time together. Just us."

"I love that idea. You sure you don't mind staying at my place? If you would feel more comfortable at the hotel, I don't want to—" Nicole was silenced by Amber's lips on hers.

"Positive, I don't mind," Amber whispered into Nicole's lips before kissing her again.

"You two are the cutest couple," Jamie said as she entered the room.

"I thought you were a night nurse," Amber said, smiling at Jamie.

"I am, but I wasn't going to miss a chance to say

goodbye to my favorite patient and couple. I come with discharge papers and instructions." Jamie held up several papers. "I can leave, but then you have to wait for a day nurse, and that could be a few hours."

"Please let me leave," Amber begged, giving Jamie puppy dog eyes.

"Yeah, please let her leave." Nicole laughed at Amber and the face Jamie was making.

"Fine. We have to go over these instructions, and I need you, Nicole, to make sure she follows them."

"I'll do my best, but she'll be going back to New York soon."

"Well, not until she gets the all-clear to fly, and she won't be given that until she finishes most of these instructions."

"Hello, I'm right here." Amber scoffed, looking between the two women.

"We know, but you don't listen very well when it comes to your health and well-being," Jamie said, causing Nicole to laugh and Amber to pout.

"Oh, stop." Nicole kissed the side of Amber's head.

"So, let's get through this so you can get out of here and I can go home. Amber, you need to take these antibiotics three times a day for ten days. Try not to move your left shoulder too much and keep the sling and brace on as much as you can stand. That will help the breaks heal. The incision spot is going to need the dressing changed daily, and you need to keep it as clean as possible. Cuddles and kissing will help pain management, but should they not be enough, here are some pain meds. Take one every four to six hours. They're going to make you sleepy. Any questions so far?"

"The cuddling and kissing. Is there a time limit on those, as well, or is it as I can tolerate it?" Amber giggled.

"We'll go with as tolerated." Jamie laughed. "Remember you were shot a few days ago, your body needs time to heal. If you're going to go for more than cuddling and kissing, be careful."

"We will." Nicole blushed as Amber nodded.

"All right. Lastly, should you develop a fever within the next ten days, you need to go to the ER immediately to have the incision site checked for infection. If you get an infection where you were shot, it can be very—and let me emphasize again *very*—dangerous."

"I get it, infection bad," Amber said.

"Well, it could cost you your kidney," Jamie said bluntly.

"Oh," Amber and Nicole said in unison.

"Yeah, so infection very bad," Jamie said.

"I'll keep an eye on her, and when she goes back, Zach will watch over her," Nicole said, feeling her heart ache at the idea of Amber leaving.

"Sign here that you agree to it, and, Nicole, you need to sign below since she's medicated that you understand it, and then you, my dear, will be free to leave." Jamie pushed the papers toward Nicole and Amber.

They signed the papers and were given copies of the instructions and the medication. They said their goodbyes, and Amber changed into the sweatpants and T-shirt Nicole had brought for her. Jamie came back with a wheelchair and wheeled Amber out of the building, and Nicole retrieved her car and met them at the front of the building. Nicole and Amber drove in silence back to the hotel to collect Amber's things.

※※※※

Zach arrived back at the hotel and grabbed Nicole's signed form out of Amber's bag and finished packing his stuff, as well as Amber's. He went downstairs to Heather's office.

"Hey, kid," Zach said as he knocked and opened Heather's door.

"Hey, Zach." Heather looked up from the paperwork on her desk.

"I'm getting ready to leave as soon as Nicole and Amber spring her from the hospital."

"I'm going to miss you." Heather stood and walked around her desk and hugged the man she had come to know and care about in such a short time.

"I'm going to miss you, too. I never thought that I could care about a group of people as quickly as I have you all. I should have known since I loved Amber almost the minute I met her."

"I never truly thanked you for taking care of her for all these years," Heather said.

"No thanks needed…she helped me, and I helped her. I wish it wouldn't have taken ten years, but I'm glad I got to know more about her and her past."

"You have my number and my email. I expect you to not be a stranger and to keep in touch."

"I will if you will," Zach said, smiling.

"Deal," Heather said as they heard a knock on the door. "Come in." The door opened, and there stood Nicole and Amber.

"Hey, you got released." Heather moved to carefully hug Amber and then Nicole.

"Hey, gorgeous." Zach moved the chair over for Amber to sit.

"Hey," Amber said softly as she sat.

"So, do I need to set up for a nurse to come in to take care of you?" Heather joked.

"Actually, she's going to stay with me until she gets the approval to fly home. Once she gets back to New York, Zach, you're going to have to watch over her," Nicole said.

"Hello, I can watch over myself," Amber said.

"Amber, you would do the same if any of us were in your spot," Heather said.

"That's different." Amber rolled her eyes.

"Bullshit." Nicole gave Amber a stern look. "The big thing is to make sure she doesn't get an infection where the incision is. If she does, they said she could lose her kidney."

"What the hell? Just from an infection?" Zach exclaimed.

"Yeah, because of how close to the kidney it was and what they had to do. Any sign of a fever in the next ten days, and she's to go to the ER immediately."

"I promise when she gets home, I will look after her," Zach said.

"I'll be fine, you guys."

"Let us worry and take care of you. You took such amazing care of me and Travis when he was sick, and when he died, you took care of me. Let me return the favor."

"You took care of me plenty of times, including that first year."

"Then you can owe me."

"Fine, I'm too tired to argue." Amber smiled back at him.

"Baby, do you want me to go get your stuff and you can wait down here?" Nicole asked.

"Yes, please," Amber said.

"I'll go with you to check the room for both of our things, and then we can get you to Nicole's to get some rest," Zach said.

"Thanks," Amber said tiredly.

Nicole and Zach went up to the room, leaving Heather and Amber alone in Heather's office.

"How are you holding up, honestly?"

"I'm tired, I hurt, I'm scared," Amber blurted.

Heather sat in the chair next to Amber and took her hand. "Hey, we all love you, and we'll always be here for you."

"I don't deserve it, you guys, any of this."

"The guilt you're feeling, you need to let it go. What happened before, it made us all the strong people we are now. It's up to us to move past and grow from it."

"Insightful," Amber said. "What my family did to Nicole…that I can't move on from."

"They did it, not you. Had you stayed, they would probably have still done it because your dad and brother would have found out you two were in love. The guilt is going to eat you up inside, and I love you too much to stand by and watch it happen."

"I love you, too, but I don't know how to let go of the guilt," Amber admitted.

"You and Nicole need to discuss what happened and what you both want for the future. I can say honestly that anyone I have ever dated, I compared to you…I know you aren't perfect. We all have flaws, but you make up for them with the kindness and compassion you have in your heart."

"Weren't you the one calling me mean not more than three days ago?"

"I was, and I stand by it, but it was in fun, and it was out of love. I wish there was a clone of you. If there was, I'd want to be with her. I know that you and Nicole are destined to be together. You may not believe it, you may not see it, but you two were made for each other."

"I believe it and feel it, I just don't see how it'll work," Amber said.

"Again, we're back to you and Nicole needing to talk."

"When did you get so smart?"

"I was a psychology and philosophy major."

"Don't those two contradict each other?"

"Shush you." Heather laughed.

"Nicole and I will talk. I'm glad you know that I have flaws, I'm not sure you see all of them, though."

"I see enough. You were the first crush I ever had. Part of me is always going to have a crush on you, I just know better than to act on it."

"I'm glad." Amber squeezed Heather's hand.

Nicole and Zach came to the door and smiled seeing the two talking.

"We're all set," Nicole said.

"Great, you two go put that stuff in the car, and I'll help Amber out," Heather said.

"See you out front," Zach said, and he and Nicole left.

"I know that you're conflicted about the future, but please keep an open mind when you two talk."

"I'll do my best," Amber said, and the two left the office.

"How do you really think she's doing?" Nicole asked as soon as the elevator doors closed.

"I think she's unsure of a lot of things right now. I know she loves you more than life, but she's scared and so full of guilt."

"I'm scared, too. I don't know how to help her get over the guilt."

"Give her time," Zach said as they gathered Amber's belongings.

"Promise me you'll keep a close eye on her when she gets back to New York." Nicole looked Zach in the eyes.

"You have my word," Zach said as they headed back down to Heather's office.

Nicole and Zach put their stuff in the car and waited as Amber and Heather slowly made their way out. Once outside the hotel, Nicole was by Amber's side, helping her to the car and getting her situated.

"Nic, sweetie, I'm okay," Amber said as she fussed over her.

"You are not," Nicole said sternly. "You were shot a few days ago, and you have a broken collarbone and fractured shoulder."

"I know, but, sweetie, they let me out of the hospital, so I must be doing better. Yes, I hurt, but once we get to your place and situated, I'll take something for the pain."

"Do you need something now?" Nicole asked as her panic rose.

"No, I need for you to give me a kiss and then get into the car and drive me to your house." Amber smiled.

Nicole leaned forward cautiously and kissed Amber before going around to the other side of the car and getting in.

"Zach and I will be by later. We'll give you two time to get situated," Heather said, surprising Zach, but also seeing relief in his eyes.

"Thanks." Amber offered a small smile to the two.

Nicole drove them to her house. It was a short five-minute drive. Once they arrived, she helped Amber inside.

"Do you want to stay in your mom's room or my room?" Nicole asked.

"I'd love to stay with you, but if it's a bother, then I'll stay in my mom's room." Amber looked down at the floor.

"I would love to have you stay in my room." Nicole tilted Amber's head up.

She helped Amber make it up the stairs and down the hall. Once inside the room, Nicole pulled back the covers on the bed and turned to face Amber.

"Do you want to curl up in your sweats, or would you like to get out of them?"

"I'd love to get out of them. I think I'd overheat if I stayed in them." Amber smiled. "I…um…will need help getting undressed, though."

Nicole blushed and smiled. "Would I be out of line to say my pleasure?"

"No, you wouldn't." Amber gave her a coy smile.

Nicole tentatively knelt in front of Amber and reached up and slipped her fingertips under the waistband of the sweatpants. She gingerly eased them down. She could feel Amber's breath catch as she watched her lowering the sweatpants. Nicole steeled herself and calmed her hormones enough to continue lowering the pants and finally was able to have Amber step out of them. Nicole's gaze trailed up Amber's body until she met deep blue smoldering eyes. Nicole rose and was pulled quickly toward Amber, and their lips crushed together in a passionate kiss. After several long moments, Nicole pulled back.

"You need to get in bed," Nicole said softly, not trusting her voice.

"Will you join me?" Amber asked.

"I don't know if that's a good idea."

"I promise to behave myself." Amber smirked.

"You behaving isn't my biggest concern. Me behaving, that's my biggest concern." Nicole smiled.

"I'm okay with you not." Amber wrapped her good arm around Nicole's waist and pulled her close.

"Behave or I'll sleep on the couch downstairs," Nicole teased.

"No, you won't. You need to be next to me, keeping an eye on me. Remember?" Amber raised an eyebrow at her and then gave Nicole a smile.

"Get in bed, and I'll go get you some water to take your meds and then tuck you in."

"Will you please lay with me? Just for a while?"

"If you get in bed now, I will." Nicole saw a relieved look cross Amber's face.

Amber got in bed and tried to adjust, but with her bad arm and side pain, she couldn't get comfortable. Nicole came back to see her struggling. She set the water on the nightstand and helped Amber get the pillow adjusted to support her shoulder and another pillow to support her side.

"Thanks," Amber said.

"I'm here to help."

Now that Amber was situated, Nicole handed her a pain pill and the glass of water. Amber took the pill and Nicole put the glass back on the nightstand before she settled herself in the bed next to Amber. Nicole put her arm around Amber's shoulders and allowed Amber to lean her head on her shoulder.

"Are you comfortable?" Nicole asked.

"As comfortable as I can get, but you holding me feels incredible."

"I'm glad because holding you in my arms is amazing."

They lay together until Amber's pill kicked in and she fell asleep. Once she was resting comfortably, Nicole eased herself out of bed and covered Amber up.

"I'll love you forever," Nicole whispered as she leaned forward and kissed Amber's forehead.

Nicole slipped out of the room and went downstairs in time to hear a soft knock on the door. She checked the peephole, even though she knew it would be Heather and Zach. Seeing them, she unlocked the three locks and opened the door for them.

"Hey," Heather said as they entered.

"Hey," Nicole said.

"Is she sleeping?" Zach asked.

"Yeah, I gave her a pain pill, and she drifted to sleep."

"Well, we were thinking that Zach would stay at my house tonight to give you and Amber some time alone," Heather said.

"You don't have to. I mean, Zach, you're leaving tomorrow, so Amber and I will have plenty of time alone, and you'll be without her for several days."

"I just don't want to intrude," Zach said.

"You aren't, and I think Amber would like to have you here," Nicole said. "I'd like it, too. It's nice for me to see you two together. I get to see her and what an amazing woman she has become."

"Thank you," Zach said.

"Jill said she would call when she's done with work to see if Amber was up for visitors," Heather said.

❦❦❦❦

"You think you're going to be able to get rid of the memories of us?" David Knight asked.

"D-daddy, you aren't going to be able to hurt me anymore," Amber said, her voice quivering.

"Wrong, little girl. We'll always be in your mind and tormenting you, keeping you in fear. Nobody will want you."

"Nicole l-loves me...Nicole w-wants me..."

"Not once she realizes how broken you are." Jeffrey Knight laughed as she squirmed to get away from him.

"No, you don't know that," Amber said as tears rolled down her face.

"Oh, we do. We'll never leave you or allow you happiness," her father said.

"No, I won't allow that."

"Oh, you don't get to choose. We're messing with you now, and you can't do a damn thing about it. If we aren't tormenting you, we'll torment that pretty little redhead of yours," Jeffrey said.

"You leave her alone," Amber snapped.

"No, I don't think we can do that."

"Nicole, Nicole," Amber called, looking around

and not finding her.

"Nicole," Amber screamed as she sat up in bed drenched in sweat.

Nicole, Zach, and Heather heard the scream and ran upstairs and opened the door to Nicole's room.

"Amber?" Nicole raced to the bed, seeing Amber dripping wet and holding her side.

"Nic," Amber panted and cried.

Nicole wrapped her arms around Amber and felt her shaking.

"Amber, are you okay?" Zach asked as he and Heather sat at the end of the bed.

Amber shook her head, and tears continued to roll down her face.

"Baby, talk to me. What happened?" Nicole held Amber close.

"I had a bad dream. My dad and brother were telling me that they were always going to be there to keep me under their control."

"Oh, baby," Nicole said. "They can't get to you anymore."

"They said that if they weren't tormenting me, they would go after you," Amber cried. "They said nobody would want me because they would keep me broken."

"Amber, that's so far from the truth. I always have and always will want you. Oh, I love you so much," Nicole cried, squeezing Amber tighter.

"Amber, all three of us love you so much and will always be here for you," Zach said as his heart broke for the pain she was in and the hold her brother and father still had on her.

"Zach is right," Heather said.

"I'm broken, though. They broke me, and I will never be right. You all deserve better." Amber shook her head.

"Amber, no! You can't believe that." Nicole pulled back and looked Amber in the eyes. "I'm yours, I will always be yours. You are mine, and you will always be mine. Face it, we're inevitable."

"I..." Amber started just as a stab of pain shot through her side, taking her breath away.

"Amber?" Heather squeaked, moving to the other side of Amber as her eyes started to roll back in her head.

"She's bleeding." Zach noticed a red mark forming below the hand on Amber's side.

"Crap, she must have jarred her incision."

"Where are the dressings?" Zach asked, panic in his voice.

"They're in the bathroom. On the counter." Nicole pointed toward the en suite.

Nicole and Heather helped Amber lie down, and Zach went to retrieve the supplies to clean up and cover the incision again.

Carefully, Nicole pulled the hem of Amber's shirt up and exposed the dressing on her side. She cautiously pulled back the dressing and took the gauze that Zach handed her and cleaned around the wound. She applied antibiotic cream and then recovered the wound with a fresh dressing. Heather grabbed a fresh shirt out of Nicole's dresser for Amber. She and Zach stepped out to give them privacy while Nicole helped Amber change.

"I don't deserve you," Amber said.

"You do, and you deserve all of us. You are so loved, and we're going to get you through this," Nicole said as they carefully sat up and Nicole removed the sling on Amber's left arm and eased her arm out of the hole and then did the same with the right arm before pulling the shirt over Amber's head. Nicole grabbed the clean shirt and put it over Amber's head, eased the left arm through the hole and then the right arm and pulled it down, covering Amber's body.

"Thank you," Amber whispered. She was ashamed that she couldn't do this herself.

Nicole smiled and helped her into her sling again and then adjusted the pillows so that Amber could lie down comfortably.

"How is that?" Nicole asked once Amber was situated.

"I don't want to sleep anymore," Amber said, her eyes pleading.

"Do you want us to keep you company?" Nicole asked. Amber nodded. "Let me get Heather and Zach, and we'll hang out in here with you. If you drift off to sleep, we'll be here to protect you."

Nicole quickly stepped out of the room to tell Heather and Zach the plan. They went and got snacks and drinks and then camped out in Nicole's room. Heather put in a movie, and Nicole and Amber cuddled together. As the movie came to an end, Zach looked back and saw that Nicole and Amber had drifted off to sleep.

"Let's get out of here and let them rest," Zach said as he and Heather cleaned up their snacks and went back downstairs.

Chapter Thirteen

Trust in Comfort

Heather called Jill and told her that she was heading home and that she should wait until the next day to come over. She said Nicole and Amber had fallen asleep, and Zach was going to make himself comfortable on the couch. After Heather left, Zach locked the door and turned the lights off. He lay on the couch and quickly fell asleep.

Nicole awoke to feel the familiar weight of Amber's head on her shoulder. They hadn't moved much throughout the night. She was pleased that Amber was able to fall asleep and stay asleep. She kissed the top of Amber's head and sighed deeply.

Amber slowly woke, feeling safer than she had in a long time. She knew it was because she was wrapped in Nicole's arms.

"Good morning," Nicole said, seeing Amber's eyes open ever so slightly.

"Fantastic morning," Amber said, her voice still thick with sleep.

Nicole adjusted and brought her lips to Amber's, barely brushing their lips together. The electric feeling of their lips barely touching caused Amber to moan as the sensation shot through her body. The longing and desire she had suppressed for ten long years came alive. Amber leaned in closer, and Nicole pressed their lips firmly together. Amber gently sucked on Nicole's lower lip, and after a couple of minutes, Nicole ran her tongue along Amber's bottom lip and was granted access. She eased her tongue in Amber's mouth, and their tongues moved together. Both women groaned at the sensation raging through their bodies. Nicole eased Amber onto her back and slowly brought her hand under Amber's shirt and ran it up her stomach, grazing the underside of Amber's breast. Amber arched into her touch, and Nicole cupped the breast in her hand, feeling the nipple harden under her touch.

"Oh, yes." Amber groaned as Nicole continued to touch her. She felt Nicole's hand go from one breast to the other, massaging and playing with her nipples. Their kisses deepened as they took turns leading. Amber ran her hand down Nicole's body and slipped it under the waistband of her underwear and cupped her now wet curls.

"Oh, Amber." Nicole moaned at the feel of Amber's hand on her wet center. "Oh, that feels so good."

Nicole carefully raised Amber's shirt more and leaned down and captured one of Amber's nipples in her mouth, causing Amber's breath to catch. Nicole sucked hard on the nipple and then moved to the other breast and did the same thing. She used her tongue to flick the rock-hard nipple in her mouth repeatedly.

"Oh, yes…" Amber panted. She started grinding her hips into Nicole's knee that had made its way between her legs and was pressing on her center. She was careful not to strain the muscles that were healing from the bullet wound.

Hearing the ecstasy in Amber's voice, Nicole moved closer to losing herself completely in her touch.

She was moving her hips in rhythm with Amber's. They both rode out their orgasms as they looked each other in the eye, feeling their connection. Nicole collapsed next to Amber. They were both panting, trying to catch their breath.

"Oh…my…god," Amber said.

"You…are…fucking…incredible." A goofy grin crept onto Nicole's face.

After several minutes, they managed to regain control of their breathing, mostly. Nicole leaned over and kissed Amber firmly on the lips.

"That was one hell of a wakeup." Amber giggled.

"I didn't hurt you, did I?" Nicole finally remembered that Amber was still injured.

"No, you made me feel more alive," Amber said, smiling sensually at Nicole. "More alive than I've felt in years."

"I love you," Nicole said before gently kissing Amber again.

"I love you, too," Amber said, smiling.

※ ※ ※ ※

Zach stirred and woke early that morning, his anxiety about leaving Amber getting the best of him and haunting his dreams. He was lying on the couch lost in thought when he thought he heard voices coming from upstairs. Zach rose to listen at the stairs and then blushed. What he heard completely eased his fears at leaving Amber there with Nicole.

Zach's phone beeped. He checked and saw a message from Heather.

Heather: Hi, Zach! How are you this morning?

Zach: I was a bit anxious about leaving Amber, but I feel better now.
Heather: What changed?
Zach: Um...I overheard her and Nicole... *blush*
Heather: Ooooohhhhh...
Zach: Yeah, I think she'll be okay here. LOL
Heather: She's in good and capable...um...hands. LOL
Zach: Bad joke!
Heather: It had to be said. Do you think everyone is up for some breakfast?
Zach: Well, they're up...and working up an appetite. LOL
Heather: I'll be by in a half hour with breakfast. You get them up. Hahaha
Zach: Sure, take the easy way out. See you soon.

Zach put his phone back on the table and looked toward the stairs. He was trying to think of a way to get Amber and Nicole's attention without going upstairs or letting them know he heard them. He decided to turn the ringer up on his phone and call it in hopes they would hear it ring.

Zach was about to call his phone from Nicole's house phone when Jill called him. He answered and told her that Heather was coming over shortly with breakfast. He heard movement from upstairs and knew they had heard the phone ring.

≈≈≈≈

Amber and Nicole were cuddling in bed when they heard Zach's phone ring and then him talking to Jill about breakfast.

"I guess that means we have to get up." Nicole looked up at Amber and smiled after seeing those blue eyes looking back at her.

"Don't wanna." Amber pouted.

"Me neither." Nicole leaned up and sucked on the lower lip that Amber was jutting out.

They both groaned at the touch, the closeness they felt being together.

"Do you need help getting dressed?" Nicole asked.

"Yeah, but I…um…need to shower, too, and I'm going to need some help with that, as well." Amber blushed.

"Oh, darn," Nicole said, laughing.

"I can try it alone…"

"No, we wouldn't want you to hurt yourself or risk you opening your incision again like last night." Nicole felt a pang of guilt for leaving Amber alone while she was sleeping. Nicole wondered if she had stayed if Amber would still have had the nightmare.

"Then to the shower it is?"

"I'll tell Zach we'll be down shortly, you just want to shower after getting out of the hospital."

"Okay," Amber said as Nicole got up and got dressed in a T-shirt and sweatpants and went downstairs.

❧❧❦❦

"Good morning," Zach said as Nicole came down the stairs.

"Good morning!"

"How are you this morning?" He turned a bit red and smiled.

"Er, I'm good. How are you?"

"I'm good. Heather and Jill will be coming by shortly. I hope that's okay."

"That's fine. I was just coming to tell you that Amber will be down in a little bit. She wants to try to shower to get rid of that hospital scent." Nicole tried not to smile too much.

"Oh…um…okay…Oh, hell. I heard you two," Zach blurted out, looking at the floor.

"You…OH…sorry." Nicole blushed at the thought of what Zach heard.

"Don't be. I wasn't going to tell you, but I'm horrible with secrets."

"Just tell me this, do Heather or Jill know?"

"Heather…"

"Crap…I'll warn Amber. We'll be down in a bit."

"Sorry."

"Don't be. I'd say I'm sorry, but I'm having a hard time buying that because I love that woman so damn much."

"Never be sorry for loving her. She deserves all the love in the world, and she feels the same way toward you. I've heard so many things about you, about dreams she had for you two…god, I want to pummel her father and brother for what they did."

"We all do, but at least they can't touch her now." Nicole put a hand on Zach's shoulder and offered him a supportive smile.

"True. Now go get her showered so I don't have to blush with Heather and Jill for too long."

"Yes, sir," Nicole said as she headed back upstairs.

Amber lay there daydreaming about the morning and how good it felt to wake up next to Nicole. She knew it was going to be harder for her to leave, but the ghosts that haunted her here weren't going to go away, ever.

Nicole came back into the room, and Amber could tell something was up.

"Is everything okay?" Amber asked, her voice laced with concern.

"Yeah…um…Zach heard us, and Heather knows, as well."

"Ohhh." Amber groaned as she put a pillow over her face. "I'll just stay up here for the day."

"He'll behave, he was blushing as much as I was." Nicole laughed.

"It isn't him I'm worried about. It's Heather that I don't want to see a knowing smirk from."

"Well, let's get you showered so we won't be doing that when she arrives. We may never live that down, either."

"Yes, ma'am." Amber smiled, her mind flashing to an image of a naked, wet Nicole.

Nicole helped Amber out of bed, and they moved into the bathroom where Nicole covered the bandage on Amber's side with protective tape so it wouldn't get wet. She helped Amber get out of her sling and brace, as well as her remaining clothes.

"You're staring at me," Amber said, feeling self-conscious.

"You're so gorgeous," Nicole said in a lust-filled voice.

"So are you." Amber pressed her body against the now naked Nicole and kissed her neck.

"We better shower."

"Maybe we need to make it a cool shower," Amber suggested.

The slightly warmer than lukewarm shower was calming for them both. Nicole helped Amber get cleaned up before she washed herself. They were admiring each other's body, but the knowledge of Zach downstairs and Heather and Jill heading over helped to quell some of their urges.

Nicole wrapped a towel around herself before she towel-dried Amber and helped her get dressed. She then got ready herself. Amber pulled Nicole close with her good arm, and they exchanged several soft kisses before they made their way downstairs just minutes before Heather and Jill arrived.

❦

"Good morning." Amber entered the living room where Zach was seated.

"Good morning," he replied but couldn't meet her eyes and turned a slight shade of red.

"Yeah, sorry you…um…heard us." Amber blushed, placing a hand on Zach's shoulder.

"Don't be. It made the fact that I have to leave today a bit easier. I know you're being well looked after," Zach said as Amber took a seat in a chair near him and Nicole brought in some coffee for herself, Zach, and Amber.

"You have my word that I'll take very good care of her." Nicole kissed the top of Amber's head as she handed Amber her coffee.

"I know, and I believe that, but it's hard for me to let go a bit. We've been connected at the hip for ten years."

"I would be the same way…but trust me, Nicole especially, and Heather and Jill will take good care of me until I get the approval to come back to New York."

"I know, I know," Zach said. "Don't push it, but get home soon!"

"Call her daily. She'll need to talk to someone other than me, I'm certain." Nicole giggled. "Plus, I doubt she's going to listen to me on the not pushing it, and I'm going to need some reinforcements."

"Oh, I should call Lucinda today," Amber said abruptly.

"Yeah, that might be a good idea. She was really concerned when I talked to her the other day."

"Nic, help me remember. I have a feeling with these pain meds my mind is going to be a bit fuzzy."

"Do you want to do it now? It's an hour later there," Nicole said.

"Yeah, do you know where my cell is?" Amber started to get up.

"Freeze. We'll leave, and you stay seated." Nicole handed Amber her phone. Amber smiled back.

Nicole and Zach excused themselves and went into the kitchen to give Amber some privacy.

≈≈≈≈

"Amber?" Lucinda said.

"Yeah, Lucinda, it's me." Amber smiled into the phone.

"It's so good to hear your voice. Are you okay? Zach said you were hurt pretty bad." The concern in Lucinda's voice made Amber feel better because she knew that Lucinda truly cared for her.

"I was, but I'll be fine. I wanted to call to make

sure you were aware that I was doing fine and to tell you that Zach will be bringing the release forms back with him today. I have to stay for another week or so. Basically, until the doctor here says I can fly."

"Why do you have to stay if you're okay?"

"I have a broken collarbone, a broken shoulder, and an incision where the bullet went into my side. The doctors don't want me to fly just yet. I should be cleared to come home in a week provided I don't get an infection."

"Well, take whatever time you need. I have the artwork, so I can start getting things ready for the show."

"Thank you. I'll be back in New York and back to work as soon as I can."

"Take care of yourself, we'll worry about the rest later. Your place in the show is safe, and it isn't for another two months. Your job is also safe, so please, just do what the doctors tell you."

"Thank you for your understanding and everything else," Amber said.

"I can't let my best new talent get away," Lucinda said as Amber heard the smile on her face.

"Lucinda, you've known me for ten years, I'm not that new of talent." Amber laughed. "I'll see you soon."

"Okay, if you need anything, just let me know. Bye," Lucinda said.

"Goodbye," Amber said and hung up.

༺༻༺༻

Jill and Heather arrived just as Amber was finishing her phone call.

"Good morning." Heather smiled as they walked

into the living room.

"Good morning." Amber smiled at the two women.

"Who would you be calling at this hour?" Heather said.

"My boss. I wanted to touch base with her and let her know I'm okay. The last time she talked with Zach, I was still in surgery. He just texted her that I was out and okay."

"Ah," Heather said as Nicole and Zach came back into the living room.

"I'm taking those damn keys away from you, Jill, if you're going to keep breaking in," Nicole teased.

"I'm a cop, Nicole. I know how to pick locks, too." Jill stuck her tongue out.

"Plus, how were we to know that you two were done with your morning adventure?" Heather grinned as Amber and Nicole blushed and Zach bowed his head.

The group enjoyed their breakfast and talked about life beyond the scope of Amber's family and her injuries. After a couple of hours, Zach reminded them that he needed to get to the airport so he could make his flight back to New York.

❦ ❦ ❦ ❦

The ride to the airport was a somber one for Amber. She knew that Zach had to get back and that Nicole was going to be with her, but for the past ten years, this man had been her security blanket and safe place.

"I'm going to miss you," Zach said as he awkwardly hugged Amber so as not to hurt her.

"I'm going to miss you, too." Amber held back tears.

"No heroics." Zach pulled back and looked Amber in the eye. "Don't push yourself."

"I promise. Do you honestly think those three are going to let me push it?"

"Well, I trust one of them not to let you push it. I somehow think the Woods sisters can be swayed."

"You're probably right." Amber laughed, knowing they could indeed be swayed.

She hugged him again before Nicole joined them.

"She's in good hands, I promise." Nicole wrapped an arm around Amber's waist, careful to avoid the bandage.

"I trust that you'll look out for her." Zach hugged Nicole. "Thank you."

"You don't need to thank me, I should be thanking you. You've kept her safe for the past ten years."

"I have, but the memory of you has kept her strong. Give her more memories to reinforce that strength."

Nicole pulled back and smiled at Zach. When he first arrived, she wanted to hate him. He had been there when she couldn't. He had Amber's trust and love. Now having gotten to know him, she cared about him and understood why he and Amber were close and that she didn't have to feel threatened. He wasn't there to take Amber from her.

They watched Zach go through security, and then Jill drove them back to Nicole's. Amber was feeling tired, so Jill and Heather left, and Nicole got Amber upstairs and gave her another pain pill. Nicole helped Amber change into a T-shirt and her panties before situating her in bed.

"Nic, will you stay with me until I fall asleep?" Amber asked, not wanting to be left alone.

"I'll stay with you until you wake up." Nicole smiled before getting changed herself and into the bed and feeling Amber cuddle up to her. To say that her heart and mind were calm would be an understatement. She felt complete and relaxed whenever Amber touched her.

Chapter Fourteen

Common Concerns

"Hey, Jill? Can we talk?" Heather asked after they helped Nicole get Amber situated.

"Sure, Squirt. Let's go back to my house, and we'll make dinner and talk."

"Great, thanks," Heather said as she fidgeted in the seat next to Jill.

The drive to Jill's house took two minutes. Once inside, Jill pulled two steaks out of the refrigerator and prepped them with salt and pepper, adding a bit of garlic powder. Jill then prepped a garlic butter to put on the steaks when they were done and resting. Heather prepared vegetables for grilling. She cut them up, added herbs, and crushed up fresh garlic to add in for flavor. She then grabbed the aluminum foil and created veggie tents, as her mom had always called them, to put on the grill to cook them along with the steaks.

"So, what's up?" Jill sat on the couch with a beer while the grill was warming.

"What do you think is going on with Nicole and Amber?"

"I honestly don't know. I mean, it seems like they're getting pretty close. They obviously slept together, so their old chemistry is still there. It isn't like Nic to just sleep with someone on a whim, even if it is Amber. Why? What has you concerned?"

"I'm afraid of what's going to happen to Nicole when Amber gets the all-clear to head back to New York. If they're rebuilding a relationship, Amber obviously has a pretty promising career in New York. She isn't going to just give that up to come back here. Even if it is for Nicole."

"So, you're afraid that Nicole is going to get hurt or she's going to leave, aren't you?"

"Yeah, basically." Heather sighed deeply and took a long drink of her beer.

"Well, that's something Nicole and Amber are going to have to talk about, little sister. We can only support them in their decisions. Don't get me wrong, I don't want Nicole leaving, but I agree that Amber isn't going to move back here with the opportunity she has right now with that art show."

"I've missed Amber a lot. I didn't realize how much because I was so pissed at her. Now that I know how much I missed her, I'm afraid she's going to go back to New York and forget all about us again."

"She didn't forget about us to begin with. I don't think she's going to stop talking to us and being a part of our lives now. Things are different. We're all different than we were back then. We have cellphones and Facebook to use to stay in touch now."

"Yeah, and time changes us all. What if she hurts Nicole? After everything she has been through…"

"That's between them," Jill said sternly.

"I know," Heather said in defeat. "I don't have to like or accept it willingly, though."

Jill got up and put her hand on Heather's shoulder. "It'll work out if it's meant to."

Jill went into the kitchen, grabbed the steaks

and veggies, and put them on the grill. She went back into the house and saw Heather lost in her thoughts. She knew Heather had always cared about Nicole and Amber. They were her best friends, and she knew that whatever happened would have a profound impact on Heather. Good or bad, that remained to be seen.

"I know it's hard because you care about them both. You need to remember, though, whatever happens, we'll always be here for them."

"I'll try to remember that." Heather hugged Jill and took another drink of her beer.

"Nicole is smart, she'll make the right choices, I believe in her for that."

"I know she is, but Amber has always been her kryptonite. As Nicole is Amber's. I just don't want either to get hurt or to lose either of them. I understand what you said about it being their choice, but part of me wants to make sure that it turns out best for both of them and for, well, all of us."

"I get that, I truly do. Unfortunately, we just have to sit back and watch how this plays out."

After a while, Jill went out and checked on dinner while Heather turned on the TV and found a movie for them to watch.

Jill returned with two plates of food and handed one to Heather as they ate and watched the movie. As the night wore on, they avoided the subject of Nicole and Amber, knowing that they had no control over things.

"Well, I should be getting home, I have an early morning," Heather said, yawning.

"All right. Hang in there, and we'll talk more as time gets closer to Amber getting approval to go home."

"Thanks for listening, Jill."

"Anytime." Jill watched Heather walk across the street and down three houses to her own place.

After their mother had died and they received the insurance money, the two women knew they couldn't live together. These two houses were far enough apart that they wouldn't get in each other's way, but close enough that they knew the other was just a minute away. Heather then used her part to pay for college and buy the hotel. Jill put herself through school and the academy to become an officer. She then opted to invest her leftovers and had been lucky in the market to have made more than she had lost.

❧ ❧ ☙ ☙

Nicole awoke to find that she and Amber were still in the same position they had fallen asleep in. Looking at the clock, Nicole saw she had slept for about three hours. She knew the pain pills Amber had taken before their nap would be wearing off shortly. Nicole was debating on waking Amber. It was good for her to rest, but if she stayed in one place too long, she was going to be sore, plus it was close to time to take care of the bandage again. She decided that she should wake Amber up.

"Baby." Nicole kissed the top of Amber's head that was resting on her shoulder. "Sweetie..."

"I'm so sorry I hurt you, Nicole. I love you... please don't hate me anymore," Amber mumbled sleepily. "I know you don't know why I left, but even from here, I can feel your hurt. I'll never let myself forget what I did to you."

"Amber," Nicole said a bit louder as she moved

her hand to rub Amber's back.

"Huh?" Amber woke up and became aware of her surroundings.

"It's time to wake up. We slept for about three hours," Nicole said, unsure if she should tell Amber what she heard.

"I was having a bad dream." Amber clung to Nicole tighter.

"I could tell. You were talking in your sleep." Nicole pressed her lips into Amber's hair.

"I'm so sorry, sweetie. D-did I wake you?"

"No, you didn't start until I tried to wake you up."

"I hope I didn't say anything bad." Amber was embarrassed and wondered what she said.

"You were apologizing for hurting me, you told me you loved me, then you asked me to stop hating you."

"Oh, that dream."

"Is that common?" Nicole's heart broke at the thought that the woman she loved had been tormenting herself like this for years.

"If I said no, would you believe me?" Amber quickly glanced up at Nicole before returning to her spot on Nicole's shoulder.

"No." Nicole smiled, and she again kissed the top of Amber's head. "But I would like to hear about it. If you're willing to tell me."

"I'll tell you about it after you take care of my bandage."

"You're afraid to tell me before, thinking I'll hurt you…"

"Yup." Amber laughed, squeezing Nicole close.

"Fine, lay on your back and lift your shirt, and

I'll go get the bandages and medicine." Nicole laughed along.

Amber lay back and pulled her shirt up, exposing her stomach. Nicole came back into the room and saw her lying there, and her breath caught.

Goddess, she's so beautiful, Nicole thought, her lips curling up in a smile.

"Like something you see?" Amber asked seductively. Nicole could only nod as she moved toward the bed.

Nicole set the bandage and antibiotic cream on the bed and leaned over and kissed Amber deeply and soundly. They both groaned into the kiss, feeling the closeness, the surge of excitement. This was something neither had felt in years. Not since they were last together ten years ago.

"You are so beautiful," Nicole said as she pulled back from the kiss, the love and devotion she had for Amber shining in her eyes.

"You still leave me breathless." Amber panted, still trying to believe that this woman really did love her and want her.

"We should get that bandage changed." Nicole pulled back from where she was leaning over Amber.

Nicole removed the old bandage and used a warm damp cloth to clean the area and then used the antibiotic cream, causing Amber to inhale deeply.

"Did I hurt you?" Nicole asked.

"No, it was just cold," Amber said, smiling.

Nicole put the new bandage on, then leaned forward and kissed the wound through the bandage, making sure not to put any pressure on the wound.

"Thank you," Amber said. "I'm sure a Nicole kiss is definitely what I need for it to heal quicker."

"Maybe if you play your cards right, I will see if Nicole kisses help your shoulder and collarbone."

"Mmm, as long as I can get that without clothes," Amber said seductively.

Nicole closed her eyes and took a deep breath, reminding herself that Amber was injured, and they needed to take it easy.

"Not fair," Nicole mumbled, clenching her thighs together, as well as her fists.

"Sorry, sweetie." Amber smiled innocently.

"Now what do you say we go downstairs and get something to eat and you can tell me about the disturbing dream you had?"

"Okay." Amber knew she wouldn't be able to get out of this conversation. Nicole helped Amber get up and stabilized her as gravity worked its magic on her shoulder. "I never knew just standing up could hurt like that. I can feel it pulling on my shoulder even with the sling on."

"I can adjust the sling for you. You might just need it to hold your arm a bit higher." Nicole carefully undid the Velcro on the sling and moved it a little and then tightened the strap so that it was higher, supporting more of Amber's arm's weight.

"That feels a lot better, thanks," she said and leaned over and kissed Nicole.

They went downstairs, and Nicole put some fruit salad in two bowls for them, and they moved to the living room. As they ate, Amber told Nicole about when she heard from Lucinda about her art being put in the next show. It was the day before she had left to come back.

"So, you had no idea that she was even watching your art?" Nicole asked.

"Not really. We had talked about it a couple of times, but there are so many artists affiliated with the gallery, and there are the artists that work there. I didn't realize she had kept an eye on things. I think my supervisor may have something to do with it. He has worked with me over the years to find new techniques and points of view. He comes across as a real gruff person, but he's just a big teddy bear."

"That sounds amazing. I hope I get to see more of your work." Nicole put their empty bowls on the coffee table.

"I'd love to show it to you. Maybe you can come to New York and see it in person." Amber glanced at Nicole out of the corner of her eye. She didn't think she could bring herself to fully make eye contact.

"I'd love that." Nicole smiled.

They adjusted on the couch so that Nicole was sitting with her back against the arm of the couch with her legs wrapped around Amber as she leaned against her on her good side.

"So, the dream. I've had it and other similar nightmares for years. The dream is always the same. My therapist thinks I need closure. Who knows, telling you may help me gain that. You aren't going to like this, I can guarantee that. Are you sure you want to know?"

"Yes, please." Nicole kissed the side of Amber's head.

"The dream starts the night that my dad and Jeffrey beat me, and I left. I see them attacking me from above, like an out-of-body experience. Then it flashes to me standing outside your window that night, and I'm apologizing for hurting you and telling you that I have to leave. After that, it shows you standing over my gravestone, crying. You look older, so I think it's been several years. You're still breathtakingly beautiful. Then I come up next to you while you're crying. That's when I tell you, 'I'm so sorry for hurting you. I love you.' I see the pain and anguish in your face, and all I can do is ask you to 'please don't hate me anymore. I know you don't know why I left, but even from here, I can feel your hurt.' You start to cry harder, and I tell you, 'I will never let myself forget what I did to you,' and then I see Jill and Erik come up and you place roses on my gravestone and turn and leave."

Nicole's heart broke as Amber told her about her dream. She placed her lips against Amber's head and kissed her as tears silently rolled down her face.

"How often do you have that dream?"

"That specific dream? A couple of times per month. This type of dream, three or four times per month," she said softly.

"Oh, baby." Nicole carefully pulled Amber closer.

They lay there holding each other for a long time. Amber was afraid to move or speak. She knew that by revealing this, it would again show how broken she truly was. In her mind, the more she revealed, the more she proved to Nicole that she was better off without her in her bed or in her life.

"Amber, I won't lie to you and tell you that your leaving didn't hurt and that I didn't like you much at times. I never hated you. I hate your father and brother, but I've never hated you. You need to forgive yourself. Baby, I can tell how much it's hurting you, tormenting you. I do not, nor would I ever, want you hurting like this."

"Nicole..." Amber interrupted.

"No, baby, let me finish. Had I known what you

went through that night and for all those years, I would have done everything I could to help you. That you know, but I'm so amazed by you and your strength to leave and stay away. I know it hasn't been easy for either of us, but I need you to tell me you honestly believe that I never hated you."

"I'm trying. Hearing you say it helps, but it's going to take me some time. I'm so ashamed, and, god, I don't know how to explain things."

"You don't have to explain them now. Just promise me that you'll think about what I've said and how amazing it feels at this moment with our bodies touching, you in my arms."

"It feels like heaven. Even when I get the pain in my side or shoulder, it isn't as bad when you're holding me."

"Good. I like hearing that," Nicole said. They fell into silence, enjoying the feel of each other, each lost in her own thoughts.

※※※※※

Erik was out walking around trying to clear his head. Since Amber's shooting, he had spent a lot of his time working or avoiding locations where she or the others would be. It wasn't that he was unhappy that Amber was back, it was that he was concerned for Nicole. He had watched Nicole struggle all those years without Amber. She was finally in a stable spot. What was she going to do if Amber didn't stay? How could she survive after all they had shared since Amber's return?

Erik was about to walk into the firehouse when he saw Jill's sheriff's cruiser pull up. About a minute later, she got out of the car.

"Erik, my man! Where have you been hiding?" Jill asked as she hugged him.

"I've been around," he replied, knowing this wouldn't satisfy her but hoping it might get her to back off a little.

"I assumed you've been around, but you haven't been by more than a couple of times to see Amber."

"I've just had some things to think about," Erik vaguely said.

"Want to tell me about it?"

"Can we walk and talk?"

"Sure, let me just grab my radio."

Jill opened the passenger side door and leaned in to grab her radio. She quickly called dispatch to let them know she didn't want to be disturbed unless it was an emergency. She locked the car door, and she and Erik headed down the street.

"So, what's up?"

"Do you think it's a good idea to have Amber and Nicole spending so much time together?"

"Why wouldn't I?" Jill was confused about where this was coming from.

"I'm just trying to look out for Nicole. Amber is going back to New York as soon as she's given the okay. I just think that with Nicole being as fragile as she has been over the years that them spending time together isn't going to help her."

"You know Amber's staying at Nicole's while she heals, right?"

"*What?*" he exclaimed. "I thought she was going to the hotel."

"Nope, Nicole decided that Amber was going to stay with her."

"Great." Erik shook his head.

The two had been walking and found themselves at the bridge near Old Miller's Pond.

"When did life get so complicated?" Erik asked.

"About the time we all became responsible adults," Jill said as they walked to the middle of the bridge and leaned on the railing, watching the water flowing underneath.

"We had a lot of good times growing up out here, didn't we?" Erik looked around the area.

"Yeah, we did. Look, Erik, I know you're concerned about Nicole, but this is something we can't interfere in. Nicole loves Amber and will do anything to help her. Even if it means she gets hurt in the process. For what it's worth, I believe Amber honestly loves Nicole still."

"I know they love each other. That was never an issue. My issue is I don't want to see my best friend's life pulled out from under her again. She won't survive that."

"Maybe you should try talking to Nicole. She's going to be the one to best allay your fears."

"Do you think Nicole would honestly listen and be objective?" Erik asked.

"You'll never know until you talk to her about it."

"You're right. Do you think you could keep Amber company while I talk to Nicole? We both know she isn't going to let Amber be unsupervised."

"Yeah, sure. Call Nicole, set up a time, and just let me know."

"Thanks, Jill," Erik said as they headed back toward town.

Nicole walked into the room with a perplexed look on her face. Amber glanced up and immediately felt her breathing falter with the look on Nicole's face.

"Sweetie, what's wrong?" Amber patted a spot on the bed next to her for Nicole to sit on.

"Erik called. He said he wants to talk to me privately tomorrow, but he knows I don't want to leave you alone, so he's bringing Jill and lunch with him."

"Did he say why he wants to talk to you?"

"No, that's the weird part. When I asked him, he just said he didn't want to get into it over the phone but not to stress on it. How the frilly hell does he expect me not to stress when he doesn't give me a single clue what it's about?"

Amber feigned a smile and wrapped her good arm around Nicole and pulled her closer.

"I don't know, sweetie, but you'll know soon enough."

"What if it's bad news?"

"Then we'll deal with it together." Amber kissed the side of Nicole's head.

"Amber, can we talk tomorrow about what's going on here? What we're doing?"

"I think that might be a great idea, provided all goes well with Erik."

Nicole leaned over, kissed Amber, and then pulled back and laid her head on Amber's good shoulder, as they lay there cuddled together but both lost deep in their own thoughts.

Chapter Fifteen

Addressing Concerns

Nicole had gotten up early. She was nervous about what Erik wanted to discuss with her and about her impending talk with Amber about the status of their relationship and where they go from here.

Nicole had cleaned the entire living room, dusted, vacuumed, and even reorganized the magazines by date. She then moved to the kitchen. She had cleaned out and scrubbed the refrigerator, including the drawers. She was now working on cleaning the stove and oven when Amber came downstairs and stood in the doorway of the kitchen.

"Whatcha doing?" Amber asked.

"What? Ouch! Shit!" Nicole yelped as she tried to raise her head while it was still in the oven and managed to hit her head on the upper element and on the interior of the oven. Amber winced.

"Careful. I'm sorry I startled you." Amber quickly made her way over to the oven.

"I hope I didn't wake you." Nicole rubbed the back of her head.

"Stand up," Amber said softly. Nicole stood, and Amber felt the back of her head to make sure there wasn't a cut. "You didn't wake me. I rolled over and tried to snuggle, but I could only find pillows."

"Sorry. I needed to keep myself busy. I decided to clean since I'm not working at the moment."

"Why aren't you working? What do you do anyway? I just realized we've never discussed that."

"How about we grab some coffee and go sit on the lanai?"

"That sounds great." Amber leaned forward and kissed Nicole. "Good morning."

"Good morning," Nicole said, pulling back from the kiss.

They both gathered their coffee, and Amber followed Nicole to the lanai. It was a very tranquil area. Amber hadn't even noticed that the hallway leading to it existed. There was a tasteful wicker table and chair set, a plush-looking swing that looked like someone had taken a Papasan sofa and hung it up. There was a waterfall feature that Nicole turned on, and with the touch of another button, the sounds of a distant thunderstorm surrounded them in the room.

"Nicole, this is incredible," Amber said as she looked around.

"Thanks. I wanted an area to escape the world. Erik helped me build most of it, but, well, you're the only person to have ever seen the fully completed room."

"You mean Jill, Heather, and Erik haven't seen this?" Amber asked as they put their coffee on the end table and curled up together in the swing.

"Nope. Are you comfortable?" Nicole asked.

"Yes." Amber moved a little closer to Nicole. "If you haven't shown this to anyone else…why me?"

"Because you and I have a different connection, and well, I wanted us to have a room or a place that was only for us. I built a lot of this with you in mind."

"Really? This is incredible."

"The thunderstorms you hear surrounding us…I actually recorded it one night so I could have something authentic sounding. I remembered how much you enjoyed listening to the rain."

"I still do," Amber interrupted quietly.

"The bamboo has always been a look that I associate with Zen architecture."

"I think this is amazing. There's a place in my apartment that I can sit and listen to the rain hitting the rooftops and leaves…every once in a while, there's a ting of it hitting a car or one of the few streetlamps nearby."

"That sounds nice."

"It is. How long have you had this house?"

"I bought it about two years after you left. It was a complete fixer-upper, but with Erik, Jill, Heather, and your mother, we got it done. The landscaping outside and the lush fake plants in here are your mother's touch."

"I recognized her work," Amber said with a hint of amusement in her voice. "Tell me about your life after I left. What did you do? Where did you go to school? What do you do for a living? I really know nothing about your life now."

"Maybe we should get some breakfast and take care of your bandage before we get into a long discussion like that. I want to know all that stuff about you, too."

"Okay, but can we come back in here?"

"Yep!"

Nicole and Amber went upstairs to take care of the bandage.

"Hey, Erik," Jill said as she entered the diner near the firehouse.

"Hey," Erik said, still wearing his EMT uniform.

"So, what time are we meeting Nicole?"

"Um, I told her we'd be there around noon and we'd bring lunch."

"So, why are we here at the ass crack of dawn?" Jill asked.

"Because you agreed to meet me after I got off work. It isn't my fault you didn't ask what time I got done." Erik laughed.

"You better hope they bring me coffee soon," Jill said, glaring at him.

Erik raised his hand to get the waitress's attention and pointed to Jill. The waitress got the message and grabbed a cup and the carafe of coffee. She came over and poured Jill her cup and refilled Erik's, as well. Erik then ordered the bacon, eggs, and pancakes. Jill ordered a veggie omelet, pancakes, and extra bacon.

"Jill, why do you order the veggie omelet and then get extra bacon?"

"Because you know it's the only way I'm going to eat those damn veggies. The bacon just masks their nasty taste. Stop laughing and judging me, Harrison," Jill said as Erik laughed and shook his head.

"That's hilarious."

"Shut up." Jill scoffed. "So, have you thought about what you're going to say to Nicole?"

"Yeah, I think so." Erik paused to take a sip of his coffee. "I'm going to tell her that I want to bring the concerns out into the open so she isn't blindsided and that I don't want to interfere, but because I care for her, I felt I should say something."

"Yeah, that's going to go over well with her," Jill said.

"What would you say?"

"Well, I didn't say I had anything better. I was just stating that no matter what we say, she isn't going to be happy hearing it. She's in dreamland with Amber being back in her life."

"I know, but something has to be said. Do you think if I truly piss her off, you can put me in protective custody again?"

"Yeah, we have the wimpy weasel cell all set for you," Jill teased.

Erik was about to respond to her comment when their breakfast arrived. They thanked the waitress as she refilled their coffee and then they ate. Erik told Jill about the oddities that he had seen overnight, and she told him what was going on in her office.

✦✦✦✦

"Um, do you think before we change the dressing, we could maybe shower?" Amber asked.

"Sure. It's probably best that we do it before we change the dressing so the new one doesn't get wet and we don't waste the antibiotic cream. I know we can always get more, but we don't have to go back to the doctor for another few days. I know that if I can avoid that place, I would feel much happier, not that it's something that you're looking to—" Nicole's babble was cut off by Amber's lips pressed against hers. The kiss started slowly as a stop to the babbling and then as they each moved their lips, the kiss became that of need and passion. They finally broke for air.

"Wanna explain why you suddenly became nervous?" Amber asked as she pressed her forehead against Nicole's.

"Well, I...I have no clue. I guess I'm worked up because of what we're going to talk about and then my mind is hyperactive in wondering what Erik wants to talk about. I'm sorry."

"You have nothing to be sorry about. If you want to put the talk off until after Erik and Jill leave, I'm okay with that. We can just shower and get ready and then go back to the lanai and cuddle. Or if there's something else you'd rather do..."

"Now who's being nervous?" Nicole giggled before leaning forward and kissing Amber.

"Let's get the shower over with and then we can figure things out," Amber said.

Nicole nodded and started the shower warming while she helped Amber get out of the sling and then carefully helped her unbutton her shirt and slid it off her shoulders and put it in the hamper. Nicole then helped Amber out of her boxers and panties.

"You realize the self-control it takes getting you undressed and not taking advantage of the proximity," Nicole said while kneeling in front of Amber.

"It takes some pretty strong self-control from this point of view, as well." Amber blushed, seeing Nicole's eyes widen and then a smirk creep onto her face.

Nicole stood, undressed, and moved to put the waterproof tape over Amber's dressing before moving them into the shower. Nicole washed Amber's hair and helped her wash up. She then washed her own hair and quickly lathered and washed her body. Amber did her best not to interrupt what Nicole was doing, but all she could think about was how gorgeous this woman standing inches away from her was.

How am I going to leave you when the doctor says I can go home? Would you ever come to visit or stay in New York with me? Amber thought as she watched Nicole rinse her body off.

"Are you done?" Nicole asked for the second time, finally jarring Amber out of her thoughts.

"What?"

"Are you done in the shower?"

"Oh, yeah, sorry."

"Where'd you go?" Nicole asked.

"I just got lost in thought. We'll talk about it later. Don't stress, either." Amber wrapped her good arm around Nicole and pulled her closer. "It was nothing bad."

Amber leaned forward and slowly kissed Nicole. It was a kiss that carried depth and meaning. She was hoping Nicole would understand how much she meant to her, even though Amber wasn't sure how to explain it all…yet.

They got out of the shower and dried off. Nicole led Amber into the bedroom and had her lie on the bed while she removed the waterproof tape and carefully cleaned the wound area. Nicole noticed that it was showing signs of healing. She quickly put the medicine and the bandage back on and then they both got dressed and headed to the lanai.

❧❧❧❧

Nicole and Amber were still on the lanai when they heard the doorbell ring.

"I guess it's time to find out what they want," Nicole said as she and Amber got out of the swing.

"Do you want Jill and me to go upstairs?" Amber asked as they made their way to the door.

"We'll see what they want and go from there."

Nicole opened the door and motioned for Jill and Erik to come in. The group then migrated to the dining room, and Erik pulled the subs and chips out of the bag, and everyone grabbed one. He had gotten two veggie lovers subs, remembering what Nicole and Amber had eaten when they were all younger.

"I can't believe you remember what type of sub I liked," Amber said, surprised.

"Well, I knew that Nic still loved them, so I took a chance you did, as well." Erik smiled.

They ate and had small talk. Erik talked about work, Jill talked about the weather for the week. Nicole was quiet, as was Amber. They held hands under the table, trying to reassure each other.

After they cleaned up, Jill and Amber went upstairs for Amber to take a pain pill and rest while Erik and Nicole went out on the front porch to talk.

⁂

"All right, Erik. What's up?" Nicole said.

"I wanted to talk to you about Amber." He put his hand up to stop her from cutting him off. "Let me just voice what I have to say before you interrupt." Seeing Nicole sit back in her seat, he continued. "I'm just worried about you getting hurt when she goes back to New York. I know you're aware that she's leaving, she has an apartment, she has a job, and an art show coming up. I just want to make sure you aren't getting too emotionally attached."

"I'm in love with her," Nicole said.

"I know you're in love with her, and I've heard her say she's in love with you. I just want to make sure you two talk about what's going to happen when she goes back. I love you...you're my best friend. I know the past ten years have been really hard for you, and I don't want you to have to go through any more emotional pain than you have already."

"I get that, and Amber and I have already discussed the fact that we need to discuss what's going on with us," Nicole said.

"Wait...you discussed the fact that you need to discuss what's going on? What the hell logic is that?"

"Shut up. It made sense to us," Nicole said, hitting his arm.

"I would hope so." He laughed.

"We actually were out on the lanai earlier..."

"Wait. *She* got to see the lanai? Nobody has seen the lanai. Did you blindfold her?"

"No, I built that for her and me if you recall." Nicole smirked. "As I was saying. We were out on the lanai talking, and she asked what I had been up to over the past ten years, what I did for a living, and we agreed we need to talk about us, as well."

"Wow, I'm sorry I didn't give you two enough credit. I was afraid you were lost in the love and lust of being together again."

"Well, there's that, too." Nicole blushed. "I'll tell you this much, loving her now is easier and more intense than it was before. We aren't kids anymore. We've both changed a lot. I don't know where this is going or what the future holds, that's something Amber and I have to discuss."

"I'm sorry, Nic." Erik bowed his head.

"What are you sorry for?"

"For not realizing that you've both grown up and aren't blinded by your love."

"Thanks. We are blinded by some things, but we're both realistic on this. When she goes, I know I'm going to be crushed. God, I love falling asleep next to her and waking up next to her. She has a life in New York and a promising career. I won't do anything to hinder that…even if it breaks my heart."

Erik wrapped an arm around Nicole and pulled her against him, putting her head on his shoulder.

"Well, you know all of us will be here for you. Um, another thing I wanted to talk to you about is, well, Jill, Heather, and I want to go up for Amber's show. Heather talked to Zach about it and about getting us tickets. I'm sure this is a given, but would you like to go with us?"

"I-I…um…I want to go, but what if she doesn't want me to go…I mean, I know she said she wants me to see her art sometime, but this show is huge for her, and I don't want to disturb her in her element."

"All right, where did the logical girl that I was just having a conversation with go? Nic, if she's going to want anyone there, it's going to be you. The one she loves."

"Sorry, I'm starting to overthink things."

"Well, I'll let it slide this time. Next time, I'm telling Jill," Erik said as they both laughed.

❦❦❦❦

"How are you feeling?" Jill asked as she helped Amber into Nicole's bed.

"It hurts, but I can definitely tell that it's getting better." Amber took a pill out of the bottle next to the bed and then held the water bottle out for Jill to open it for her.

"I'm glad you're starting to feel better." Jill opened the water bottle and handed it back to Amber. She took her medicine, and Jill closed the bottle for her again.

"So, what's Erik's concern?"

"W-what? What makes you think Erik has concerns?" Jill looked around the room, avoiding Amber's eyes.

"I'm not stupid. I would actually be surprised if none of you had concerns."

"You would?"

"Yeah. I know how protective you are of Nicole and everything she's been through over the years. So, what are his concerns? Or what are yours? Or even Heather's?"

"You're more direct now than you used to be." Jill laughed. "The concerns are all the same. We don't want to see Nicole get hurt when you go back to New York. We also don't want you to drop out of our lives once you go back."

"Nicole and I have a lot to talk about. We need to discuss what's going on between us, what we want for the future. Are we still compatible?"

"Well…um…I'm guessing you're still compatible if you're sleeping together. By the way, did your doctor say that sort of activity was okay to do at this juncture?"

"Yes, we still love each other. She is and always has been my everything…but we both have our own lives now, as well."

"So, have you thought about discussing this stuff with her?"

"Yeah, we were out on the lanai earlier, and we

decided that later today or tomorrow we're going to have that heart-to-heart discussion. You know the one that says what we've been up to for the past ten years, where we want our life to go, where we want *us* to go or if there is even an us. Why are you looking at me like that?" Amber saw Jill's wide-eyed look and gaping mouth.

"You were out on the lanai? What the hell! None of us has ever seen that damn area, and you just get to waltz out there and see it? Nicole has some serious explaining to do," Jill said.

"Yes, I was out there, and anything further, you have to take up with Nicole."

"Fine. So, what are your feelings for her?"

"You already know that. I'm in love with her and always have been."

"But what about the future?"

"I can't say until Nicole and I talk. That's something we need to decide together," Amber said.

"Yeah, but you have to have something in mind for what direction you want things to go."

"I do, but until Nicole and I talk, I'm not saying anything."

"Well, poop. Fine. So, what's it like living in New York?"

"At first, it was scary, but I found this amazing brownstone after being in the city for a couple of years. It's on this quiet tree-lined street, and there are only two units in the building. My landlords live below me. They're this cute little old couple."

"That sounds nice. Are the places as small and expensive as they always say they are on TV?"

"Most are, but again, I have these amazing landlords."

Nicole and Erik finished their talk and headed upstairs to check on Amber. Nicole knocked, and the two entered the room.

"Hey, baby," Nicole said as she went over and kissed Amber.

"You all done with your talk?" Amber said.

"Yeah," Nicole said, smiling back at Amber.

"So, what were you two gossiping about?" Erik asked.

"Amber was telling me about New York," Jill said.

"So, did you two get your concerns all worked out?" Amber offered Erik and Nicole one of her lopsided smiles.

"Jill! What the hell?" Erik exclaimed.

"It wasn't that big of a secret. I figured it out all by myself," Amber said.

"Yeah, we got them worked out. The big thing is that you and I need to sit down and discuss stuff." Nicole took Amber's good hand in her own.

"I wanna know why Amber gets to see the lanai and the rest of us don't," Jill said, pouting.

"Because it was created for her and me." Nicole stuck her tongue out at her friends.

"Fine, be that way then." Jill pouted again.

"We will." Amber laughed as she tried to stifle a yawn.

"All right, I think it's time to go. Amber needs her rest," Jill said.

The group said their goodbyes, and Nicole escorted Jill and Erik out, giving them each a hug, then went back upstairs and found Amber fighting to stay awake.

"Why are you fighting the meds?" Nicole curled up next to Amber.

"Because we were going to talk…" Amber said, yawning again.

"Sleep now. When you wake up, we'll go out on the lanai, I'll turn on the thunderstorm and waterfall, and we'll talk."

"I love you, Nicole," Amber said.

"I love you, too." Nicole leaned in and kissed Amber and then allowed her to curl up next to her as they both drifted off to sleep.

Chapter Sixteen

The Talk

Amber woke up feeling the warmth of Nicole's body next to her. By the even breathing, she could tell Nicole was still asleep. Amber eased out of bed and made her way to the bathroom. She was still a little groggy, but not so unstable that she would need to wake Nicole. Amber used her good arm to splash water on her face to try to fend off the residual affects from the medication.

"Amber?" Nicole stretched out on the bed and found it empty.

"I'm right here," Amber opened the bathroom door, came back into the bedroom, and sat next to Nicole.

"Are you all right?"

"Yeah, I just wanted to splash some water on my face. The meds linger, and I don't like how that feels."

"Are you hurting? Did you sleep well?"

"I'm okay, I can tell it's healing. I slept pretty well. I had this amazing snuggle buddy," Amber said, offering a smile. "Did you sleep well?"

"Yeah, I did." Nicole took Amber's hand in hers and played with her fingers. "Are you hungry?"

"No, not really. I'm actually feeling a bit anxious about the talk we have coming up."

"Why are you anxious?"

"I...I don't know. I'm partially afraid that I'll say something to hurt you, and that's the last thing I want to do."

"I understand that. I have the same fear, but we need to talk. Right?"

"Being an adult isn't fun sometimes." Amber laughed as she brought Nicole's hand up to her mouth and kissed the back of it.

"No, it isn't. Let's go get something to drink and then head out to the lanai."

Amber nodded in agreement. They made their way downstairs and eventually into the lanai.

֍֍֍֍

Jill and Erik went to visit Heather at the hotel after they left Nicole's. They knew she would be waiting to hear how the talk went.

"Hey, Squirt," Jill said as they entered Heather's office.

"Hey." Heather looked up from her computer. "How'd it go at Nicole's?"

"It went really well, actually." Erik sat in the chair across from Heather.

"Really?"

"Yeah," Erik said and then he and Jill filled Heather in on their respective talks with Nicole and Amber.

"Did either offer any other information?"

"Not a word," Jill said.

"Well, that isn't helpful. When are they going to talk?"

"Today, when we left, they were going to take a nap and then talk later."

"Sure, nap." Heather laughed, making air quotes.

"Actually, Amber took a pain pill, so I think they were legitimately going to nap," Jill said.

"So, when Amber gets the okay to go back, do you see this going well or not?" Heather asked.

"I don't know. Nic says they're different people and adults, so she knows it'll be hard, but they're being open and honest," Erik said.

"I guess we're just going to have to wait and see."

※※※※

Nicole and Amber were finally situated in the swing, and they were enjoying the sounds of the rain while they gathered their thoughts.

"So, who's going to go first?" Nicole said hesitantly.

"I totally think you should." Amber giggled.

"Oh, really?" Nicole smiled.

Amber captured Nicole's lips in a heated kiss.

"Please." Amber kissed Nicole again.

"Knight, are you bribing me with kisses?" Nicole said when they finally broke for air.

"Is it working?"

"Yes, damn it," Nicole said as they both laughed. "Fine, I'll go first."

"Thank you."

"So, Life since you left. It has been hard, stressful, lonely missing you. I guess I'll start from the beginning. Erik called the day after you left. He told me your mom was hurt bad. I thought for certain you would either be at the hospital or show up there. Now I know and understand why you never did."

"You mean my mom never told you what

happened? About my dad and Jeffrey beating me up that night? About her telling me to leave?"

"No, she just said you left, but she never said why. There were times when she claimed she didn't remember what happened to you or what caused you to leave."

"I don't understand why she wouldn't tell you that."

"Maybe she thought at that point if we knew we'd try to find you and bring you back. After your mom got out of the hospital, she moved in with me. I was renting this house at the time, and eventually, I bought it."

"How were you affording it? We were barely out of school," Amber said.

"Well, I had this big surprise planned for you before you left. I wanted to tell you that I had started my own company, and I was doing freelance software development and making pretty good money doing it. I'm actually still doing it. I got a few government contracts, so I can't discuss most of what I do, but they pay well and allow me the opportunity to work when I choose and play around, as well. For fun, I created a couple of games for the Apple and Android platforms."

"That's incredible, Nic. You always were so much smarter than the rest of us. For a long time, I wondered what it was you ever saw in me," Amber said, not meeting Nicole's eyes.

"Hey, look at me." Nicole lifted Amber's chin until their gazes met. "I saw an amazingly smart woman who had the heart of an angel, the body of a goddess, and she didn't care that I was a geek."

"You have to know that I was in love with you long before we got together," Amber admitted, giving her a lopsided grin.

"Good, because I was in love with you before we got together, as well," Nicole said, laughing. "Shortly after your mom moved in, my parents were killed. It was a really hard time for me. Even though my parents were absent, they were still my parents. I hit a pretty low spot. I mean, my parents had just died, you were gone, and we had no clue where you were or if we'd ever see you again. Just as things started to settle down, Mrs. Woods got sick and died, then the stuff with your dad happened. Again, as things started to calm down, your mom got sick. It was sort of a waterfall of bad luck. Don't get me wrong, there were good times in there, but the bad really seemed to overshadow the good."

"I'm sorry I wasn't here. I can't believe I missed all that. Mrs. Woods was always so nice to me. Your parents, I really only met them a few times, even though we've been friends since we were five," Amber said.

"Nicole, I understand that you and Amber enjoy spending time together. I just don't understand why that Jill Woods girl hangs around you two," Sharon Brooks said.

"Mom, we've known each other since we were five. It has always been Amber, Jill, Erik, and me as a group."

"That Harrison boy is trouble. He's going to end up sleeping with one of you and ruining your lives," Sharon said, shaking her head.

"No, he isn't. Jill doesn't like him that way."

"Well, you had better not sleep with him. Wait until you find a guy that loves you."

"I'm already dating the someone who loves me and who I'm going to build a future with."

"What do you mean? Your father and I haven't met anyone. You only talk about your little group."

"I've been dating Amber for a year now. I love her, and she loves me. Once we graduate, we're going to get a place together."

"Over our dead body," Sharon said before storming out.

"I remember your mom and my mom having a heated argument about us moving in together after school," Amber said, smiling.

"Yeah, that wasn't fun. Your mom had a good laugh when she moved in instead of you. She always teased me that I just wanted one of the hot Knight females to live with." Nicole laughed.

"What about your life over the past ten years? What did you do when you left? Why did you choose New York?" Nicole asked.

"After I left here, as cliché as it sounds, I hopped on a train and just rode until I felt safe. Interestingly enough, New York City was where I felt safe."

"You rode until New York City and got off because you felt safe? Seriously?" Nicole laughed. "Baby, did you bump your head after the doctor looked at you?"

"Yeah, I know. With all those people, I wasn't going to stand out. I could hide in the shadows and be free of the fear."

"I don't know how you could possibly think you were hiding in the shadows. You're much too beautiful." Nicole laughed before kissing the side of Amber's head.

"You, my love, are biased," Amber said, giving Nicole a chaste kiss.

"Yes, I am." Nicole pulled Amber into a heated kiss. "Now continue."

"Mmm, can't we just kiss instead? I love the feel of your lips on mine."

"Nope! Talk first, kissing later."

"Fine. After I got to New York, I found a place to stay and started to go to the galleries. There were never many people there, so while I healed, I didn't have to deal with the looks or the questions that came with the injuries. That was when I met Zach and got the job as a replicator. I spent a lot of time with Zach and Travis until he passed away. Zach was devastated. I think we pretty much lived together from a month after we met until I found the brownstone I live in now two years later."

"Living in a brownstone sounds nice. What's your place like?"

"I'm really very lucky for the place I have. It's the upper half of the house and it's huge. There are three bedrooms, three baths, with roof access. It's an amazing open layout. There's a large bay window in the living room that overlooks the street. I like to sit at it and listen to the rain. Depending on the storm, if I open the windows on each side of the house, I can get something that sounds a lot like this." Amber motioned around the lanai. "One of the rooms I converted into a studio to do my painting and film processing."

"You still process your own film?"

"Yeah, I'm still that picky about my prints," Amber said as they laughed together.

"Um, as I recall, that wasn't the only reason you processed the prints yourself." This caused Amber to blush.

"Aren't you glad those aren't the ones that

Lucinda saw and wanted to show?" Amber watched Nicole's eyes widen as she blushed.

"So...um...do you have lots of friends in New York?"

"Not really. I have Zach, Jessie, and a few others, but otherwise, I keep to myself."

"What do you do for fun?"

"For a while, Zach, me, and a few others used to go out to the club to dance, but I just didn't enjoy it as much. Without you there to dance with me...I didn't want to dance with anyone else. You always filled my dance card."

"Erik and Jill did the same thing. They would drag me out or even set me up on dates, and ew, no thanks. Not that they chose bad people, it wasn't you."

"I hate the idea of leaving you soon," Amber blurted out and then averted her eyes.

"What?" Nicole asked.

"I hate the idea of leaving you. I know you have your work and your life here, and I have my job and the art show going on in New York, but lying here in your arms feels incredible. It's the closest to being home I've felt in ten years."

"I know, I feel it, too." Nicole pulled Amber closer and kissed the top of her head. "I guess we keep avoiding the subject of the future, don't we?"

"Yep, I know I have to go back to the doctor in a couple of days. I'm scared to go."

"Why?"

"Because then reality sets in, and I have to leave here..."

"I don't like reality!"

"Nic, will you come to my show?"

"Of course," Nicole said.

"I mean, not just to see it and be supportive. Will you be my official date for it?"

"And how is that different from me coming to the show?"

"Well, there's a dinner the night before, a gallery walk-through, then you'd be my arm candy." Amber laughed. "Mostly, though, you would have to stick with me instead of with Zach or if the others were to come. Plus, there's an after party that I hear is pretty intense."

"Hmm, arm candy for a gorgeous woman or hanging with the people I've seen daily for years… that's a hard choice, Ms. Knight."

"I'm serious. I'm scared that when I leave… that you and I are going to go back to being distant strangers. I woke up earlier because of it."

"That isn't going to happen. I just got you back in my life, I'm not letting you go again." Nicole squeezed her tight. "I love you too much to lose you."

"I…" Amber started to say when the emotions overwhelmed her, and she did the only thing she could think of. She rolled onto her back and pulled Nicole on top of her. "Make love to me, Nic. Make me feel the intensity of our love and our bond."

"My pleasure." Nicole growled as her predatory instincts took over, and she lost herself in Amber.

※ ※ ※ ※

"So, how long do we give them before we start calling or stopping by?" Erik asked, his leg nervously bouncing.

"We give them as much time as they need." Jill glared at him.

"Are they going to call us when they're done

talking?" Heather asked.

"You're as bad as Erik. We didn't set up anything. I think we just have to patiently wait for them to contact us. This is a huge discussion for them. The outcome of this can change a lot for all of us, but we don't have a say in it."

"Yeah, and they're both very good at avoiding talking. Well, at least they were the last time they had to have a serious talk," Erik said.

"Oh, I remember that very well. *You* weren't the one that walked in on them." Jill blushed.

"Huh?" Heather said.

"Oh, Nicole and Amber were supposed to be discussing college and what they were going to do with their future. You know, get a place together? Move away? What they were going to be when they grew up."

"Okay." Heather noticed that Erik's eyes had glazed over.

"Well, I knew they were supposed to be talking, but I still stopped by to see what they were up to. Mrs. Brooks let me in and told me they were upstairs. I figured it had to be safe to go up there, hell, Nicole's parents were there. I was *very* wrong. I got up there, I knocked, and I heard something. I couldn't make out what was said, so I stupidly opened the door and, well…I will just say they had a very spirited sex life."

"Really? Was it kinky?" Heather asked as a smile crept across her face.

"Ugh, I say it again…you are as bad as Erik." Jill hit her arm.

"Ow, brute." Heather rubbed the spot.

"Wimp." Jill laughed.

"Do you think Nicole would move to New York if Amber asked her to?" Heather asked.

"I don't know. I hope they discuss that, as well," Jill said before hitting Erik hard in the arm, causing him to jump and cry out.

"Ow, brute," Erik said, rubbing his arm.

"You are both such wimps. Did you have a nice mental vacation?" Jill laughed.

"Right up until the police brutality started."

※ ※ ※ ※

Nicole and Amber had just finished their second round of lovemaking and were trying to catch their breath.

"You know if you are this good at making love while injured, I'm going to be in real trouble when you have the use of both of your hands." Nicole snuggled closer.

"Mmm, I can't wait." Amber ran her hand down the front of Nicole's body. "You are pretty darn good yourself. Have you been practicing?"

"Only when I dream of you." Nicole rolled on top of Amber and pressed their bodies together.

"I like your dreams," Amber said in a sultry tone.

"You should, you star in them regularly," Nicole said before Amber kissed her hard, causing them both to groan.

※ ※ ※ ※

"Hello, Zach," Lucinda said as he entered her office.

"Good morning, Lucinda."

"How's Amber?"

"The last I heard from her, she was doing better.

She has a doctor's appointment in a couple of days. I think that's the one where they'll give her the okay to fly."

"What happened down there?"

"Amber will have to explain," Zach said, smiling sympathetically. He knew he could explain it, but this wasn't his story to tell.

"She's safe, though, right?"

"Yes, she's being very well cared for." Zach smirked. "Here are the forms she had signed."

"Thank you. When you learn when she'll be back, please let me know."

"I will. Have a good day."

Zach left the office and went to the studio to start work. He had never liked working in the studio without Amber being there. He hoped she would be back soon, but he was also concerned about what state she would be in mentally having to leave Nicole.

Chapter Seventeen

The Doctor

Amber and Nicole made their way out of the lanai and into the kitchen to make something to eat after their extended lovemaking adventures. Amber looked through the cupboards and refrigerator and decided she would try to make dinner. She knew she was leaving soon and felt it was the least she could do. Nicole sat at the island and watched as Amber whipped up their dinner. Amber set plates and cutlery at the island.

"How long should we make the gang wait to find out what we talked about?" Nicole took a bite of the pancake taco Amber had made for them. "Oh, my god, this is amazing."

"I'm glad you like it." Amber smiled. "I always loved cooking for you. As for how long we make them wait, why don't you invite them over for breakfast tomorrow and we'll make some more breakfast tacos and we can talk things over?"

"That sounds like a good idea, then the following day, you have to go see the doctor," Nicole said sadly.

"Hey, beautiful." Amber lifted Nicole's chin with a finger. "I'm sad about the idea of leaving you, but we agreed we're still going to be a part of each other's life. You're going to be my smoking hot date to my art show. If you play your cards right, there may even be breakfast in bed."

"And a tour of your brownstone?"

"I planned on you staying with me. I'm sorry if I didn't make that clear to you, but when you're in New York, I want you as close to me as possible."

"Oh," Nicole said, embarrassed.

"What's going on in that head of yours?"

"What if now that you've gotten us all back as friends and stuff…what if you start to get on with your life and find someone else? Not that I think I'm the perfect person, but I love you so much, and I just want you. I've always wanted just you. I can't ask you to want me, and I can't ask you to…I don't know what I'm thinking. I'm mostly afraid of losing you again once you go back to New York."

"I love you. I know that making this work, and trust me I want us to work, will be difficult. I don't know how we're going to do it, but I'm not giving up hope or the idea of us. You're the love of my life, and I think we're the only two that can say that they met the love of their life at the age of five even if we didn't know it then."

"You make it sound so romantic." Nicole giggled.

"It is, in our quirky way." Amber leaned forward and kissed Nicole. "Why don't you call the gang while I clean up and put the dishes in the dishwasher, then maybe we can cuddle and watch a movie or TV."

"I can clean up while I call them. We need to change your bandage, so why don't you go get that together, and I'll be up when I'm done."

"Okay," Amber said.

Amber kissed Nicole and then headed upstairs. She was feeling pretty sore after their amorous activities that afternoon, but she knew she couldn't tell Nicole about it. Nicole would blame herself, and she couldn't let the end of her time there be marred by negativity. It was going to be hard enough leaving in a few days, and Amber knew from how she was feeling that she was going to get the okay to go home. It was then that she realized that New York was home for her now. Even though the love of her life lived here and this was where Amber had spent the first part of her life. She had lived in fear and could never call this place home. Yes, a small-town girl in a big city, there was the fear and the unknown, but those were things that Amber could control and had overcome. She had made a life there, and she was excited to get back to it but more excited about showing it to Nicole when she came up for the show.

After Amber left the room, Nicole gathered the dishes and rinsed them and loaded the dishwasher. She then grabbed her phone and called Jill. Nicole explained that they had talked and that they just wanted to spend a quiet night together, but she said she and Amber wanted the gang to come over around nine the next morning to discuss their decision.

Jill tried to get additional information out of her, but Nicole knew if she gave in, she would never get off the phone. After hanging up with Jill, Nicole sat there for a minute thinking about Amber going back to New York. Nicole admitted to herself that yes, she would know where Amber was going and would get to see her off, but she was trying to convince herself that it was better than the way Amber had left before. Nicole knew she was going to see Amber again in less than two months, but she had grown used to sleeping next to her. Nicole shook her head to clear the thoughts. She couldn't ruin the night and the remaining time that Amber had here with her fears and doubts. Nicole collected herself, called Erik and Heather, and then went upstairs to tend to Amber's wound.

Morning arrived, and Nicole and Amber showered together as had become their ritual. Once they were out and dressed, they moved to the kitchen. Nicole sat at the island helping Amber prep for breakfast and sipping her coffee. Amber had opted for orange juice instead of coffee. A knock on the door before the doorbell rang alerted them that their friends had arrived. Nicole told Amber to stay put and that she would get the door. Amber got her miniature assembly line set up for cooking and assembling the breakfast tacos.

"Amber, goddess of food," Erik said as he entered the kitchen followed by the three women.

"G'morning, Erik." Amber hugged him. "Did you bring your appetite?"

"Does he ever leave home without it is a better question." Heather walked over and hugged Amber.

"Hi, Amber." Jill hugged her before joining the others at the island.

Nicole got everyone a cup of coffee and a glass of orange juice while Amber made the eggs, sausage, bacon, and pancakes. Once the cooking was done, Amber cautiously assembled the tacos. Pancakes as the shell, crumbled sausage for the meat, scrambled eggs for the lettuce, diced tomatoes and chilis for spice, then cheese, bacon, and syrup to top it off.

"Baby, these are better than last night," Nicole said with her mouth full.

"Amber, will you marry me and be my live-in

housewife?" Heather said.

"Hey! Back off, Woods." Nicole pointed a fork toward Heather.

"Sorry, Heather, but..." Amber started.

"You couldn't handle her." Nicole blushed, knowing that Heather was kidding but still feeling territorial.

"Wow, Nicole. That's quite a proclamation." Jill laughed.

"I didn't say anything that wasn't true," Nicole said smugly.

"All right, if you plan for me to ever cook for any of you, let's get off the subject of my prowess in the bedroom."

"Baby, your prowess isn't just in the bedroom," Nicole whispered into Amber's ear. The words mixed with Nicole's warm breath on her ear caused Amber to blush and shiver with desire.

"Subject change," Erik called, feeling left out of the sexual banter.

"So, what did you two discuss yesterday?" Jill tried to steer the conversation back to neutral ground.

After refilling everyone's drink of choice, Nicole and Amber explained how they had discussed what the past ten years had been like, and Amber invited everyone to come to the gallery showing. They all told her they would try, but sometimes, it was hard to get away. What Amber didn't know was that Zach had already arranged for them to surprise her at the show.

After their talk, they decided to go for a walk, and the group took a picnic lunch and went out to Old Miller's Pond and spent the day reliving their childhood. Sitting by the tree, talking, laughing, Nicole and Amber kissing. All but Nicole and Amber went swimming. Amber still needed to protect her incision, and Nicole didn't want her sitting out alone.

"Sweetie, you can go swim with the others, I don't mind watching. I can dip my feet in the water and still be nearby," Amber said.

"Why don't we both go dip our feet in the water? I never had fun swimming without you anyway."

"You just liked me in my swimsuit." Amber raised an eyebrow.

"I'm not blind or an idiot. Hell yes, I loved you in your swimsuit." Nicole leaned closer and kissed Amber on the cheek and then whispered in her ear, "I prefer you out of the swimsuit."

"Play your cards right, Brooks, and I'll show you my birthday suit tonight," Amber said before kissing Nicole passionately.

"Damn, get a room, you two." Heather laughed. "We're in the water to cool down, not have you heat it up."

"I only have her lips for a bit longer, I'm going to kiss them as much as I damn well can," Nicole said as she pulled back from the kiss.

The group laughed. The sun was starting to set before they left the pond. They dropped Nicole and Amber off first and told them to call after Amber's doctor's appointment the next day. The two women agreed and went inside.

☙ ❧ ☙ ❧

"They're both going to be devastated," Jill said as they left Nicole's house and headed home.

"Yep," Heather and Erik agreed.

"Do you think they realize how devastated they're going to be?" Heather asked.

"Yep, and they're fighting to hide it from each other." Erik received shocked looks from the two women. "What? I can be observant and insightful. I'm just shallow because I'm a man? Pffft, whatever."

"I, er…" Jill stammered.

"You're the eyes of the group. You always have been," Heather said as she wrapped an arm around Erik's shoulder and sidearm-hugged him.

"She's right. You were the one that saw the whole Nicole-Amber romance before the rest of us," Jill agreed.

"Thank you." Erik laughed as they headed to their homes.

⁂

"Today was fun," Amber said as soon as they got inside.

"Yeah, it was a lot of fun having everyone together at the pond." Nicole pulled Amber close.

"Can we cuddle on the lanai again after we shower?" Amber asked.

"Of course." Nicole led them into the bathroom, and they showered and put on their pajamas.

Once they were settled on the lanai listening to the sound of the thunderstorm, they became lost in their thoughts. It wasn't until later that Nicole felt Amber shaking that she noticed something was wrong. Nicole had been so lost in her own head that she had no clue how long Amber had been crying or why.

As they lay together, Amber started to cry, realizing how much she had missed everyone and what her family had truly cost her. There were so many years that were gone that they would never get back. She had missed out on their twenties together. When they were old and gray and discussing their life, they would have this gap. She hated her father and her brother for costing her that, for costing her the few remaining years with her mother and those years with Nicole. There was a full decade they weren't getting back, ever.

"Baby, why are you crying?" Nicole asked.

"Loss" was all Amber could sputter out.

"What do you mean loss?"

"We lost so many years and so many people, not to mention the emotional and physical traumas. And it's all because of my father and my brother. Two people who couldn't give a rat's-fucking-ass about if we were hurt or what we lost. How is it that people like that can be allowed to take so much and get away with it? What gave them the right?" Amber asked, anger in her voice now.

"We gave them the right," Nicole said, feeling Amber stiffen with her words.

"What?" Amber was confused by Nicole's statement.

"We gave them the right when we didn't stop them from hurting us, when we didn't stop them from separating us. We're the ones that made the choices and allowed them to control us. That doesn't diminish what they did, but it's the truth."

"You're right, and it's more that I gave them the right than anyone else. I was too scared to speak up, too scared to stand up to them, too weak. God, I don't deserve anybody's forgiveness or friendship." Amber stood and walked to the edge of the lanai and looked out into the darkness.

"Whoa, Amber." Nicole quickly sat up and followed her. "You had been used by them from before you knew how to protect yourself or fight back. You didn't know you had choices. We're all at fault, but your brother and father are most at fault for orchestrating the circumstances that caused it all to happen. And they are and will continue to pay. They also can't hurt us anymore. Now come lay back down with me, my love." Nicole led Amber back to the swing and lay her down again and cuddled with her.

The couple drifted off to sleep in the swing, both holding on to the other tightly.

Morning brought a heavy feeling in both women's hearts. They were going to find out when Amber was going to be cleared to leave. Then they were going to have to admit completely and not just say the words that Amber would be leaving.

Few words were said as they ate breakfast, got dressed, and prepared to go to the doctor. Jill, Heather, Erik, and Zach all tried calling the girls, but each received a text message back stating they would talk to them later, they needed time to process what today truly meant. Each person respected their wishes, but they knew there was no way the two women were going to be able to handle what the day meant.

Nicole drove them to the hospital, and they walked hand in hand from the parking ramp to the clinic in the hospital. Amber looked around. It was only a week earlier that she was here and fighting for her life. For Nicole, this place had so many horrible memories and one good one. The one where Amber lived and she was able to keep her as a part of her life.

"Amber Knight?" the nurse said.

Amber nodded and started to get up when she saw the conflicting emotions playing across Nicole's face.

"Sweetie, please, come with me." Amber offered her good hand. Nicole smiled and nodded, taking Amber's hand and following behind her and the nurse into the exam room.

After taking her vitals, the nurse left the room, and Nicole and Amber held hands but sat in somber silence.

"I love you," Nicole whispered without looking up.

"I love you, too." Amber softly squeezed Nicole's hand.

The doctor entered the room and understood what the nurse meant when she warned him that the moods were low.

"Amber, Nicole, hello," the doctor said.

"Hi," they both answered.

"How are you feeling?"

"Better, a couple of tweaks of pain when I move wrong, but otherwise okay," Amber said.

"And the drainage?" He pointed for her to lie down on the table.

"The first night, she caused it to bleed after having a nightmare, but there hasn't been anything since then...well, not anything that you hadn't warned us of," Nicole said.

The doctor tested the tenderness of Amber's side, looked over the wound, and was pleased with the progress of the healing. He then took Amber to get an X-ray of her shoulder and collarbone to check the healing there. While they waited for the films to be developed and read, they sat close together, Nicole occasionally kissing the side of Amber's head. Once the results were ready, the doctor took them back to the exam room to talk.

"Well, I must say, you're healing remarkably well, Ms. Knight. It's as if your bones were trained to heal quickly," the doctor said, seeing both women flinch at his statement.

"She was abused by her father and brother from age four until eighteen when they almost killed her, and she got away," Nicole said, her voice full of venom, sorrow, and pain.

"I'm sorry, I didn't know. I shouldn't have said what I did. Please, both of you, forgive my insensitivity and ignorance."

"It's fine," they said.

"Well, with the way you're healing, you have your wings back and can return to…um…New York," the doctor said, reading her chart and where she was from. "You'll still have work restrictions, but as long as you abide by them and keep up with the antibiotics, you should heal perfectly."

"How long will I be in the brace and sling?" Amber said.

"With the way you're healing, I would say the brace about three more weeks and the sling I would recommend starting to wean yourself off it in about a month. Most importantly, I want you to follow up with your regular doctor before anything. Have them check to make sure there's no infection once you complete the antibiotics, then have your collarbone checked before taking off the brace and then get checked again before weaning from the sling. I know that sounds like overkill, but we want to ensure that your body has the best opportunities to heal and to make sure you don't have issues in the future. Can I count on you to do that?"

"She will." Nicole looked sternly at Amber.

"Yes, sir." Amber knew that between Nicole and Zach, she wasn't going to stand a chance. "I also need to have you put all those instructions into a note for my employer."

"Really?" he asked surprised.

"Yeah, she's a bit of a stickler for detail, and well, one of Nicole's co-conspirators works with me and seems to have told my boss that I'm notorious for not following instructions, and that if they had them, they would make sure I followed them."

"Zach rocks," Nicole said.

"Did they want me to email them or mail them, as well?" The doctor smirked.

"Yeah, here are the email addresses." Amber pulled a piece of paper out of her pocket and handed it to the amused doctor.

"I'll make sure this gets off to them today. You're free to leave as early as tomorrow."

"Thank you," Nicole and Amber said.

Everyone stood, and they shook the doctor's hand. He handed Nicole the updated prescriptions for antibiotics and pain pills.

"Oh, Ms. Knight. You're healed enough that you can stop wearing bandages unless you notice leaking, and you can take baths again."

"Thank you," Amber said, smiling back at him.

The pair left the hospital and dropped off the prescriptions to be filled before heading to Nicole's house to make the arrangements for Amber to return to New York and for Zach to take over the care and protection of Amber.

Chapter Eighteen

Making Plans

After leaving the doctor's office, Nicole and Amber headed back to Nicole's house so Amber could call Zach and Lucinda and make her plans to fly to New York. The car was filled with mixed emotions from both women. They were happy that Amber was healing and that there was no infection or complications, but they were struggling with the idea that they were going to be apart.

"What are you thinking about?" Amber asked as they entered the house and moved to the living room.

"I'm thinking about a lot of things," Nicole said, avoiding Amber's question.

"Nicole, please, don't withdraw from me," Amber said.

"I'm sorry. I'm just trying to process the fact that *yea* you're doing better and *boo* you're leaving." Nicole sat on the couch next to Amber.

"Sweetie, I know how you feel. I'm conflicted, too." Amber took Nicole's hand and brought it up to kiss the back of it.

"You need to call Zach and Lucinda. Do you want me to call the gang?" Nicole got up from the couch.

"That'd be great. Um, Nic?" Amber waited for Nicole to turn and look at her. "I love you."

"I love you, too." Nicole turned and kissed

Amber.

After Nicole left the room, Amber took a deep breath and called Lucinda. Amber explained what happened at the doctor and that Lucinda would be getting an email from him. Lucinda was amused that Amber did ask for the email, and she was pleased to be getting her back before the show and that Amber was healing so well. Lucinda told Amber that although she couldn't wait for her to return, she understood that there were things going on in Eagle Peak, as well. She told her that since it was Tuesday, she would expect Amber back at work on Monday.

Once Amber got off the phone with Lucinda, she called Zach and gave him the news of her return and what the doctor had to say. Zach told Amber to let him know when her flight would be in, and he'd pick her up. She said she would take a cab, but he insisted on meeting her at the airport. Amber finally conceded and told him she would text him the flight details as soon as she got them worked out. They then talked about how things were going with Nicole and their decisions for the future.

※※※※

While Amber was making her calls, Nicole went into the kitchen and called Jill, Erik, and Heather, and told them that Amber had been given the okay to fly again and that she would be leaving soon. The group agreed they should have a farewell party once they learned Amber's flight plans. Everyone was concerned with how Nicole was dealing with Amber leaving. Nicole said she wasn't sure. At the moment, she was numb. She promised that if she needed to talk, she would call them. After she was done with her calls, she headed back into the living room where Amber was just hanging up with Zach.

※※※※

"So, how soon does Lucinda want you back?" Nicole sat next to Amber.

"Monday morning," Amber said, smiling.

"Don't tease me…"

"I wouldn't tease you about something like that." Amber said before kissing Nicole. "She said she'd like me back sooner, but she understands that I have things going on here, as well."

"Yea me! I suppose that means we need to make your flight arrangements, so you can tell Zach and I can tell the gang. The rest of the time, I'm not letting you out of my sight."

"I'm okay with that." Amber smiled.

Nicole and Amber went into Nicole's office and booked the flight for Sunday afternoon, getting her home around seven p.m. Nicole knew Amber was going to be tired, but she selfishly wanted to spend every possible minute with Amber that she could.

Amber called and told Zach her flight schedule, and he said he would be there to pick her up. Nicole called Jill, and she suggested they have a sleepover whatever night worked best for Nicole and Amber. Nicole and Amber decided on Friday night. They both knew Saturday would be their last night together for a while, and there was no way they wanted to share that with anyone else. After they were done calling the others, the women made a late lunch together. As they finished lunch, Nicole received a call involving her work.

"Baby, I have to take this," Nicole said as she saw the caller ID.

"I understand. I'll be upstairs in my mom's room." Amber kissed Nicole's cheek.

Nicole smiled as she watched Amber walk away, and then she turned her attention back to her phone call. Nicole spent about an hour on the phone before making her way to the room that had once been occupied by Amber's mom. She saw Amber lying on the bed holding a picture of Nicole and Karen.

"We should go through the photo albums your mom put together before you leave. You can take the journals with you if you'd like," Nicole said as she entered the room and sat on the bed next to Amber.

"I'd like that. Is everything okay with work?"

"Yeah, I'll have to do some stuff a little bit later, but for now, I'm all yours."

"Yea." Amber put the picture on the nightstand and turned toward Nicole. "I think that after your work is done, I want a candlelit bath with you, then I want us to go to the lanai and cuddle."

"I think that sounds like a good plan. Did you want me to see if one of the gang is around while I work? Not that you can't just hang out or entertain yourself, I just know they're going to miss seeing you, and I don't want you to think that I'm monopolizing you. I know I want to spend every minute I can with you and…" Nicole babbled before Amber started to giggle. "You're laughing at me."

"No, I have just missed your babbling so much. I love you, sweetheart, and I would like to see if Heather can hang out for a bit. If you need me out of the house, I can go to the hotel."

"I'll call Heather quickly." Nicole grabbed her phone out of her pocket and called. They worked out that Heather would swing by and hang out with Amber while Nicole worked. Heather was excited at the chance to spend more time with Amber.

※※※※

After Heather arrived, Nicole told them she would be as quick as she could, but the company she was making the changes for tended to be indecisive. Heather and Amber said they understood and told her to do what she needed to and that they would be hanging out. Nicole kissed Amber before leaving the room.

"You two seem homey," Heather said.

"That isn't a bad thing." Amber smiled at the idea of being homey with Nicole.

"I didn't say it was. It's nice to see her smiling and know that it's because she's happy and not just pretending to be."

"I'm sorry that I hurt her and all of you. I regret hurting Nicole the most, though…" Amber's voice trailed off.

"You weren't left with a choice, we all know that. You also aren't going to do something stupid like that again anyway," Heather said.

"No, I'm not."

"You don't have to answer this, but how did you deal with getting over what your dad and brother did to you? Mentally, I mean."

"I didn't for a long time, and then Zach left me no choice but to see a therapist. I've seen her pretty much every other week for five years now. Shit, I just remembered I never canceled my appointment with my therapist nor my dinner plans with Jessie. We usually have dinner after my therapy appointments."

Heather helped Amber find her phone, so she could call to cancel her appointment and dinner plans.

"Hello, Amber?" the woman on the other end of the line said.

"Hi, Jess," Amber said.

"Are you okay? Is something wrong? My receptionist said you wanted to cancel our dinner plans for tomorrow," Jessie Burke said.

"I'm fine," Amber said.

"Liar," Heather said a little louder than she intended, and Jessie heard her.

"It sounds like someone disagrees with you."

"Yes, she does. I'm in Eagle Peak."

"Now you need to explain some things to me," Jessie said.

Amber put Jessie on speakerphone because holding the phone up hurt after a while.

"I have you on speakerphone, and my friend Heather is here listening. She's the one who called me a liar.

"I'm glad she's there to keep you honest. Stop stalling, Amber. What's going on?"

"The short story is, I'm getting to do the art show coming up that we've talked about. I had to come back here to get some release forms signed. That led me to become reacquainted with Heather, Jill, Erik, and Nicole," Amber started.

"Oh, boy," Jessie said.

"Amber?" Nicole came into the room and saw Amber put a finger over her lips to silence her.

"Yeah, there's a lot we'll need to discuss when

I get back. After reconnecting with them, I had an unfortunate run-in with my brother. I'll be okay, but again, more stuff for us to go through—"

"Damn it, Amber, you're stalling. Heather, what isn't she telling me?"

"She isn't telling you that her brother hit her with the butt of a gun, and he broke her collarbone and part of her shoulder. Then the jackass shot her," Heather said.

"*What?*" Jessie exclaimed as Amber groaned.

"I'll be fine, I just got cleared today to fly home."

"Amber, I've been one of your best friends for over five years. Why the hell didn't you call me sooner?"

"It all happened so quick. I left New York fourteen hours after I learned about being in the art show. Then I got here and ran into Heather, then Nicole, then the others."

"How'd it go with Nicole?"

"She's here in the room, as well. She just came in. I'm staying with her until Sunday when I fly back."

"Hi," Nicole sat next to Amber.

"Hi, Nicole. Is there anything else I should know?" Jessie asked.

"Amber's mom lived with me for several years before she passed away," Nicole said.

"Oh, hell. Amber, you get back Sunday and go back to work Monday, correct?"

"Yes, ma'am," Amber said.

"Monday after work, you and I are getting together, understood?" Jessie ordered.

"Yes, ma'am," Amber said again.

"Heather, Nicole, you are my witnesses that she agreed to be there."

"You know, you're mean and evil," Amber said.

"That's why we're friends and you've dragged your happy ass out to dinner with me every other week for five years."

"No, it's your sunny disposition." Amber laughed.

"Whatever. I have a someone waiting. I'll see you Monday night. Nicole, Heather, it was nice to talk to you. I hope someday to meet you both."

"Goodbye," they all said, and Amber hung up.

"She seems interesting," Nicole said.

"Yeah, she was almost my therapist, but I found her business card taped to the bathroom stall in a gay bar."

"Seriously?" Heather said, her mouth gaping open.

"I already had scheduled the appointment to see her when I found her business card one night when Zach and I went out dancing. It turned out one of her patients didn't feel she had her attention, so she stole a bunch of her business cards and taped them up in random places."

"What'd you think when you saw it there?" Nicole asked.

"I was ready to cancel the appointment, but Zach said he'd heard good things about her, so I kept the appointment. We didn't mesh well as patient/therapist and then I ended up getting to know her because she lives in my neighborhood. Are you done with your work, sweetie?"

"It's compiling, so I had a few minutes and decided to come and see if Heather was behaving herself."

Heather stuck her tongue out at Nicole.

"Sweetie, you know there's a better way to get back at her, right?"

"Huh?" Nicole said.

Amber grabbed the front of Nicole's shirt, pulled her in close, and kissed her deeply and passionately. Both women groaned from the sheer intensity of the kiss.

"Mean! Cruel! Not fair," Heather said, pouting.

"You're right, that's definitely a better way to get back at her. I should get back to my program," Nicole said before kissing Amber again.

After Nicole left, Heather told Amber about the couple of short relationships she had, and Amber told her about New York and some of the bars she had gone to. It was about another hour before Nicole came out of her office and said she was finally done. Heather said she had to get back to the hotel, but they both suspected it was an excuse to allow them time together without them feeling guilty about it.

※ ※ ※ ※

Nicole led Amber by the hand upstairs and into her bedroom. Nicole went into the bathroom and started the water running for their candlelit bath. After lighting the candles, she went back into the bedroom where her breath caught as she saw Amber sitting on the edge of the bed. Nicole closed the distance between the two of them and kissed Amber before helping her to undress. Then she allowed Amber to undress her. They moved together into the bathroom. Amber pulled Nicole close and kissed her. Once the kiss broke, Nicole turned the water off and relaxed into the tub. After a moment, she motioned for Amber to have a seat between her legs. Amber sat and leaned her back to Nicole's front and felt her arms wrap around her waist.

"I'm going to miss my bathing buddy," Nicole said before kissing Amber's neck, trying to control her emotions and her thoughts.

"I'm going to miss this, too. I'm going to miss just being near you." Amber felt the reality of leaving not by necessity, but by choice.

"Who would have thought that after ten years apart we would have fallen so in sync again?"

"I knew from before our first kiss that you and I were meant to be together. I'm sorry it's taken so long to get back to us."

"It wasn't your fault what happened to you. I'd wait forever if I thought there was a chance that I could spend my life with you," Nicole said before kissing her way down Amber's neck.

"Mmm, that feels good. Nic, um…" Amber's voice trailed off.

"What's troubling you, baby?" Nicole pulled Amber closer. "Talk to me."

"I'm…okay…I'm not so much troubled as unsure how to ask you something."

"You can ask me anything," Nicole said.

"The show is in six weeks. I'm wondering if you could come up earlier than just before the show. I know you have responsibilities here, but I really want—no, need—you there with me."

"When do you want me to come? I mean how early?"

"Three weeks…" Amber said sheepishly, knowing that Nicole had obligations here.

"Hey, remember, we're each other's safe spot. You don't have to ever hide from me."

"Okay…um…my confession is that I'm scared that by leaving you I'm going to lose you. I know I told you we weren't going to be out of each other's life and everything, but it scares the shit out of me, too. Part of me is afraid that once I leave, you'll have time to think about things and resent me for leaving and not coming back for so long."

"I have the same fears. I'm afraid you'll go back to New York and forget about me and this place because the bad memories are going to outweigh the good ones."

"Oh, Nic." Amber turned so she was facing her. Amber stared at Nicole for a long minute before bringing a hand up to cup her face. "Sweetie, you are the best thing in the world that has ever happened to me. I wouldn't have survived all those years of abuse and the years of loneliness had it not been for you… knowing that you were a part of this world is how I survived."

"Amber," Nicole breathed as tears rolled down her face. Nicole couldn't make her mind work. She was suddenly overcome with emotion. Sitting in front of her was the woman she had loved since before she knew what it meant to be in love.

Amber pulled Nicole to her and held her as she allowed her emotions to come out. After Nicole calmed down, Amber got them out of the tub and dried off before moving them into the bedroom and onto the bed.

"How is your shoulder?" Nicole asked.

"Better."

"Amber, help me forget the world out there exists," Nicole said.

Their gazes locked, and Amber knew what Nicole needed. Amber felt the pull deep inside her, and she hungrily captured Nicole's lips. Amber pulled Nicole's body to her own and ran her hands up and down Nicole's body, feeling the flesh beneath her touch. Nicole was groaning and moving with Amber's touch. Every sound from Nicole only increased Amber's need and wanton desire. It wasn't long before they were both completely consumed with each other.

※※※※

Nicole and Amber isolated themselves from the group until Friday afternoon, wanting to spend as much time as they could together. Both were dreading Sunday. They had worked out that Nicole would come to New York in three weeks. This would allow her to be at Amber's last doctor's appointment and allow her to see what Amber's life was like.

While in their self-imposed isolation, Nicole and Amber went through the photo albums that Amber's mom had put together, and they reminded each other of stories revolving around the pictures.

"Remember this one?" Amber pointed to a picture of her, Nicole, Jill, and Erik dressed up for Halloween when they were about eight years old. They were dressed as characters from *The Wizard of Oz*.

"Ugh, yes. Jill made a good Glinda. Erik was so cute as the Tin Man. He got in a lot of trouble for taking his dad's funnel for putting oil in the car. You were so gorgeous as Dorothy."

"I loved how the green makeup made your eyes stand out. You were the cutest Wicked Witch of the West."

"What about this picture?" Nicole said, smiling. The picture was from just before Nicole and Amber started dating. Nicole had sneaked into Amber's room to surprise her and found her asleep at her desk. Amber had been studying and had put her head down and fallen asleep. Much to her dismay, she was a drooler, and there was a big puddle of drool next to her head.

"Where did my mother find that? I thought I burned all those *and* the negative," Amber said.

Nicole didn't say anything, she just had a smug smile on her face.

"What did you do?"

"I had a copy hidden. You looked so cute, and I had such a crush on you..."

"So, are there other photos I need to be aware of?" Amber teased.

"None that I'm going to own up to at this point." Nicole laughed.

They continued going through the album and reached ones from after Amber had left.

"Tell me about this one." Amber pointed to a picture of her mother and Nicole all dressed up.

Nicole left the room and returned with a small award statue. "That was taken the night I won this."

Amber took the statue from Nicole and saw the plaque said *Entrepreneur of the Year* and Nicole's name.

"Sweetie, that's amazing." Amber set the award next to her and kissed Nicole.

"Thanks. I took your mom as my 'date' for two reasons. One, she had been so supportive with my business and helping me. Two, it felt like you were there with me. Well, a part of you at least."

They continued going through the albums for a long while. Amber loved hearing the stories regarding the pictures of Nicole and her mother after she left. It also served as a reminder of how much she had missed.

Nicole held Amber while she read her mother's journals and cried at the loss of such an amazing woman.

※※※※

Friday arrived, and Nicole and Amber knew they were going to have to go to Jill's for the group farewell party. It wasn't that they didn't want to see everyone, but they were enjoying the time with just the two of them.

"Jill said we should come over around four today," Nicole said as they were making lunch.

"Okay," Amber said quietly.

"What's wrong, baby?" Nicole wrapped her arms around Amber and leaned her chin on the uninjured shoulder.

"The reality that I'm leaving soon is setting in. Plus, I've really enjoyed our alone time."

"I know, but I'll be coming to New York in three weeks," Nicole said before kissing the side of Amber's head.

"I know, but I'm still going to miss you."

"No more than I'm going to miss you."

The couple finished their lunch and then went to pack the stuff they would need for the night. Once they were done, they cuddled on the lanai until it was time to leave.

Chapter Nineteen

Slumber Party Fun

Nicole and Amber were almost asleep cuddled together on the lanai when Nicole's phone alarm went off, notifying them that it was time to head over to Jill's. Nicole shut the alarm off as Amber cuddled closer and nipped at Nicole's neck.

"Mmm, that isn't going to make going to Jill's easier," Nicole said.

"I wasn't trying to make it easier. I was enjoying where we are now," Amber said as Nicole turned her head and pressed their lips together.

After kissing for several long minutes, they pulled apart, and Nicole looked into Amber's eyes and saw the sadness there.

"What's the matter, baby?" Nicole asked.

"This feels so perfect, and I'm going to miss it when I leave," Amber said.

"I'm going to miss it, too. We're just going to be apart for three weeks, and then I'll be coming to visit you."

"I know, and trust me when I say that knowing that will be the only thing that will keep me going."

"How about I promise that we'll talk daily, and we can even video chat?" Nicole ran her hand through Amber's hair.

"That helps."

"Let's get over to Jill's, then when we get back tomorrow, we can come in here and cuddle again."

"Okay."

They got up, got their stuff, and headed to Jill's house.

☙ ☙ ❧ ❧

"Jill, do you have everything?" Erik called as he finished setting up the living room for the party.

"I think so." Jill finished up in the kitchen.

Jill and Erik had decided that they were going to go all out. They wanted Amber to know it wasn't just Nicole who loved her and was going to miss her. Jill had gone out of town to a restaurant they used to frequent and gotten all their favorites. She picked up decorations, and Erik had come over and helped her decorate the living room with banners and streamers. There were even a few helium balloons with *We'll Miss You* and *We Love You* written on them.

"Jill? Erik?" Heather called as she entered the house.

"In here," Jill called back from the kitchen.

Heather entered the kitchen, carrying a large cake in her arms. Erik took it from her and set it on the counter. He looked at the cake and saw there was a pond and tree that looked like Old Miller's Pond, a collection of paintings and a paintbrush, and *Don't forget how much we love you* written across it.

"Where'd you get this?" Erik asked.

"Sidney's aunt makes special order cakes, and Sid talked her into doing a rush order cake for me."

"Amber is going to love it," Jill said.

"What time are they supposed to be here?"

Heather asked.

"Any time now."

Just then, they heard a car pull up and made their way to the front door to greet the two women. The first thing they noticed was the sullen mood they were in.

"Hey, Amber! Hey, Nicole," Erik said as they walked up to the door.

"Hey," they said.

Erik wrapped them both in a hug, being careful not to hurt Amber's shoulder and collarbone. They hugged for a minute before he released them, and Heather wrapped them into a warm hug. Heather, while hugging them, whispered that she loved them both and she knew how hard this was, but she knew it would just make them stronger. When they pulled back, Amber wiped a tear away and looked Heather in the eyes and gave her a smile. Jill hugged Nicole and then Amber before blindfolding them both and escorting them into the living room. She removed the blindfolds, and the two gaped at the fully decorated room.

"This looks amazing," Amber said as she looked at the banner, the balloons, and the pictures of their childhood strewn around the room.

"You guys were busy today." Nicole laughed.

"You have no idea." Erik beamed.

"Why do I smell Dante's Grill?" Amber asked.

"First off, how in the hell did you recognize Dante's food?"

"Jill, I moved to New York, I didn't die. And if the food tastes the same as it used to, it's my all-time favorite and you never forget that." Amber laughed. "Now why do I smell Dante's? I know the one here closed."

"Because I went there and got all our favorites."

Jill smiled, seeing the shock on Amber and Nicole's face.

"That's a three-hour round-trip drive," Nicole said.

"Not really. You see, when you turn on that loud siren thingy and those pretty flashing lights on top of my car, it cuts the time down considerably."

"You abused your power as sheriff for me?" Amber feigned shock.

"Damn straight."

"She is not, and stop trying to make her that way," Nicole joked, pulling Amber into her arms and kissing the side of her head.

"Yeah, am not, and you can't make me." Amber stuck her tongue out at Jill.

"That's such an old and horrible joke," Heather said.

"So." Nicole stuck her tongue out, too.

"Mmm, Nicole tongue," Amber said before quickly capturing Nicole's tongue with her teeth.

"Mmm." Nicole groaned.

"Ew, nasty." Jill turned and went into the kitchen to get the food.

Everyone laughed and then found places to sit. Heather in one of the oversized chairs. Erik on the loveseat. Nicole and Amber curled up together on the couch. When Jill returned, she set the food on the coffee table and handed out plates. Everyone filled his or her plate.

"I can't believe you went and got all this." Amber looked over the spread.

There were beer-battered onion rings, French fries, steak sliders with grilled onions, chicken strips, cheese curds, fried pickles, grilled cheese, jalapeño poppers, and potato skins.

"Well, at least I'm a paramedic. With the amount of fat and grease in this, someone's arteries are hardening." Erik laughed.

"Well, it is a special occasion, and it's allowed," Heather said.

They ate, and Jill said she asked one of her deputies to order and then she went to pick up the food. She said the man who took the order laughed so hard he was crying when she arrived to pick up the food. He said he expected some big burly man and instead he gets a petite woman with a sheriff's badge, nonetheless.

After they ate, Jill put the leftovers in the fridge to keep until later when they were looking for munchies.

"So, are you getting excited about your show?" Heather asked.

"Yeah, it's going to be a lot of fun. And I'm going to have the hottest date there," Amber said, and Nicole blushed.

"What do you mean?" Jill looked between the two women.

"Amber invited me to come up to New York as her date for the art show."

"That's cool," Heather said.

"I'm actually going up there in three weeks and staying through the show," Nicole said.

"You are?" Erik was surprised by that. "Isn't the show in like six weeks?"

"It is," Amber said. "I want Nicole to get a chance to see what my life has been like and for us to spend some time getting to know each other out of the shadow of fear and memories we have here."

"I don't know what to say. I mean, I'm glad you two are going to take the time to rebuild your relationship, and I know you still love each other, but, Nic, does this mean you're moving to New York?" Erik looked at Nicole.

"No, it doesn't mean that. We haven't discussed anything further than we love each other. I have commitments that are going to keep me here for a while anyway."

"Okay, this is going in a direction that is *not* going to help us at all. Let's move back to the fun," Jill said.

"I agree. So, have you heard from Zach since he's been back?" Heather asked.

"Yeah, he's been whining via text daily."

"What's he whining about?" Erik asked.

"The fact that he's trapped in a room with boring people mostly. We all share a large room, and there aren't many that have a sense of humor. Okay, it's only Zach and me. So, when the other is gone, life is very boring."

"That sounds horrible," Nicole said.

"It can be. We just try to schedule our vacations at the same time," Amber said.

"Okay, movie time." Heather jumped up and grabbed the three movies they had rented for the night. "We have *Jumanji, Much Ado About Nothing,* and—"

"Much Ado!" Nicole and Amber said.

Heather popped the movie in, and everyone got comfortable and started to watch. It wasn't long before Amber started nipping at Nicole's neck while she was lying in front of her on the couch.

"Behave," Nicole said quietly.

"Do you really want that?" Amber ran her tongue up Nicole's neck and sucked on her earlobe.

"No." Nicole turned to face Amber and captured

her lips.

The two lay there kissing for a long time before they heard three loud coughs.

"Some things never change." Jill laughed, remembering all the times when they were teens and they would start a movie and Nicole and Amber would end up making out.

"You realize you two aren't still teenagers, right?" Heather joked.

"We have a lot of time to make up for." Nicole pulled away from Amber's lips and heard a disappointed whine.

"Plus, I'm leaving soon," Amber said as Nicole started to pout.

"Well, I think it's dessert time," Jill said.

"I'll get it." Erik jumped up and skipped out of the room.

He returned with the cake. Amber was surprised by the detail that was put into the cake and loved it. Amber and Nicole took several pictures before they carved it up and ate it. After the cake, they decided that Nicole and Amber couldn't be trusted not to go back to making out if they watched another movie, so they pulled out Life and Monopoly. Amber chose Monopoly. They sat down to play, and Nicole was the banker. As the game progressed and properties were bought, houses and hotels were added, Amber got low on funds. She landed on one of Nicole's properties that was maxed out with a hotel, and Nicole smiled.

"You owe a lot for that," Nicole said.

"How about I work it off in *some* way?" Amber said seductively.

"Maybe we can work something out." Nicole waggled her eyebrows.

"Nuh-uh, no way! That is not fair," Erik said.

"If you two are going to make those types of deals, they have to be available for everyone," Heather said.

"That's fine. You, Jill, and Erik can have the same deal." Amber laughed.

"Ew," Jill and Heather said in unison.

Heather tossed a house at Amber, who flung it back, and it bounced off Heather and hit Erik. After a minute, someone grabbed a pillow, and things escalated into a full-on pillow fight. Nicole and Jill ganged up on Erik until they got his pillow away from him, then they went after Amber, who was quickly subdued due to her injuries, allowing them to turn their attention to Heather.

"I don't think this is fair. Two against one..." Heather pleaded for their sympathy.

"You didn't seem to mind when they went after Erik and me," Amber said.

"That was different," Heather retorted. "It wasn't me they were going after."

Before anyone could say anything else, Nicole and Jill pounced and pinned Heather down and tickled her. Heather squirmed and tried to get away but couldn't. Nicole and Jill had always been a troublesome pair when they worked to get someone. After a while, they eased up and let Heather sit up. She had tears in her eyes from laughing.

"You all are mean." Heather pouted, crossing her arms.

"And yet you still love us," Amber said.

"Maybe," Heather said.

The board game forgotten, the group turned on the Xbox and played video games to pass the time.

Amber challenged Erik to darts. He won, but barely. They all played a few games of bowling. After several hours of video games, they decided to call it quits and get some rest. Nicole and Amber slept on the air mattress again, while Heather and Erik each took a guestroom upstairs, and Jill had her room.

※ ※ ※ ※

After everyone had gone to bed, Nicole and Amber lay awake and very aware of how close they were.

"I want you," Amber whispered into Nicole's ear before running her tongue along the edge of her ear and sucking on her earlobe.

"Everyone is just upstairs." Nicole groaned as Amber's hand caressed her breast.

"Then I guess you had better be quiet." Amber growled as she ran her tongue along Nicole's neck.

"Oh, god, you do not play fair…oh, hell…take me," Nicole breathed as she turned to face Amber.

Amber captured Nicole's lips and pulled her body close to her own. They both groaned at the feel of the other's body. Amber slipped her hand under Nicole's T-shirt and ran it up and down Nicole's back, occasionally dipping it into her panties and squeezing her butt.

Nicole ran her hands along Amber's body and under her shirt. Her hand traced Amber's curves up her body and cupped one of Amber's breasts, gently massaging the breast and tweaking the erect nipple.

"That feels so good," Amber said as she broke the kiss.

"You feel so good," Nicole said as Amber brought

her hand to the front of Nicole's body to massage Nicole's breast. "Oh, god, yes."

Nicole rolled Amber on her back and covered Amber's body with her own. Their hips rocked in a familiar rhythm.

"I love you," Amber whispered.

"Mmm, I love you, too," Nicole said.

Nicole nudged Amber's shirt up and ran her tongue around Amber's nipple before taking it in her mouth and sucking on it.

"Oh, god, yes," Amber whispered, arching her chest up.

Amber used her good arm to snake down Nicole's body and slip inside her shorts and panties.

"Ohh, Amber." Nicole groaned as she felt Amber's fingers touch her.

"Shh," Amber said, trying to remain quiet.

"You're making that very hard." Nicole growled before leaning forward and kissing Amber deeply.

Just as they were getting into a strong rhythm, the hall light turned on, and Jill came down the stairs. Nicole grudgingly rolled off Amber, so they wouldn't get caught. Not that their ragged breathing didn't give them away,

"Sorry...I left my phone down here," Jill said as she scurried into the living room smiling at the two women.

"It's okay," Amber managed to get out as her hormones were still in overdrive, and she wanted Jill gone.

"Okay, good night again," Jill said, smiling at them and heading back upstairs and turning the light off.

"That was close." Nicole turned to look at Amber.

"Yes, it was." Amber rolled on her side and slipped her hand back inside Nicole's shorts and two fingers inside.

"Oh, fuuu—" Nicole squeaked as her hips moved with Amber's thrusting.

"I love how you feel." Amber moved her hand faster.

"Oh, Amber," Nicole said softly.

The hall light came on again, and Amber halted her thrusting but stayed inside Nicole.

"Sorry," Heather said. "Water run."

"It's okay," Nicole said.

Heather grabbed some water and headed back upstairs. As soon as Heather was out of sight, Amber started moving her hand again. She used her thumb to quickly stimulate Nicole's already sensitive bundle of nerves.

"Don't stop…dear god, don't stop even if someone comes down those damn stairs again." Nicole moaned.

Amber could feel Nicole's release was near. She sped up her thrusts, hitting Nicole's sweet spot, and then just as she was getting ready to scream out, Amber leaned over, pressing their mouths together, and swallowed her scream.

"As soon as I get control of my limbs, I'm going to take you," Nicole panted.

"Mmm, as much as I want that, I don't know that we'll get that kind of free time, but when we get back to your place tomorrow." Amber growled.

"Oh, god, yes." Nicole smiled as the hall light went on again.

"Sorry," Erik said.

"How much did they pay you to come down

here?" Nicole joked.

"Nothing...but Jill did threaten to make me scream like a girl in the middle of the night, and Heather said she was going to tape it and show the guys at the station," Erik said, blushing.

"Why?" Amber asked.

"Why what?" Erik squeaked.

"Why do you keep waking us up?"

"Oh, come on, you two aren't that quiet... you never were," Jill said from the top of the stairs, laughing.

"You're dead to me, Woods." Nicole blushed as Amber buried her head in Nicole's neck.

After they got done teasing Nicole and Amber, everyone went to bed. Nicole reached over and pulled Amber close.

"I'll make it up to you when we get back to my place." Nicole kissed the side of Amber's head.

"I can't wait." Amber kissed Nicole's neck before lying back down to go to sleep.

☙☙❧❧

About four in the morning, Nicole and Amber heard the stairs creaking and looked over to see Erik and Heather sneaking down.

"Where the hell are you two going?" Amber shined the flashlight from her phone at the two.

Heather jumped, and Erik screamed like a girl, causing everyone to roar in laughter. Jill came down the stairs to find out what all the noise was.

"We got hungry, so we were going for leftovers," Erik said. "And might I say, Ms. Knight, that was *not* nice of you."

"That was freaking hilarious," Nicole said, wiping the tears from her eyes.

"I have to agree with Nicole," Amber said.

"Of course you do," Erik said deadpan.

"I'll go warm up the leftovers, you set up the next movie and put a pillow between those two." Jill motioned toward Nicole and Amber.

"Yeah, like a pillow would stop us." Amber scoffed.

After Jill returned with the leftovers, the group ate and watched the movie. Amber and Nicole refrained from making out, but they cuddled close. After the movie ended, everyone went back to bed to get more rest.

Sunlight breaking through the curtains woke Nicole and Amber. As they started to get up, they heard the others moving upstairs. Everyone convened in the kitchen, and Amber, with some help from the others, made them a breakfast of French toast, eggs, funky-shaped pancakes, bacon, and sausage. They ate and then everyone said their goodbyes to Amber. She promised to keep in touch, and Heather threatened to not let Nicole come to New York if she didn't.

After their goodbyes, Nicole and Amber went back to Nicole's house to spend what time they had left together.

Chapter Twenty

Saying Goodbye

"What are you thinking about?" Amber saw Nicole lost in thought.

"Do you want me to invite them to the airport tomorrow?"

"I don't think I could handle it. I'm already a wreck at the thought of leaving you. Oh, sweetie, do you want them to come with so you have someone there for you?"

"Maybe Jill, if that's okay." Nicole looked sheepishly at Amber.

"Of course." Amber kissed the tip of Nicole's nose. "Call her and then let's go upstairs to Mom's room. Maybe you could hold me while I just spend time where she was."

"Whatever you want, love." Nicole called Jill and arranged for her to pick them up the next day and take them to the airport.

Nicole and Amber made their way to Karen's room and got the journals together for Amber to take back with her. Nicole also slipped in a couple of pictures of her and Karen for Amber to find when she got home. Then they cuddled for a while and moved to Nicole's room.

Nicole and Amber planned to spend the remainder of their time making love, cuddling, and talking about life.

"Do you remember our first kiss?" Nicole asked as they lay facing each other in bed.

"That's a trick question, my love. Are you talking about our first one as a couple or the very first time we ever kissed?"

"The very first time."

"Yeah, I do. Spin the bottle at eight wasn't the same as it was when we were teenagers." Amber laughed before leaning forward and kissing Nicole.

"No, it wasn't. It was when I knew I never wanted to kiss a boy, though."

"It was when I knew you were the only one I ever wanted to kiss." Amber blushed.

"Wait, you've…"

"Been in love with you since we were eight. Yes. I didn't know what it was or what it meant, but I knew you were the only one I wanted. *Even* when you had that crush on Jill."

"You knew about that?" Nicole squeaked.

"Sweetie, everyone knew about that. I'm just glad it only lasted for a couple of weeks."

"Jill knew?"

"Yeah, she did. Do you remember our first kiss as a couple?"

"Yep, in the treehouse in Erik's backyard right after you agreed to go out with me," Nicole said, grinning.

"We had a lot of firsts in that treehouse. First kiss, first hickey, first groping, almost the first time we made love," Amber said.

"Mmm, yeah, but I'm glad you decided to wait until later that night for us to make love. In the tent out at Old Miller's Pond under the stars was perfect."

Amber kissed the tip of Nicole's nose. "It was."

Nicole and Amber started kissing, and after a while, Amber rolled Nicole onto her back and slipped her hand under her shirt and teased the already stimulated nipples pressing against the silky fabric. As Amber did this, Nicole pulled them into a heated kiss. Amber slipped her arm out of the sling and moved her hand out of Nicole's shirt so that she hovered over Nicole before adjusting to lie between Nicole's legs. She flexed her hips so their warm centers pressed together.

"Oh, Amber." Nicole moaned. "What about your shoulder? Baby, be careful."

"It's fine, I promise I won't be up here long enough to hurt it more," Amber said before capturing Nicole's lips. Amber continued to grind into Nicole's center, making them both wetter.

Nicole slid her hand down Amber's body and nudged down Amber's shorts and panties. Amber took the hint and slipped out of her shorts and panties as Nicole removed her own. Amber reached over and helped Nicole out of her shirt and bra before removing her own. Amber positioned herself between Nicole's legs again and leaned over and kissed her soundly. She then trailed kisses along Nicole's jaw and down her neck, sucking on Nicole's pulse point. Nicole groaned and threaded her fingers into Amber's hair and held her in place for a minute before releasing her. Amber continued down Nicole's body, stopping to tease Nicole's nipples with her mouth.

"Harder," Nicole urged.

"Mmm." Amber groaned into Nicole's breast as

she did what she was told.

As Amber sucked on a nipple, she brought her hand up to tease the other one. Nicole arched into Amber's touch. Amber switched to the other breast and continued to make Nicole squirm.

"Amber." Nicole's hips moved as she tried to get some friction, something to rub against.

"Are you wet enough?" Amber asked, causing Nicole to moan.

"I need…" Nicole panted and felt as though she were going to explode.

Amber looked up and saw the desire in Nicole's eyes, and after a moment, she kissed her way down Nicole's body before lying between her legs and kissing her lips. As Amber gave Nicole an intimate kiss, she slipped her tongue in and tasted her wetness and groaned at the taste. Amber wanted to make this last a long time, but she knew there was no way after tasting Nicole that she could. Amber lapped up the juices as Nicole bucked her hips, panting and calling out Amber's name.

Amber sucked on Nicole's already sensitive bundle of nerves, causing Nicole's breath to catch. Amber felt Nicole place a hand on her head, holding her in place. Without easing up the pressure on Nicole's clit, Amber slipped two fingers inside her and slid them in and out. Nicole's hips moved to the rhythm Amber set. Nicole grunted and groaned as Amber brought her closer to her climax.

Amber moaned into Nicole's sensitive clit, the vibration causing Nicole to shiver with desire. She never got tired of the intense way that Amber loved her.

"So close," Nicole breathed.

Amber sped up her actions, taking Nicole by surprise and quickly bringing her over the edge and into immense pleasure.

"Oh, fuck, oh, yesss," Nicole said as loud as she could.

"I love how you taste," Amber said as she continued to lap up the wetness.

"Come up here." Nicole gently pulled on Amber's head.

Amber crawled up Nicole's body and kissed her gently while she tried to regulate her breathing.

"I love you, Nicole Brooks."

"I love…you, too." Nicole rolled Amber onto her back. "My turn."

"Oh, yes." Amber groaned.

Nicole knew that Amber was always so turned on after she came. She teased Amber's breasts briefly before continuing down her body and resting between her legs. Nicole could see how wet Amber was, and she groaned at the sight. Nicole hungrily lapped and nibbled on Amber's warm tender center. Amber was moving her hips rapidly.

"So…close." She panted.

Nicole moaned, and the vibration from that on Amber's clit was enough to send her over the edge. She came hard, calling Nicole's name.

Nicole allowed herself to be pulled up Amber's body. They rolled onto their side and kissed for several minutes.

"That was amazing," Amber said.

"As cheesy as it sounds, every time with you is amazing."

"I love cheesy." Amber kissed Nicole.

After basking in the afterglow of their lovemaking,

Nicole helped Amber back into her sling.

"Do you think we can spend the rest of the time until you leave in bed?" Nicole asked.

"I'm okay with that," Amber said.

❦❦❦❦

Morning arrived, and Nicole and Amber made their way to the kitchen and made breakfast. Neither was truly hungry, but they knew they had to eat. They had spent most of the last twenty-four hours in bed. They hadn't made love the full time, taking an occasional break.

"I can't believe you have to go back to New York today." Nicole buttered the toast.

"I can't, either. I'm going to miss you." Amber wrapped her good arm around Nicole from behind and kissed her neck.

"Remember not to push yourself when you get back to work," Nicole said.

"I won't. Zach and Lucinda have already talked with my supervisor about my restrictions. I will also schedule my follow-up with my doctor and my therapist Monday…plus I'm having dinner with Jessie on Monday night."

"She seemed really interesting." Nicole laughed.

"She is. Nic, would you go see my therapist with me when you get to town?" Amber asked hesitantly.

"Of course. I'll go anywhere with you." Nicole turned in Amber's arms and kissed her. "I'm really going to miss kissing you and cuddling."

"I'm going to miss that, too. I can't believe how much has changed in two weeks."

"I know. I never imagined I would be this close

to you again."

"I dreaded coming here when Lucinda told me I had to get the release forms signed. I had no idea if any of you were still around or if you would give me the time of day. After a bit of yelling, here I am, in your house, in your arms…" Amber said as her eyes filled with tears. "I love you so much, Nicole. I'm so sorry I hurt you."

"We both know that had you not left, you would have been killed. Not that returning didn't almost get you killed," Nicole said with a shudder. "Dr. Scott, my therapist, always says not to dwell on the past. It's over and done with, and there's nothing you can do about it. Well, I think that's good advice to live by right now. So, no more talking about the past or about being hurt. From now on, we talk about the present or the future."

"I love you," Amber said as she pressed their lips together in a kiss that she hoped would convey the depths of her love for this woman.

❧❧❧❧

"Hey, Jill, what brings you by?" Erik said as he saw her enter the firehouse.

"I have to pick up Nicole and Amber soon to take them to the airport. I'm really not looking forward to them having to say goodbye and what it will do to Nicole."

"Yeah, I know what you mean." Erik led them to a corner of the upstairs rec room that had a sofa and two chairs.

"I know Nicole is going to New York in a few weeks, but that's scary, too."

"I know. Nicole in the big city doesn't sound

right. Although, I never would have pictured Amber thriving the way she has, either. We're just going to have to keep an eye on Nicole until she leaves. Dr. Scott is supposed to be back this week, so if we need to get her in, we'll be able to."

"That's good. I have to pick them up in a couple of hours."

"Do you want me to come with?"

"No, Nic was adamant that it just be me. Maybe you can stop by and see her later, though."

"That I can do. Tell Amber not to be a stranger."

"I will. I gotta stop by the PD before I go. I need to finalize the paperwork on Jeffrey."

As Amber's departure time neared, she and Nicole pulled inside themselves. Amber wasn't sure what she was feeling outside of the sorrow of leaving Nicole. She sat in one of the chairs by the window in her mother's room looking at the pictures on the dresser and the view outside.

"Mama, I can feel you near me when I'm in this room. I'm so sorry I didn't get to say goodbye or to be here to help you," Amber said aloud. "I'm glad you had Nicole, and you got to see why I love her so much. I have to go back to New York today, and I'm so worried about leaving her. I love her so much and…and I just want everything to work out. No, I can't come live back here…but she has her job and commitments, as well as her friends, well, our friends. I'm a bit shocked that they let me back into their lives. I never thought I would see them again or be a part of any of this again. How am I going to survive the next three weeks waiting for Nicole to join me?"

"The same way I'm going to survive you not being here," Nicole said softly as she entered the room, seeing Amber jump. "I didn't mean to scare you, eavesdrop, or interrupt."

"It's okay." Amber pulled Nicole onto her lap. "I was just talking to Mom. I feel so close to her in here."

"You were probably the most thought about person in this room, so feeling close to her here makes sense. We'll get through this time apart. We'll talk on the phone, video chat, text, email, whatever we have to."

"I know, it's just going to be hard."

"You just need to remember that I love you," Nicole said.

"I love you, too." Amber pulled Nicole closer. "Jill's going to be here soon, isn't she?"

"Yeah, she is," Nicole said softly.

Amber looked around the room again before she and Nicole went to make sure they had all of Amber's stuff packed. Amber was surprised that she was still going to be able to get away with not checking any bags. She hated going to baggage claim after a flight. They were always so crowded, and everyone was pushing and shoving because they were in a hurry to get out of there.

While they were waiting for Jill to arrive, Nicole and Amber curled up on the couch and held each other.

⁂

Jill pulled up to Nicole's house and took a deep breath before exiting her car. As she walked toward the front door, she looked in the window and caught a glimpse of Nicole and Amber lying together on the couch.

Jill rang the doorbell and was prepared to wait for them to answer. She was surprised when Nicole opened the door a few seconds later. Nicole's eyes were red-rimmed. She knew Nicole had been crying. When Jill followed Nicole into the living room, she saw Amber, whose eyes also showed signs of crying.

"I'd ask how you two were doing, but the red-rimmed eyes give that away." Jill sat on the chair while Nicole and Amber sat close together, their bodies touching to give them both comfort.

"We need to leave, don't we?" Nicole asked.

"Yeah, I'm sorry to say, but we do need to get going," Jill said.

The three women got into Jill's Jeep. Nicole and Amber sat in the back so they could hold on to the last bit of time together. Jill couldn't tell who this was hurting more, but she hoped they weren't going to suffer mental breakdowns.

When they arrived at the airport, Jill took Amber's two bags and walked ahead of them. Nicole took Amber's hand, and they made their way to security where they were going to have to say goodbye.

"I love you, Nicole." Amber wrapped her arms around her neck.

"I love you, too." Nicole wrapped her arms around Amber's waist. "Text me when you land and call me tonight before you go to bed. I don't think I can handle not hearing your voice."

"The moment I can text from the plane, I will, and I'm going to need to hear your voice, too, before I go to bed. It's going to feel weird going to sleep without you holding me or me holding you."

"Weirder for me since we've been sharing my bed. I do, however, get to smell you on the pillow. I hope it lasts for three weeks." Nicole pulled back to look Amber in the eyes.

As the two kissed, Jill heard a guy catcall and whistle. Jill pulled her badge out and offered to give him a place to stay for the night. The guy laughed until his friend pointed out to him that it was a sheriff's badge. The man apologized and moved on. Neither Nicole nor Amber had heard or were aware of the exchange. They were lost in their kiss.

After they broke from the kiss, Amber hugged Jill and told her to take care of Nicole while they were apart. Jill promised she would.

Amber hugged Nicole again and then pulled out her ID to go through security.

"Remember, you promised to text me and call me," Nicole said.

"You're going to be on my mind the whole time. I won't forget."

Jill and Nicole watched as Amber went through security. They waved as she turned and headed toward the gate. Jill took Nicole out to where they could watch the plane take off.

Amber slowly walked to the gate, her heart aching. She was trying hard not to cry. It wasn't long after Amber made it to the gate that they called her flight. As Amber sat and watched the plane taxi out, she thought she saw Nicole and Jill watching. She pressed her hand to the window.

I love you, Nicole. I will see you soon, Amber thought.

I love you, Amber. You're my soul mate. I can't wait to see you again, Nicole thought as she watched the plane taxi and take off.

❦❦❦❦

Jill drove back to Nicole's house. Nicole hadn't said much since Amber had passed through security.

"Are you going to be okay? Do you want me to stick around for a while?" Jill asked as they pulled into Nicole's driveway.

"Thanks, but I just want to be alone for a while," Nicole said.

"I'm worried about you."

"I'm sad. I miss her already. I just need time to process. The love of my life returned and was here, in my house, in my arms, and now she's gone again."

"But you're going to see her again…in three weeks even," Jill said.

"That's the reason I'm still functioning. If I knew I wasn't going to see her again or if it was going to be longer, you'd be taking me to the hospital psych ward," Nicole said with a small laugh. "I just need some time to get my emotions under control. If I can't control things, I'll let you guys know."

"All right, but let me know when you hear from Amber. I want to make sure she gets back to New York all right." Jill hugged Nicole.

Nicole nodded and got out of the car and went inside. She went right to the lanai and curled up where she and Amber had spent so much time.

❦❦❦❦

Amber rested her head on the window as the plane took off. The man sitting next to her slept and occasionally snorted in his sleep.

"Are you all right, ma'am?" the female flight attendant asked as she made her walk through the cabin. She had noticed Amber's head hung and the sorrow in her eyes when she boarded the plane.

"Yeah," Amber said. "I just had to leave someone I love deeply."

"I'm sorry. If you need anything, please, let me know."

"Thank you." Amber smiled at the woman.

As the flight descended into New York, Amber felt some of the heartache ease. She felt safe here. She didn't have the lingering memories to torture and torment her.

The plane landed, and Amber sent Nicole a text that she was in New York and she would call her later. Nicole replied that she was glad she made it safely and she looked forward to Amber's call.

The flight attendant helped Amber get her bag from the upper compartment and helped her get off the plane without her arm being bumped. Amber again thanked the woman and walked up the ramp to the terminal. As Amber reached the main part of the airport, she saw Zach standing there. She hurried to him and leaned into his chest as he wrapped his arms around her.

"I know it hurts, but she'll be here in a few weeks," Zach said as he held Amber until she was ready to go to the car.

Zach drove Amber back to her place. They rode mostly in silence.

"Thanks for picking me up," Amber said as they pulled up outside her brownstone.

"Of course. I know it hurts now, but it will get

better." Zach gently squeezed Amber's hand.

"I know, I just need to get settled and call Nicole. It'll be easier then."

Zach nodded and helped Amber get her stuff upstairs. He told her to call if she needed anything; otherwise, he would be over in the morning to get her for work. She tried to tell him he didn't need to, but he was having nothing to do with it.

Amber was just about to call Nicole when she heard a knock at the door. She made her way over and looked through the peephole and saw it was her neighbor.

"Mrs. Phelps, hello," Amber said.

"Amber, hi. I heard someone moving around on the stairs earlier, and I wasn't sure if it was you or not. Are you all right?" the woman asked as she noticed the sling.

"I will be. I'm sorry I was gone so long. I know you and Mr. Phelps were looking after my plants. Thank you so much."

"You know you're like a daughter to us. Was your trip successful?"

"More than I ever imagined," Amber said as a smile crept across her face.

"Maybe we can sit down and talk this week. I'd love to hear about it."

"I can't wait to tell you about it."

"If you need anything, dear, just let us know." The older woman hugged Amber and headed back down the stairs.

Amber closed the door and went back to the couch to call Nicole.

Chapter Twenty-one

Daily Living

Nicole jumped when the phone rang. She looked at the caller ID and smiled when she saw it was Amber.

"Hey, gorgeous."

"Hi, love," Amber said. "How are you doing?"

"I miss you," Nicole admitted. "How was your flight?"

"I miss you, too. The flight was long. I missed you the whole way. I still do. Zach met me at the airport, and after I got home, Mrs. Phelps, my landlady, came up to check on me."

"That was sweet of her. What are you doing right now?"

"I'm curled up on the couch, looking at a picture of you and me. What are you doing?"

"I'm out on the lanai. It reminds me of you, plus your scent is still on a couple of the pillows." Nicole hugged one of the pillows close to her.

"I miss the lanai. Do you have to work tomorrow?" Amber tried to get on to a subject that hurt less.

"Yeah, I have a couple of meetings. I also think Jill and Erik will be watching me like a hawk, so I'm sure lunch and dinner are taken." Nicole laughed. "What does your day look like?"

"It'll be busy, so I don't dwell on the fact that you

aren't here."

"This will be a long three weeks, won't it?"

"Very long. I love you, Nicole."

"I love you, too, Amber."

They discussed what Amber thought her dinner with Jessie would be like. Amber explained that she would get a lecture for not advising her that she was going to Eagle Peak and that she was injured while she was there before she called to cancel their dinner plans. Nicole told Amber that she could call her, and she would help her get through the dinner. Amber said she'd keep that in mind. They both yawned, having been up all night making love and trying to maximize their time together. They said their good nights and I love yous before hanging up and going to bed.

≈≈≈≈

Morning arrived, and Amber got up and saw a text from Nicole.

Nicole: I love you! Have a great day. Know you will be in my thoughts all day.

Amber: I love you, too! You will be in my heart and thoughts all day.

Nicole: Message me if you get time.

Amber: I will. You message me, too.

Amber showered and got dressed for work. She was just about to make breakfast when she heard a knock at the door. When she opened it, she saw Zach standing there holding coffee and doughnuts.

"Good morning." Zach smiled as he entered the apartment.

"Good morning." Amber followed him to the

breakfast bar.

"How are you feeling?"

"Physically or mentally?"

"Both."

"Physically, I'm a little stiff. Mentally, I miss her. I think it's harder than it was the first time being away from her."

"It'll get better, I promise." Zach put a hand on Amber's shoulder.

"I just have to survive three weeks. Then she'll be here."

The two ate and drank their coffee. When they were done, Zach drove them to work. It wasn't often that he used his car, but today, he thought it would be easier. It was a smoother ride for Amber, and they were going to need it for getting to Jessie's office where they were meeting before dinner.

When they arrived at work, Amber was told to clock in and go up to Lucinda's office. When she got to Lucinda's office, her secretary announced her, and she went in.

"Amber, it's good to have you back," Lucinda said as Amber entered.

"It's good and hard to be back." Amber smiled, taking a seat across from Lucinda.

"I can imagine. If you need anything to make it easier for you to work, just let me know."

"I will. And thank you again for being so understanding and accommodating while I was gone."

"You've been a valued member of our team for ten years, and you'll be one of our featured artists. I don't want to keep you from work. I just wanted to welcome you back and make sure you were all right."

"Thank you again," Amber said and headed

downstairs to work.

※ ※ ※ ※

Nicole got up and made some coffee and texted with Amber before she had to shower and get ready for her first meeting. As Nicole was getting out of the shower, she heard her phone beep. Nicole saw she had a text from Jill that she and Erik were bringing breakfast and would be there shortly.

Just as Nicole was getting downstairs, she heard a knock on the door. She answered and saw Jill and Erik standing there.

"Hey, guys," Nicole greeted as they entered, and everyone went into the kitchen.

"How are you doing, Nic?" Erik asked.

"I miss her, but I'm okay. We texted a bit earlier."

"Text or sext?" Jill waggled her eyebrows.

"Text. Like I would tell you the other." Nicole rolled her eyes.

"So, what do you have planned for today?" Erik asked.

"I have a couple of meetings and some coding to do. I also have to start planning for my trip to see Amber."

"That's three weeks away," Jill said.

"No, it's less than three weeks, and I'm going to be gone for a while, so I need to get stuff lined up around here, as well."

"I'll come to water your fake plants," Erik offered.

"Great." Nicole laughed. "I actually want you two to look in on the house and stuff."

"That's a given," Jill said.

"I have to get to work. Call or text if you need anything today," Erik got up and hugged Nicole.

"So, how are you really doing now that he's gone?" Jill asked when they were alone.

"I'm surviving. I miss her. I know I'll get to see her soon and that helps, but she's still my everything."

"You two were always perfect together. From what I saw before she left, you still are. It'll work out. I'm sure of it. Have you thought about giving Dr. Scott a call?"

"Yeah, but then I talk myself out of it." Nicole smiled.

"You should see him. At least to touch base. A lot has happened, and it could help you to talk to him."

"I'll think about it." Nicole glanced at the clock. "Crap, I have to get going soon. I have a meeting with one of the government agencies I do work for."

"Well, call, text, or stop by if you need anything." Jill hugged her.

"I will."

Jill left, and Nicole quickly cleaned up and headed off to her meeting.

❧❧❧❧

When Amber finally made it to her painting station, she saw that her boss had given her several small paintings to work on so she didn't strain herself her first day or week back.

"Welcome back," her boss said.

"Thanks. Sorry I was gone so long," Amber said softly.

"You're back now, and that's what's important. For the next couple of weeks or until I get a release from your doctor, we're going to have you doing little paintings. You're one of my best painters, so please, get well soon," he said before turning and walking away.

Amber laughed to herself as she watched him walk off. Zach came over and helped her get ready to paint. Once Amber started painting, her reflex memory kicked in, and it was as if she hadn't been gone at all. The day went by quickly, and Zach helped Amber clean up. As they were walking out, Lucinda stopped them. She asked Amber how many would be with her for the artist party for the art show. Amber said there would be two.

"What?" Amber said as she and Zach walked out of the gallery.

"Nothing," Zach said.

"I'm not moving until you tell me what that smile was for."

"Fine. You glow when you think about Nicole. It's cute. Now come on or you'll be late for your dinner with Jessie."

"Yeah, I'm going to move quicker to get someplace where I'm going to get lectured and possibly yelled at." Amber laughed.

The drive wasn't long, and for once, they made good time. Amber walked into the building and took the elevator to the twelfth floor. Amber checked in with the receptionist who told her that Jessie would be right with her.

Dr. Jessie Burke opened her office door with a glare already fixed on her face. Amber looked up and saw this and blanched a little. Jessie just shook her head slowly.

"Amber, my office now."

Amber got up, bowed her head, and walked past Jessie and into her office. The office was decorated with a couple of high-back leather chairs, a sofa with several pillows on it, fake plants, and dark wood throughout.

She wanted her clients to feel as relaxed as possible, so it was easier for them to open up and talk about their problems. Amber sat on the sofa, still not looking at Jessie.

"How are you doing?" Jessie asked, in a much softer tone, and she had a genuine look of concern on her face.

"I've been better, but I'm healing," Amber said, still not meeting the other woman's eyes.

"I have no clue where to start tonight. I heard so little when I was on the phone with you, Heather, and Nicole. Where should we start?" Jessie placed a hand on Amber's good shoulder.

"Lucinda is going to put me in the next art show at the gallery," Amber said. "She chose a couple of photos that I needed to get release forms signed for so I could legally show them."

"Which sent you to Eagle Peak?"

"Yup. When I got to the hotel, I ran into Heather, who I found out later owns it."

"Did she recognize you?"

"Yep, right away. I thought for certain that changing my hair color—"

"Wait, you aren't a natural blonde?" Jessie interrupted, surprised by this revelation. She had prided herself and was usually good at spotting those people who colored their hair.

"Nope, I'm a brunette just like you. It turns out, my eyes give me away." Amber laughed. She proceeded to tell about seeing Nicole and the others, the meeting in her room, Jill slapping her, and then learning about what happened to her mother after she left. Amber told Jessie about her father tormenting Nicole and the emotional toll that took on her. She told her about the episodes Nicole had, what had triggered them, and what had brought her out.

"Wow. This is going to take a while, I can tell. I'm ordering us dinner. Do you want me to give you a ride home tonight?"

"Since you live a block from me, yeah I'll ride with you," Amber said. "Do you want to go back to my place to finish this? This is going to take a while, probably even more than you're thinking it will."

"Yeah, I think we should." Jessie laughed.

As Jessie ordered dinner for them, Amber messaged Zach and told him she would call him later. She told him they were going to go back to her place to finish talking. Jessie came out of her office, and the two made their way to her apartment so she could change her clothes before they went to Amber's apartment.

"Amber? Is that you?" Mrs. Phelps peeked her head out the door.

"Yes, it's me," Amber said as she and Jessie stopped in the hall.

"Okay, good. Oh, and I see your girlfriend is back," Mrs. Phelps said. "You two are cute together."

"Mrs. Phelps, Jessie is my friend, not my girlfriend."

"You're too beautiful to be single," Mrs. Phelps said.

"I-I'll explain when we sit down in the next couple of days." Amber gently squeezed the old woman's hand. Mrs. Phelps nodded and went back inside.

Once inside Amber's apartment, the two women sat on the sofa to continue their talk and eat dinner. Amber talked about the letter her mom wrote, about going to the pond to read it with Nicole, and about their first kiss in ten years. Amber then let Jessie read the letter from her mom. She hadn't seen her friend cry before, but this seemed to push her over.

"That's a sweet letter." Jessie handed it back to Amber. "So, you and Nicole? Your brother? Where do we go next?"

"Nicole…you'll get to meet her soon." Amber grinned and blushed.

"Really?"

"Yeah, she's coming up in a few weeks to spend some time together. She'll be my date for the show."

"So…are you two together again?"

"Yes." Amber blushed. "We are. She still loves me."

"Like that was ever in doubt." Jessie laughed. "Everyone loves you."

Amber talked about the encounter with her brother, about getting shot, and about her time with Nicole. Amber glossed over the other people in Eagle Peak, her main focus was, always had been, and always would be Nicole.

"I can't believe you went through all this and didn't call me until you canceled our dinner plans," Jessie said.

"There was a lot going on. I was so overwhelmed."

"I can imagine. Now what's it like being back in New York?"

"Lonely. I miss Nicole and can't wait for these damn three weeks to be over, so I can have her here."

"And then what?" She knew this was a hard question and Amber probably had no answer, but sometimes friends needed to pose the touchy questions.

"I don't know what. I just know that she'll be here, and I'll be happier and complete."

"You have to have some idea or a plan in mind. What do you want to happen?"

"I want her to stay, to move in, and be with me forever. Is it realistic? I don't know. She has a career, and yeah, some of it can be done from here, but she has a life there, too. I know I can't go back there," Amber said.

<center>~~~~</center>

Nicole's meetings had gone by slower than she thought they ever could. She thought for a while she was going to fall asleep in one of them. She knew that would have been bad since there were just three of them in the room. She didn't understand why some government officials had to be so boring. After she finished her meetings, she had lunch with Erik, Jill, and Heather.

"How's your day going?" Erik asked as they sat for lunch.

"Boring! I miss Amber, but I haven't lost my mind…yet," Nicole said. "You guys don't need to worry as much as you are. I know she's okay. I'm going to see her in less than three weeks. I feel better than I have in years."

"That's great, Nic, but we still worry that you're going to get lonely or depressed without Amber being here," Jill said.

"I don't doubt that I will, but that doesn't mean you need to worry that something bad will happen to me. I know logically that I just have to wait it out until it's time for me to go to New York."

"Have you thought about the future? Did you and Amber talk about your plans?" Heather asked.

"I've thought about it, but I don't feel like sharing my thoughts right now. And Amber and I did talk about the future, but we wanted to wait and see what happens when I go up there. We may do a long-distance thing, we may not. I know I love her, and she loves me, and right now, that's going to sustain us."

The group finished lunch. Nicole said her plans for the night were spending some time alone and waiting for Amber to call. The others said they didn't think that was a good idea, but she said it was what she wanted.

༄༅༄༅

Jessie held Amber for a long time while she cried out her frustrations.

"We'll get you through it, Amber, I promise," she said. "Maybe you should start seeing your therapist weekly until Nicole gets here. I think you're going to need it when the glow of having just seen her wears off."

"I guess it wouldn't hurt," Amber said as she heard a knock at the door. "Can you get that? I need to go fix my makeup."

"Yeah, sure. Are you expecting anyone?" Jessie asked.

"No. It's probably Mrs. Phelps again." Amber laughed as she hurried out of the room and Jessie answered the door.

Jessie opened the door to see a redhead standing there with a suitcase.

"Hello, is this Amber Knight's place?" Nicole asked.

"Yeah, she's in the other room. Is there something I can help you with?" Jessie asked.

"Who was or is it?" Amber asked as she came back into the room.

"Um," Jessie opened the door a bit wider for

Amber to see.

"Nic? Sweetie?" Amber rushed toward the door.

"Yeah, baby." Nicole opened her arms and wrapped them around Amber.

Jessie stepped back and watched the interaction between the two.

"Not complaining, but what are you doing here?" Amber asked before pulling Nicole into a slow sensual kiss.

"Mmm, I couldn't handle being there and knowing you were here," Nicole started before quickly kissing Amber.

"What about work? Jill? Erik? Heather?"

"I took a short leave of absence from work. As for the gang, they sort of don't know that I left. I had lunch with them, and, baby, I missed you so much, I just hopped a flight and came here. I figured I'd call them when we decided if it was okay for me to be here or not."

"Of course it's okay for you to be here."

"Knock, knock" came a voice from the doorway.

Nicole and Amber turned to see Mrs. Phelps standing there holding a cake.

"Hi, Mrs. Phelps," Amber said, her arm wrapped around Nicole's waist, holding her close.

"Oh, you have more company. I'm sorry to interrupt."

"You aren't. I'm glad you came up. *This* is my girlfriend, Nicole. Sweetie, this is Mrs. Phelps."

"I've heard a lot about you." Nicole extended her hand toward the older woman.

"Amber, is this the woman you've told me about over the years?" Mrs. Phelps said.

"Yes." Amber took the cake out of the woman's

hands, only to have it taken out of her hands by Jessie, who put the cake in the kitchen.

Mrs. Phelps pulled Nicole into a hug and whispered in her ear, "She loves you so much."

Nicole smiled and whispered back, "I love her, too."

"Amber, I hope you enjoy the cake. I love seeing you smile, my dear," Mrs. Phelps said as she hugged Amber and headed for the door.

"Thank you! I still want to do coffee or tea in a couple of days."

"We will." Mrs. Phelps left, closing the door behind her.

"Nic, I…um…forgot to introduce you to someone." Amber laughed before kissing Nicole.

"Huh?" Nicole said.

"Nicole, this is Dr. Jessie Burke, one of my best friends. Jess, this is the love of my life, Nicole."

"It's nice to finally meet you." Jessie shook Nicole's hand.

"It's nice to meet you, too. Thank you for taking care of her over the years." Nicole wrapped her arms around Amber's waist from behind and kissed the side of her head.

"Well, I'm going to go home. I see I'm no longer needed as a shoulder to cry on," Jessie said.

"Thank you for being here tonight. I'll call you tomorrow," Amber said.

"It was nice to meet you," Nicole said.

"It was nice to meet you, too, Nicole. I'll call Zach when I get home and tell him you'll see him tomorrow. I somehow think that talking to him is one of the last things you want to do tonight," Jessie said.

After Jessie left, Amber pulled Nicole over to the

couch, and they sat close together.

"I can't believe you're here."

"She seems nice."

"She's a good friend. Wait, are you jealous?"

"A little," Nicole admitted. "She has been here for you, and she isn't exactly unattractive."

"Sweetie, you're the only woman I've ever wanted," Amber said before kissing Nicole.

After a heated makeout session, Nicole's phone rang. Nicole groaned as she reached for it.

"Hi Jill," Nicole said, trying to hide the groan.

"Nicole Marie Brooks, where the hell are you? Erik and Heather both went by your house, and you weren't there. I've called most of the hospitals in the area and had a bolo put out on your car," Jill snapped.

"Jill, relax. I'm in New York with Amber."

"I'm sorry, I think I heard you wrong. Can you please repeat that? Wait, let me put you on speaker, so Heather and Erik can hear it, as well."

"Nic? Are you okay?" Erik asked when Jill had her on speakerphone.

"I'm fine. I'm in New York with Amber," Nicole said, feeling Amber kiss the side of her head.

"Seriously?" Heather said.

"Hi, guys," Amber said cheerfully.

"When? Why? Huh?" Jill said.

"After lunch, I was missing Amber so much. I took a short leave of absence from the government contract stuff, hopped on a plane, and came to New York. I took a very scary cab ride to Amber's house, I about had a heart attack when an attractive woman answered her door, and now I'm sitting curled up on the couch with the most beautiful woman in the world."

"And you couldn't tell us you were leaving?" Erik asked.

"I just did it."

"So, Amber. Who was the attractive woman answering your door?" Heather asked playfully.

"Jess, my friend." Amber laughed.

"She's attractive? Is she single? Does she date women?" Heather said.

"Yes, she's attractive, yes, she's single, and yes, she dates women, and no, you cannot date her," Amber responded.

"Well, why not? It isn't like you're going to date her," Heather said as the others laughed.

"Listen, you guys know I'm okay, and it has been a long day. Why don't I call you sometime tomorrow?"

"All right, but don't you ever run off like that again," Jill said.

"She won't. I won't let her," Amber said.

They finished saying goodbye, and Nicole put her phone on the table.

"Are you sure you aren't mad about me just showing up?"

"Sweetie, I hardly slept last night because you weren't holding me. Now let's lock up and go into the bedroom and you can help me shower and get ready for bed."

"Yes, ma'am," Nicole said as they stood and took her stuff into Amber's room.

The couple showered together and dried each other off before slipping into bed for some naked snuggles.

Chapter Twenty-two

Together Again

"Amber?" Nicole said as they lay in bed naked trying to fall asleep.

"Yeah, sweetie?" Amber had almost been asleep in Nicole's arms.

"What am I going to do while you're at work tomorrow?"

"Well, you can hang out here…" Amber started.

"You aren't afraid I'll rifle through your things?"

"I expect it. I did at your place when you were gone," Amber joked. "Honestly, sweetie, I trust you, and if you want to rifle through my stuff, wear my underwear on your head…well, if you're going to do that last part, I would like to be here to get pictures. You can do whatever you want. I'll see if maybe Wednesday you can shadow me at work."

"You can do that?"

"It wouldn't be the first time someone had a visiting family member come for a day."

"I don't want to invade your personal space. Which I should have thought about before I jumped on a plane and headed here, but I missed you, I love you, and I didn't know what to do with myself without you there. I'm sorry if I'm—" Nicole babbled before she was cut off by Amber's lips on hers. After a couple of minutes of kissing, Nicole started to relax.

"First, I missed you, and I love you, too. Next, you aren't invading my personal space because had I thought you would do it, I would have asked you to come back with me. Now stop talking silly, or I'm going to have to put on clothes. And I don't mean a skimpy negligée. I'm talking sweatpants and a sweatshirt."

"To sleep in?"

"If you keep talking like that, yes. Now kiss me."

Nicole didn't need to be told twice to kiss the woman she loved. Nicole pressed their lips together, hearing a groan from Amber as her tongue made its way into Amber's mouth. They kissed for several minutes before Nicole pulled away and looked deep into Amber's eyes. Deep enough to see her soul and see that she meant what she had said and that their love was stronger than she knew.

❧ ❧ ❧ ❧

Morning arrived, and Nicole tried to stay out of Amber's way while she got ready for work. Nicole had perched herself at the breakfast bar. As she looked around the apartment, she loved all the "Amber" tweaks that made the space warm and comforting. The pillows by the window to curl up on and read or listen to the rain. There was the desk and laptop in one corner of the room, and down the hall, Nicole knew there was Amber's art studio. Amber's art covered the walls. It was one of the first things Nicole checked out while Amber was getting dressed.

"So, what did you decide to do today, cutie?" Amber asked as she entered the kitchen, placing a kiss on Nicole's head before making breakfast and getting coffee.

"I thought I might do some work. I have a couple of programs I need to make some progress on. Do you have Wi-Fi or are you wired internet?"

"Wi-Fi. I like to sit over by the window with my laptop and read or surf. Do you want some toast? I know I don't need to ask if you want coffee."

Nicole smiled and nodded. While her computer was booting up, Nicole went to get a cup of coffee and found herself pinned between Amber and the counter. Amber had a hand on each side of Nicole with her back against the counter.

"Hi." Amber leaned in and sucked on Nicole's neck.

"Helloooo. Oh, god, Amber." Nicole moaned. "You can't do that and then leave me, baby."

"Sorry," Amber said, her lips brushing against Nicole's ear. "I want you to think about me when I'm gone."

Nicole let out a whimper before turning her head and pulling Amber into a searing kiss. Amber let out a moan and pressed her body even closer to Nicole's. Things were heating up when the doorbell rang.

"Damn it," Amber mumbled as she grudgingly pulled away from Nicole to answer the door. She knew it was Zach picking her up for work, but she was enjoying the closeness with Nicole more.

"Good morning," Zach said as Amber opened the door and motioned for him to come in.

"Morning," Amber said, hoping she wasn't still flushed from her session in the kitchen with Nicole.

The two made their way to the kitchen where Nicole was buttering the toast and sipping on her coffee.

"Good morning," Nicole said, smiling at Zach.

"Good morning, Nicole. I was surprised when Jessie called last night and told me you were here."

"Why is that?" Nicole asked as Amber took a piece of the toast Nicole had buttered.

"I'm surprised it took you that long to get here," Zach said, smiling.

"I had a couple of meetings I had to attend before I could leave. I did get here as soon as I could, though," Nicole said.

"Are you about ready, Amber?"

"Yeah, go down, and I'll be there in a minute."

"Okay. It was good to see you again, Nicole. I'm glad you're here."

"Thanks. Good to see you, too."

Amber waited for the door to close behind Zach before kissing Nicole and pulling her close.

"I love you. This is your place, as well as mine, as far as I'm concerned. Do as you want. I'll be home as soon as I can. Text me and let me know how you're doing. We'll go out tonight and I'll show you around. If you need anything, Mrs. Phelps is just downstairs. She'll talk your ear off, but she's the sweetest little old lady."

"I love you, too," Nicole said, enjoying the closeness with Amber. "I'm just going to work on my programs if you'll give me your Wi-Fi password."

"Oh, yeah…um…it's my Nicole. Spelled M-y-N-1-c-0-l-e…" Amber said, blushing as she looked down.

Nicole tried as hard as she could, but she couldn't help but laugh. "Really?"

"I told you in Eagle Peak, you were always on my mind no matter how long I was gone or how far apart we were." Amber smiled as Nicole realized how true that was.

"I love you. You better go before Zach leaves you here."

"I love you, too. I'll call you on my lunch break. Text me when you want."

With that, they kissed again, and Amber headed out. Nicole stood in the kitchen dumbfounded that what she had believed of Amber was not true at all. She really had been in her thoughts over the years.

※ ※ ※

"So…" Zach said as they headed off to work.

"What?" Amber asked.

"Start talking. What is she doing here?"

"She missed me…she didn't like being away from me."

"Did you know she was coming?"

"Hell no. I had no clue. I, however, am not going to complain, either. I need her here or with me. I've always needed that."

"Happiness agrees with you. So, what are you going to do now? Are you going to ask her to give up her life in Eagle Peak?"

"We have a lot to talk about. I only know that I'm happy she's here and that I can't wait for today to be over with."

"I'm happy for you then," Zach said.

Once they arrived at work, Amber spoke to her supervisor and Lucinda and got approval for Nicole to shadow her the next day.

※ ※ ※

After Amber left, Nicole logged in to her

computer, then called Jill.

"Hello?"

"Hey, Jill," Nicole said.

"Nicole! What's up?"

"Not much. Amber left for work a few minutes ago, so before I started working, I thought I would call and touch base."

"I still can't believe you just jumped on a plane and flew to New York City without telling any of us."

"Well, I missed her and couldn't handle the idea of living without her."

"I know, I know. So, what are you going to do while she's at work?" Jill asked.

"I have some work to do, and once she gets home, she said she'd show me around. Oh, I got to meet the little old lady from downstairs. She's so sweet. She whispered that Amber really loves me when she hugged me last night."

"Aww, so Amber told her about you?"

"Apparently, she meant it when she said she thought about us over the years," Nicole said, her voice cracking a little.

"Hey, you're there with her. No need for the voice crack."

"I know. This may sound stupid, but she gave me her Wi-Fi password, and it's just too damn cute."

"Oookay…explain," Jill said, skeptical.

"Her password is my Nicole."

"You don't think she set that since she was here?"

"She was home twenty-four hours before I got here. I don't think changing the password was a high priority for her."

"Yeah, good point."

"I'm going to get some work done. I'll touch base

with you guys in a few days, okay?"

"Okay. We love and miss you."

"I love and miss you guys, too."

After they finished their goodbyes, Nicole connected her phone to the charger and sat on the pillows next to the window to work.

Nicole had worked for a few hours when she heard a soft knock at the door. She set her computer aside and moved to the door. Nicole opened the door to see Mrs. Phelps.

"Hello, Nicole," Mrs. Phelps said.

"Hello, Mrs. Phelps." Nicole smiled at her. "Amber is at work today."

"Oh, I know, dear. I heard her and that nice boy Zach leave. I wanted to talk to you. Is now okay?"

"Yes, ma'am."

"Good. Would you like to come downstairs? I can make us some tea and cookies."

Nicole followed her downstairs. They entered the apartment, and Nicole was instructed to keep the door open so Mrs. Phelps could hear the mailman. The two sat at a little table in what appeared to be a breakfast nook.

"You sit, dear, and I'll get the tea," Mrs. Phelps said.

"I can help if you need it," Nicole offered.

"No, dear, you sit. I've been getting tea in this house for sixty-five years. It used to be my parents' house."

"It's a beautiful house. Amber told me that she lived here for most of the time she's been in New York.

I'm so grateful you and your husband have been here for her."

"Oh, she's such a lovely girl."

Mrs. Phelps asked Nicole several questions about her life and her intentions with Amber. She asked how strong Nicole felt their love was. Nicole said she felt it was stronger than it had been when they were younger. Mrs. Phelps explained that they were more mature and knew what they wanted and what they were willing to sacrifice to get what they desired.

"Have you talked with Amber here before?" Nicole looked around. She felt as if she were enveloped in a large hug being with Mrs. Phelps.

"She and I have had so many talks at this table. She has told me a lot about you."

"She has?" Nicole said, surprised.

"Did you think that after she left you, she forgot about you?"

"Yes, ma'am." Nicole lowered her head.

"Well, she didn't. She told me all about you, and let me see, Jill, Erik, and Heather. Did I get it correct?"

"Yes. I'm still learning a lot of things that she never let us in on growing up."

"Give her time. She'll tell you all she can." Mrs. Phelps covered Nicole's hand with her own.

"She may even tell you what she can't handle, either," Amber said, smiling from the doorway.

"Amber," Nicole squeaked.

"Hi, sweetie." Amber entered and kissed the side of each woman's head. "What have you been up to, Mrs. Phelps?"

"I'm just trying to get to know the woman who holds your heart. I think she's lovelier than you described. What are you doing home? What happened to your arm, dear?" Mrs. Phelps noticed the sling again.

"I came home to have lunch with Nicole, and my arm…" Amber let out a deep sigh before continuing. "My brother is what happened. I'll be okay. I have a broken shoulder and collarbone, as well as a surgical incision from where he shot me."

Nicole's eyes filled with sorrow as she saw the pain in both women's faces.

"Oh, dear sweet Amber. Whatever you need, Max and I are here for you."

"You both have always been here for me. I'm so grateful. Would you be upset if I borrowed your tea buddy for a little bit?"

"You two go enjoy your lunch. Nicole, when she leaves, if you feel like coming back down, you're more than welcome."

"Thank you for the tea and for helping me to learn more about the woman I love." Nicole hugged Mrs. Phelps before Amber took her hand and led her upstairs.

<hr>

Nicole and Amber entered the apartment, and Amber pulled Nicole over to the couch.

"Hi," Amber said, smiling at Nicole as she pulled her onto her lap.

"Hey, gorgeous."

The two leaned together into a soft kiss. The kiss lasted for several minutes before they broke apart.

"So, you were getting to know my landlady, huh?" Amber gave Nicole a lopsided smile.

"Well, you know I was trying to get you some added perks."

"Don't let Max hear you say that." Amber laughed. "He has a thing for blondes and redheads."

"I think you need to move."

"Yeah, not going to happen, my love. Being close to Max and Edna is what has kept me going for years."

"She's a really nice lady. I didn't meet Max."

"You will. How has your day been?"

"Good. I got my programs done and then Mrs. Phelps came up, and we had tea, and I got to know another side of you. I couldn't love you more, though."

"I love you, too, sweetie." Amber kissed Nicole.

"Are you ready for lunch?" Nicole stood and pulled Amber toward the kitchen.

"Yep."

The two made buttered rice and frozen veggies for lunch. Amber hadn't had time to shop for groceries since her return from Eagle Peak. She was grateful that Zach had cleaned up her refrigerator for her while she was gone. She could just imagine the food that had expired.

After eating lunch, Amber had to head back to work, but she told Nicole that they would go out to shop for food, and she would show her around after she got home.

Amber arrived back at work with minutes to spare. She punched in and quickly got a new canvas for the painting she was starting. She hated doing the fluff pieces, but they did still help her hone her skills, and she understood that with her arm in a sling it was the best solution.

"Zach, thanks for offering to let me borrow your

car at lunch." Amber handed him his keys. "I ended up taking a cab, it was easier than trying to drive one handed.

"My pleasure. Was Nicole surprised?"

"Yeah, she was. I found her having tea with Mrs. Phelps."

"You better keep an eye on her...you know Mr. Phelps likes redheads more than blondes."

"Oh, I know. I think Mrs. Phelps can keep him in check after fifty-plus years together."

"True. So, what are you two doing tonight?"

"Grocery shopping and then I thought I'd show her around a bit."

"Are you going to the club?" Zach asked.

"No, not tonight. I want a couple of weeks with her before I subject her to that." Amber laughed.

The rest of the afternoon dragged on while Amber waited to go home. Once the day was done, Zach dropped her off and said he would pick them up in the morning. Amber thanked him and made her way upstairs. She entered the apartment and smelled the aroma of fresh garlic bread, spaghetti, and meatballs.

"Mmm, it smells amazing in here," Amber said as she made her way into the kitchen.

"I'm glad you like it. Max and Edna showed me a store nearby so I could make you a nice dinner."

"You're the best." Amber placed a sensual kiss on Nicole's lips before sticking her finger in the sauce and teasingly licking it off.

"Oh, god...That was not nice." Nicole felt a surge of desire threaten to overtake her.

"My bad." Amber laughed before she took ahold of Nicole's hand and dipped a single finger into the sauce and did the same with one of her own fingers.

Amber then took Nicole's finger in her mouth and sucked on it as she allowed Nicole to do the same with hers. Both women let out a loud moan, and their eyes glossed over. "Yeah, that was my bad, too…very bad."

Nicole just stood there gripping the side of the counter, trying to kick-start her brain back into functioning.

"You keep that up, and we aren't leaving the house tonight," Nicole warned once she regained her composure.

"You like it when I'm playful." Amber wrapped her arm around Nicole's waist and rested her chin on Nicole's shoulder.

"Yes, I do. I did get some stuff, so we technically don't need to leave tonight, either." Nicole turned in Amber's arm and wrapped her own arms around Amber's neck.

"Mmm, dinner and a night of lovemaking sound appealing to me." Amber growled into Nicole's ear.

"How soundproof is this place?"

"Max and Edna never heard my nightmares, and I know Zach said I was good at screaming in those."

"Well, let's eat and test it with screams of pleasure."

"Dear god, yes," Amber said before hungrily capturing Nicole's lips.

They ate dinner and cleaned up before heading to the bathroom for a couple's bath and night of passion.

Chapter Twenty-three

Art and Therapy

Morning arrived earlier than Nicole or Amber realized it would. They had spent most of the night and early morning hours lost in each other. Amber showered and allowed Nicole to sleep in a little longer. Once she was ready for work, she woke Nicole and told her to shower while she started coffee and breakfast.

"Amber? What should I wear today?" Nicole entered the kitchen wrapped in a towel.

"I...er...yummy." Amber growled.

"Focus." Nicole laughed.

"Oh, I'm plenty focused." Amber pulled Nicole closer and kissed her deeply. "Just wear a nice pair of jeans and a nice shirt. If you need one, I have one that will fit you."

"Thank you."

Nicole headed back to the bedroom to get dressed. While she was gone, Amber finished making breakfast. After eating, the two sat on the couch kissing until Zach arrived to take them to work.

⁂

"Amber, who do you have visiting today?" Lucinda asked as she walked up to Amber's station.

"Lucinda, this is my girlfriend, Nicole. Nicole, this is Lucinda Baer, the gallery curator."

"It's really nice to meet you," Nicole said, smiling and extending her hand.

"It's nice to meet you, as well. The photograph of you that Amber has in her collection is one of my favorites. I must say that you have great taste, Amber. I believe she's more beautiful now than she was when you took that picture."

"It's all Amber's talent making the picture look good." Nicole blushed.

"No, sweetie, you are more beautiful now," Amber said with pride.

"Well, Amber, I'll let you get to work. Would you mind if I borrowed Nicole for a little bit?"

"No. Is that okay with you, Nic?"

"That's perfectly fine," Nicole said, nerves taking hold of her.

"Great. I promise not to keep her too long." Lucinda led Nicole out of the replicating area.

Amber glanced in Zach's direction, receiving a supportive smile from him.

❧ ❧ ☙ ☙

Nicole followed Lucinda through the gallery and up to her office. Nicole was surprised at the elegance of the gallery. She loved the rich woods and warm feeling. As they entered the office area, Nicole noticed that the colors and feeling continued.

"Hold my calls," Lucinda said as they passed her assistant's desk and entered her office. "Have a seat, please."

"Thank you." Nicole sat in the chair across from

Lucinda.

"Relax, Nicole. I just wanted to see how Amber's really doing. I know she's good at putting up a front. I've watched her do it for years."

"You care about her a lot, don't you?"

"Yes. Ever since the day I offered her a job with us, I've kept an eye on her and done what I could to help her grow and succeed."

"If you don't mind me asking, why?"

"There was a look in her eyes that made me want to protect her. She looked so lost and listless. It didn't hurt that she has a wicked amount of talent."

"She always has," Nicole said, beaming with pride.

"How long have you two known each other?"

"We've been friends since we were five. As for knowing each other, well, I'm learning that there's more to Amber than any of us knew."

"Zach told me about some of it. I won't pry, but I want you to know that if Amber needs anything, I'm here to make sure she gets it."

"I appreciate that, and I know she does, as well. I know your faith in her and putting her in the art show has done amazing things for her confidence. She beams whenever she talks about it. I think she's a bit nervous, though," Nicole said.

"She's talented and has earned it. Did you get to see the pieces that are going in the show?"

"She showed me the proof."

"Well, that won't do. Follow me." Lucinda led Nicole into the warehouse section of the gallery. They went into a secure, locked area, and Lucinda flipped on the lights. "Here's the layout I've been playing with."

Nicole stood in awe of the artwork in front of

her. There was a large black and white picture of her surrounded by pictures of Heather and Erik, as well as paintings that Amber had created.

"Wow," Nicole whispered. "You're right. The proofs did not do her work justice."

"Have you seen any of her work?"

"She has a few pieces up in her apartment, but I've only been in town for two days."

"Well, if she doesn't show you her work by the end of the week, let me know and I will."

"Thank you."

"I just wanted a chance to talk with you. Thank you for allowing me that. I'll take you back to Amber now," Lucinda said as they left the secure area.

"Thank you for taking the time to talk with me and for looking out for Amber over the years."

"It's been my pleasure. I've seen her smile more in the past couple of days than I ever have. Even though she was sad Monday, I could still see a glow in her. You've done something for her that nobody else can. Please, don't break her heart."

"I have no intention." Nicole smiled as they entered the replication room, and she saw Amber look up and smile in their direction.

※※※※

While Nicole was off with Lucinda, Amber received a call back from her therapist, Dr. Dyer, asking her to come in after work for a session. Amber agreed, although she wasn't happy about it. Amber wanted time to reconnect with Nicole and for them to grow together, even to discuss a future together. She knew that going to see Dr. Dyer was needed, though.

Amber had finished a small painting before Nicole and Lucinda came back. She was starting on another when they walked up to her station.

"Hey," Nicole said, smiling at Amber.

"Hi." Amber smiled back.

"Thank you for letting me borrow Nicole for a bit, Amber," Lucinda said. "Nicole, it was great to meet you. If you need anything, please let me know."

"It was nice to meet you, too. Thank you for showing me Amber's show pieces and for taking the time to talk with me."

Lucinda smiled at the two women, turned, and headed back to her office. Amber turned back to the painting she was just starting and explained to Nicole what she was doing and the reasons she was doing it.

During lunch, Amber and Nicole walked to the deli across the street and got a sandwich and a bowl of fruit. While they ate, Amber told Nicole about her call from the therapist and said they would be going to her office after work. Nicole said she was okay with it and that she was looking forward to meeting with Dr. Dyer.

☙☙❧❧

The cab pulled up outside Dr. Dyer's office building. Nicole and Amber entered, and the security guard smiled at Amber.

"Hi, Tony," Amber said.

"Hi, Amber. How are you doing?" the burly security guard asked.

"I'm good. Tony, this is my girlfriend, Nicole. Sweetie, this is Tony."

"It's really nice to meet you," Tony said.

"You too," Nicole said as she shook the man's

hand.

"What time is your session?"

"In about ten minutes."

"I'll be here when you get done, and I'll get you a cab."

"Thanks, Tony. Tell Trevor hi for me, and I hope to see him Friday or Saturday," Amber said as she took Nicole's hand.

"I will."

Nicole and Amber made their way into the elevator, and as they rode it up to Dr. Dyer's office, Nicole looked at Amber questioningly.

"Tony has been the security guard here for as long as I've been coming. His partner, Trevor, owns the club I was thinking we'd check out this weekend. That is, if you're up for it."

"I look forward to it." Nicole gave Amber a chaste kiss just as the elevator dinged.

"Hi, Amber," the receptionist said as they entered Dr. Dyer's office.

"Hi," Amber said softly and averted her eyes.

"It's been a while since I've seen you. You're looking good today."

"Thank you."

"Did you want something to drink or anything?" the receptionist asked.

"No, thanks."

Nicole and Amber sat in the lobby. Nicole glared in the direction of the receptionist. "Who was that?"

"Nobody, sweetie. Just let it go," Amber said.

"Does she do that often?"

"She isn't usually here when I come in. Dr. Dyer had her schedule switched because she didn't understand the boundaries."

"She still doesn't," Nicole snipped.

Nicole was about to say something else when Dr. Dyer appeared and motioned for them to come in. The two women rose, and Dr. Dyer could sense the tension.

"Is everything okay?" Dr. Dyer sat in the high-backed leather chair, and Nicole and Amber sat on the couch almost near each other.

"Fine," Amber said, not making eye contact.

"Nice try, Amber. Nicole, what's going on?"

"Hey, this is my session, not hers."

"Well, if you aren't going to tell me the truth, I'll seek it out."

"Fine, whatever," Amber said dismissively.

"Your receptionist needs to learn professional boundaries," Nicole said curtly.

"I'm sorry about that. I try to keep her on days that Amber isn't coming in, but I thought it would be good if I got you both in since you were in town and I'm certain that things are good but confusing." Dr. Dyer made eye contact with Nicole to show her sincerity.

"Can we just move past it? Please?" Amber asked softly.

"Sure," Dr. Dyer said, and Nicole smiled and moved closer to Amber so that they were touching.

"So, outside of that, how have things been going?"

"Nicole is here." Amber smiled. "She doesn't hate me."

"I never hated you," Nicole said.

The three women discussed Amber's return and Nicole's need to be here with her. They discussed the emotions that came with her sudden appearance. Nicole mentioned her talk with Lucinda and what it was like to see the pieces that were going in the show. Dr. Dyer pointed out the three pieces of Amber's artwork she had in her office. Amber blushed as the two women discussed her artwork. Nicole talked about what had transpired with Amber's father and that since she had talked with Amber, she hasn't had any terrors or episodes. Dr. Dyer agreed with Dr. Scott, Nicole's therapist, that having faced her fear and telling Amber about what happened gave her some closure. Dr. Dyer asked if they would be willing to do weekly sessions to try to move Amber out from under her past. They both agreed to it.

"Nicole, what is the biggest change you've seen in Amber?" Dr. Dyer asked.

"Physically or mentally?" Nicole asked.

"Both."

"Physically, I would have to say her being a blonde. She's always been the most beautiful woman I've ever seen or known. Mentally, I'm still learning the truth about her and what she kept hidden from us for all those years."

"I really can't picture you as a brunette."

"I have pictures. I can bring them next time," Nicole offered.

"No, you can't." Amber smiled.

"Maybe," Nicole said.

"Well, let's call it a night and I'll see you back here Monday night."

"Sure," both women said.

Nicole and Amber left the office, ignoring the receptionist as she tried to talk to Amber. Dr. Dyer witnessed the events and advised the receptionist that she was fired for being unprofessional after receiving numerous warnings for making clients feel uncomfortable.

Nicole and Amber were exhausted by the time they made it back to Amber's apartment. They made something to eat and crawled into bed together. Amber held Nicole, and they drifted off to sleep.

Amber was wandering through the woods. The moonless and starless night coupled with the tree cover made it so that she could barely see what was in front of her. She couldn't tell if she was headed to safety or back into harm.

"Bitch, get back here" came a booming voice out of the darkness.

"We're coming for you," another voice boomed.

Amber looked around. She hoped to see some sign of life, something to help her escape. She ran forward, stumbling over tree roots and the uneven ground.

"Amber? Baby?" Nicole's voice rang in the night.

"Nicole?" Amber whispered.

A flash of lightning lit up the sky; Amber saw her father and brother behind her and Nicole on the horizon. Amber raced forward, and as she did, the figure in front of her changed from Nicole, the love of her life, to her father and brother, two people who wanted to take away her life.

"Keep running toward us, bitch." Jeffrey growled.

Amber turned and ran in another direction. Looking up, she saw Nicole standing in front of her brother and father.

"No, you leave her alone," Amber called, racing toward them. She stumbled over some roots and fell to the ground.

The next thing Amber saw was Nicole at her side,

reaching down and helping her up.
"*Nicole, go. It isn't safe for you here.*"
"*I'm not leaving you,*" Nicole said.

Amber had been holding Nicole while they slept. As she started thrashing around, Nicole's head slid off her shoulder, and she was now lying facing away from Amber.

"Nicole...run..." Amber said in her sleep. "RUN!"

Nicole woke to hear her name.

"Amber?" Nicole said as she sat up.

Amber was running again. Running from the two men who had tormented her for her entire life. As she ran, she saw another flash of lightning followed by a loud crack. Amber felt something rip through her body.

Amber bolted upright and screamed out, "NO!"

Nicole was startled by the sound of Amber's voice. The fear and panting sent shivers down her spine.

Amber sat there shaking in fear and trying to catch her breath from her dream.

"Amber? Baby?" Nicole slowly reached toward Amber. The moment her hands touched Amber, she collapsed into Nicole's lap crying. Nicole held Amber close and comforted her.

Amber cried herself to sleep, and Nicole held her until the alarm went off.

"Are you okay?" Nicole asked, breaking the silence.

"Yeah, I'm sorry about last night and a little embarrassed."

"You have nothing to be sorry or embarrassed about. Do you want to talk about it?"

"Yeah, but I need to call and tell them I'm not going to be in today, and then tell Zach not to pick me up."

"Okay." Nicole got up to give Amber some privacy to make her calls. While Amber was on the phone, Nicole went to make coffee.

After calling work, Amber went into the kitchen and grabbed a cup of coffee. She led Nicole to the sofa, and they sat and cuddled together. After several minutes of silence, Amber told Nicole about the dream and how realistic it felt. Nicole held her and listened.

"Do you often get nightmares after going to therapy?" Nicole asked.

"I haven't in years. I did when I first started, though."

"Well, after seeing Jeffrey and being back there, I would think that would be enough to cause them."

"I hadn't thought about that. I think that could be a reason for it. Wow, brains and looks. I'm going to have to keep an eye on you."

"Promises, promises." Nicole laughed as she pulled Amber close and kissed her. "Do you want to go back to bed?"

"Actually, I have something I'd like to show you." Amber stood and extended her hand to help Nicole up.

The two women went back to a closed door at the end of the hallway. Amber opened the door and led Nicole inside. Nicole looked around and saw the paint tarp on the floor and several paintings around the room. There were paintings on the wall, some leaning against the wall, and four on easels.

"Wow," Nicole said as she looked around the

room.

"When I used to have nightmares, I would come in here and paint until the fear went away or until I was too exhausted to think."

"These are amazing." Nicole moved to look at the paintings leaning against the wall.

"Thanks." Amber blushed. "I know it isn't the most comfortable place, but will you sit in here while I paint?"

"Of course. Let me grab my laptop and I can do some programming while you paint."

Nicole pulled Amber into a probing kiss before exiting the room to get her laptop. Amber stood there trying to regain her breath and clear her mind. She was still standing there when Nicole came back in.

"You okay, baby?"

"You know what kissing me like that does, right?"

"Yup," Nicole said, smiling proudly. "But if it's an issue, I can stop kissing you like that."

"No, I didn't say that. I was just verifying that you knew what it did to me."

After Amber regained control over her hormones, she got her paints ready and started working on one of the canvases. Nicole made herself comfortable in a bean bag chair. She positioned herself so that she could still watch Amber, but it wouldn't appear as if she were staring at her.

Chapter Twenty-four

Night at the Club

The next couple of weeks passed without any trouble. Nicole and Amber fell into a comfortable routine. They got up and ate breakfast together. Amber got ready and went to work while Nicole sat at Amber's desk and worked on her programming. Once Amber got home, they made dinner together, and then went for a walk or cuddled on the couch. Amber sometimes laughed at how domesticated they were. They had planned to go out so Amber could share with Nicole some of the things she enjoyed, but life crept into those plans. There were a couple of nights that Nicole was exhausted, some that Amber was exhausted, and then there were a few nights for both that nightmares had plagued them. Both were reluctantly pleased that they were nightmares and not the night terrors that had traumatized them for years.

❧ ❧ ❧ ❧

"Hey, Nic," Jill said.

"Hey, what's up?" Nicole leaned back in the desk chair.

"Are you ever coming home?"

"Eventually, I'll have to…but for now, I'm enjoying my time here with Amber."

"But I miss you…" Jill whined.

"I get that. I miss you guys, too, but Amber's show is in a few weeks. You and the gang are still planning on coming to it, right?"

"Yeah, we are. Zach wants us to tell Amber that we aren't coming so we can surprise her. I'm not sure if she'll see that as rejection or not. What do you think?"

"I think surprising her will be fun. I'll make sure she doesn't get too down."

"Ew, don't need to know about your sex life." Jill scoffed playfully.

"Whatever. You're just jealous that I'm actually getting some from a smoking hot blonde," Nicole teased.

"She looks good as a blonde, doesn't she?"

"She looks gorgeous no matter what."

"You're biased, Brooks."

"Completely! And hopelessly and helplessly in love."

"I'm happy for you two. Are things better for her in New York?" Jill asked.

"Mostly. We've been going to see her therapist together. Sometimes, I go in, and other times, I sit in the waiting room. We've each had some nightmares, but not the night terrors that we were having."

"That sounds like an improvement."

"It is. Mrs. Phelps and her husband are awesome, too."

"Who are they?"

"They're the little old couple that owns the brownstone that Amber lives in."

"Oh, yeah. Do you see a lot of them?"

"I do because I work from home. They truly care about Amber. They call her their daughter even. I think it helps her feel like she has a family that cares about her. They were all she had for years."

"They didn't have to be," Jill mumbled.

"No, they didn't, but they were, and that helped her survive."

"I'm happy about that, but come on. Aren't you a bit hurt that she didn't have the faith in us that we would be there for her? We were a family."

"Yeah, it hurts," Nicole started. "I've also learned a lot about Amber and how she learned to cope with what happened to her growing up, and I understand her reasoning. Just know it wasn't personal that she closed us out. She honestly did it to protect us. The mental torture they did on her was more extensive than the physical shit."

"That's a scary thought. Oh, Jeffrey's trial was this week. Bastard will not be seeing the light of day until he dies."

"That's good. Did they put him in the same prison as his dad?"

"He's headed there next week. Not soon enough if you ask me!"

"How are things going there?"

"Pretty much the same. Heather found a new girl she's wooing. Erik and Lori are on speaking terms again. After she heard about what went on with Jeffrey at the hotel, she decided Erik was worth another try."

"What about you?"

"Nothing other than work going on with me. I'm content with that right now. How's work going?"

Nicole explained about the setup she had at the apartment and the schedule she had worked out. She had all but one client transitioned so she could connect to them from New York. She had even picked up a couple of new clients courtesy of connections from Lucinda. They agreed to talk in a few days to plan out getting together after Amber's show.

After hanging up, Nicole looked at the clock and saw she had five minutes before her tea time with Mrs. Phelps. It had become a daily event for them, something they both looked forward to and time they cherished together.

❧❧❧❧

Amber had finally been cleared by her doctor to return to normal work provided she took a five-to-ten-minute break every two hours and she kept up with the physical therapy exercises.

"Stupid arm," Amber mumbled as she worked with the exercise band the physical therapist had given her.

"How's it going?" Lucinda asked as she approached Amber in the breakroom doing her exercises.

"Painfully good?"

"Do those words really go together?" Lucinda laughed.

"No, they truly don't. I know it's just going to take time for my arm to get back in shape, but these exercises hurt." Amber laughed as she wrapped the exercise band up. "How are you today?"

"I'm doing well. I was hoping that after lunch you and I could sit down and discuss your show, how we're going to set up the display, and what information you would like us to include in the bio for the program."

"Bio?"

"Yes, we put that in for all the new artists. It

gives the attendees the illusion that they know the artist better. Don't worry, though, it isn't going to be anything extremely in-depth. And I promise that we won't put *anything* in there that you don't approve of."

"Thank you. I really appreciate everything you have and are doing for me, Lucinda."

"It's my pleasure. You've always shown such potential. The work I've seen from you in the past year and especially the past two weeks has been incredible."

Amber blushed at the compliment. Her confidence had improved over the years, but she was still far from a confident person. She had hopes of achieving it, but she didn't delude herself into believing that it would happen.

The two women talked for a couple of more minutes before Amber had to get back to work. Lucinda told Amber that she would work out with her supervisor when the best time for them to meet was.

Amber arrived home to find Nicole lost in thought at her computer. Amber knew how intense she was when she was working, but this was even more so. Nicole's fingers hadn't even slowed down when Amber called to her when she came in the door or when she walked over and kissed the side of her head. Amber glanced at the screen, and the cryptic code Nicole was typing looked like random words mixed with punctuation and special characters. Amber had no clue if Nicole was really typing something or if her fingers were just pressing buttons.

While Nicole worked, Amber made dinner and took a bowl of chili to the desk for Nicole should she ever come out of her code coma. Amber took her bowl and sat on the pillows she had in the far corner of the room. It was one of her favorite spots to sit and watch out the window. She had slept many nights in this spot listening to the rain and thunder. After she finished her dinner, she set the bowl on a small table nearby, pulled out a sketchpad, and started to draw.

Nicole finally finished her code and saw the bowl of chili sitting on the desk. She looked around the room and saw Amber sketching. She smiled to herself realizing that Amber looked the most at peace she had ever seen when she was sketching or painting. She wondered how long Amber had been home. And if she should disturb her or not.

"You can come sit by me and eat your dinner." Amber smiled, never taking her gaze off the sketchbook.

"Are you sure it wouldn't distract you?"

"I welcome all distractions of the Nicole variety."

"Well, in that case…" Nicole grabbed her bowl and sat next to Amber who had set down the sketchpad. "Why'd you stop?"

"Well, I was hoping for a kiss from a hot redhead—" Amber's words were cut off by Nicole's lips pressed against her own. "How was your day?"

"It was good. I talked to Jill, had tea with Mrs. Phelps, and I even figured out how to fix a program glitch that has driven me nuts for months."

"Sounds like a good day. Do you have more work to do, or are you done for the night?"

"I'm done for tonight, but I'm going to need to work tomorrow night to update the code for a couple of clients. How was your day?" Nicole finished eating and set her bowl next to Amber's.

"Not bad. I had a meeting with Lucinda to discuss

the show. I'm not sure if I'm getting really excited or if I'm scared."

"I say it's excitement. You're so talented, and Lucinda and the rest of us support you and can't wait to see your amazing work on display."

"You're just excited to see your picture at the center of all the other artwork," Amber teased.

"That's just an added perk. Seriously, though, baby, I'm very proud of you."

Amber blushed, and the two shared a comforting kiss. After the kiss, Amber and Nicole decided that tonight was the best night they had to go out dancing. Amber wanted Nicole to get to know Tony and Trevor. They had planned to go several times before but were too tired or too busy. Amber knew she needed to show Nicole one of the few places she felt completely safe.

※※※※

After paying the entrance fee, Amber took Nicole's hand and led her through the crowd to the bar toward the back of the club. Amber talked briefly with the bartender and received two drinks. She handed one to Nicole, and they made their way to an empty table near the bar.

"Do you come here often?" Nicole asked as she felt Amber take her hand as they watched the people dancing.

"Not lately. Zach and I would come here because I never felt comfortable in straight clubs. I didn't like guys always coming up to me and wanting to dance. I barely can dance with Zach. I know he and I know we're just friends dancing, but I'm still uncomfortable at times."

"So, do you just people watch?"

"Not exactly," Amber said with a smile, looking past Nicole.

Nicole turned to see what Amber was looking at, and she saw Tony making his way over toward them. As he reached the table, Amber jumped up and hugged him.

"It's about time I see you here," Tony said. "Hi, Nicole. I'm glad Amber finally brought you out here."

"Hi, Tony. It's mostly my fault that it's taken so long. I've kept some odd hours with work."

"What do you do?" Tony asked, his interest genuine and comforting to Nicole.

"I'm a computer programmer."

"She's being modest. She owns her own programming business," Amber interjected proudly.

"Wow, that's impressive. How long have you and Amber known each other?"

"Since we were five." Amber blushed. She was glad that it was dark in the club so Tony couldn't see how red she was.

"Really?" Tony smiled, raising an eyebrow. "Wait. Nicole…this is…"

"Yes, Tony. This is the love of my life." Amber wrapped her arm around Nicole, pulled her close, and kissed the side of her head.

"Wait until Trevor finds out." He giggled. Nicole smiled at the giggle.

"You're such a schoolgirl," Amber teased.

"Hush you," Tony said as the three of them laughed.

As they talked, Tony and Nicole got to know each other. Amber smiled, pleased at how well Nicole was fitting in with her friend. As they talked, the

DJ started a remix of an eighties medley. Tony and Amber shared a look, and they each grabbed one of Nicole's hands and pulled her onto the dance floor. They danced throughout the full remix, and when a slow song started, Amber pulled Nicole into her arms. Their bodies melded together as they danced. Tony went to find Trevor to bring him to meet this woman who Amber had told them about for years.

"Are you having fun?" Amber asked as she held Nicole close and leaned their foreheads together.

"I'm with you. Of course I am."

As they danced, they shared a couple of chaste kisses. After the dance, they returned to their table and slid their seats closer together. Nicole and Amber were talking softly when Amber felt a large hand on her shoulder. She knew instantly who it was and smiled.

"Hi, Trevor." Amber smiled, looking up at the man towering over them.

"Hey, sexy," Trevor said. "I've missed you."

"I'm sorry it's been so long. I had to go back to Eagle Peak for a bit."

"Is that where this happened?" Trevor pointed to Amber's shoulder.

"Yes." Amber looked down as she felt Trevor gently squeeze her shoulder and Nicole squeeze her hand.

"Do I need to make someone pay?"

"No, it's been taken care of."

"All right, but if you need me to at any point, you know I have connections. Now who is the beautiful woman sitting here?" Trevor motioned toward Nicole.

"Trevor, this is Nicole. Nicole, this is Trevor. He owns the club and is Tony's partner."

"Hi, it's very nice to meet you." Nicole offered

her hand but was engulfed in a warm hug instead.

"I'm so happy to see you here and to finally get to meet you. Tony was right, you make her glow," Trevor said.

"Paws off my girlfriend." Amber playfully pulled Nicole from Trevor's embrace. Nicole looked at her with shock and gratitude.

"Thanks," Nicole said softly.

"Nicole, should you need anything ever, call me and I'll do whatever is in my power to assist. No matter what it is." Trevor handed Nicole one of his cards.

"Thank you."

"You make it sound like you're a mobster." Amber laughed.

"You know the mob only wishes they were as stylish and amazing as I am." Trevor kissed Amber on top of her head before sauntering away.

"He's…sweet," Nicole said, trying to choose her words properly.

"He's amazing. He and Tony have been there for me for years."

"Hey, Amber," a female voice said from behind them.

"Crap," Amber mumbled as she quickly moved closer to Nicole and pressed their bodies together.

"What's wrong?" Nicole whispered, feeling Amber tense.

"S-stay close…" Amber stuttered as Nicole wrapped an arm around Amber's waist and held her closer.

"Well, hello there, gorgeous," the brunette said, directing her attention to Nicole. "My, my Amber, who do we have here?"

"This…" Amber started.

"Nobody you need to be concerned with. If you'll excuse us," Nicole said dismissively.

"Now, there's no need to be rude. Amber and I go way back, and I'm just being friendly."

"Back off, Beth," Tony's voice boomed from behind Nicole and Amber.

"Oh, Tony, I'm not hurting anyone. I was just trying to find out who Amber's gorgeous friend here is and see if she wants to hang out with someone who knows how to have fun."

"I think I know Amber well enough to know that isn't what you were trying to do and that you really don't know a damn thing about her," Nicole defended.

"Oh, yeah, redhead and feisty. Come with me, baby, and leave this bore here." Beth reached for Nicole's hand.

"Keep your hands away from my girlfriend, Beth," Amber snapped, stopping her hand.

"Girlfriend? Seriously? Don't lie, Amber, it doesn't become you. Plus, how long could you two possibly have been together?"

"Twelve years," Nicole snapped.

"No, I've known Amber for several years, and she has been single, so, really, babe, don't lie to me."

"Technically, we've been together for twelve years, *babe*." Nicole sneered. "We never broke up. Even if we had, there's no way I would be interested in something like you when I have this sexy woman here."

Amber blushed, and Tony giggled.

"Really, Tony? Man up," Beth snapped.

"Just leave, Beth," Amber said, exasperated.

"I'll leave when, I'm sorry, what's your name, beautiful?"

"Nicole, my name is Nicole."

"Well, Nicole. I would be honored if you would please join me for a dance," Beth said.

"No, thanks." Nicole brushed her fingers along Amber's jawline before leaning in and kissing her soundly. Their bodies melded together as if the rest of the world no longer existed.

"I think we need to go home," Amber said, her eyes a darker shade of blue and her breathing ragged.

"I agree." Nicole gave Amber a chaste kiss.

The two women said goodbye to Tony and ignored the now shocked and aroused Beth.

"Want a threesome?" Beth asked as the two women started to leave.

"You wouldn't have the stamina to keep up," Amber said, causing Trevor and Tony to laugh and Beth to just stand there with her mouth open.

"What the fuck just happened?" Beth said in disbelief as she watched them leave.

Nicole pulled Amber out of the club, and they hailed a cab.

Chapter Twenty-five

Therapy

As the art show got closer, Amber felt her anxiety building and scheduled a couple of appointments with Dr. Dyer when Nicole wasn't with her. It wasn't that she didn't want Nicole there, she was afraid of what she would bring up and what Nicole would think.

"Amber, you know Nicole isn't going to judge you on your past," Dr. Dyer said as she and Amber sat in her office.

"I know. I just don't know if I'm ready for her to hear how bad things really were. I just got her back," Amber said softly.

"I know, but if you want this thing to work between you two, you need to be open with her. There are going to be triggers that she'll need to be aware of so she can help you. I'm sure she has her own triggers. You both have some serious scars from the past that you're going to have to overcome, and to be honest, you're going to have them throughout the remainder of your life. I'm not saying there will be issues, but the past isn't going away."

"So, you're saying that you aren't going to make it all go away?" Amber said, laughing.

"If I could do that, I would either be really busy or really bored. You've come a long way since Nicole came back into your life. You now need to decide if you're going to bring her into the thick of it all or keep her on the outside of the heart of what you're going through."

"That's a lot easier said than done."

"Anything worth having and doing always is. What scares you about bringing Nicole into that inner circle of knowledge?"

"I'm afraid mostly that it's going to change our relationship. That she's going to pity me and either stay out of guilt or leave me because she'll realize how fucked up my family has made me."

"Seriously?"

"What? You don't think her learning the stuff that happened to me will change things between us?"

"No, I don't. There are a lot of relationships that I could say that it would affect them, but what you have with Nicole will only grow stronger. There are people who are destined to be together, that were made for each other. I believe from what I've seen of the two of you together, and what you have told me over the years, that you belong together and nothing in your past or future will keep you apart."

"So, you're saying you think we should skip the rest of this session and I should bring Nicole in with me to let her hear all the crap I had to survive and hide from her over the years."

"I'm saying that I think it would be good for both of you. I can only offer my opinions. You're the one that must live with the fallout, and if you think you and Nicole are going to make a true go at this, maybe we should bring her in. I'm not saying we can't discuss things, I just don't think it's best going forward that you exclude her."

"Okay. Well, since I'm here, why is it that I'm so upset that Jill, Heather, and Erik told us they can't make it to the art show?"

"They can't? Well, that stinks. Did they give you a good reason?"

"Work was the main reason. I know we aren't close friends like we used to be, but I had hoped they would be here. They said when I was getting the releases signed that they would be here. I know Nicole is upset by it, too. She isn't letting on that she is, but I can tell."

"Maybe it is work or maybe it's just that they're still coming to grips and understanding on things. You were gone for a long time. I know there was a good reason and extenuating circumstances, but you were gone, and that may be playing a part in their decision not to come. You and Nicole need to not let it affect you and your relationship. You know that Nicole, Zach, and Jessie will be there."

"I know and I'm grateful that they will be. Mr. and Mrs. Phelps will be there, too."

"From what you have told me, they love you like a daughter. I'm not surprised that they will be there for you." Amber decided to call it a short session and promised to bring Nicole with her the next day. Dr. Dyer was pleased with the session and knew that she wasn't wrong about the relationship between Nicole and Amber. They could make it through these hard parts and still come out as a couple.

※ ※ ※ ※

Amber arrived home to find Nicole on the phone with a client. Amber quietly slipped into the bedroom to change, then went into her art studio to paint.

"Hi, beautiful," Nicole said after she finished her

call.

"Hey, sweetie." Amber smiled up from the canvas. "I hope I didn't interrupt your call."

"Of course not." Nicole made her way over to Amber and placed a soft kiss on her cheek. "How was your day?"

"It was good. How was yours?"

"Eh, it wasn't bad. I got a lot of coding done for my one client. Tomorrow, I have to be on a conference call with one of my larger clients. I did some prep work for that meeting."

"Sounds interesting. Would you be available to see Dr. Dyer with me tomorrow? I stopped in to see her today, and she thought it would be good if you came in for the next session."

"Of course. My meetings tomorrow are all in the morning, so I can be there any time after one o'clock. Why did you see her today? Is everything okay?"

"Great. It would be a four o'clock appointment, so that should work out well. I saw her because I was having a hard time dealing with the fact that the gang said they would be there for the opening and now they aren't coming. I didn't want you to be concerned, so I didn't say anything," Amber said, seeing the concern on Nicole's face. "She thinks that you coming in to discuss my concerns about the gang not coming and then maybe discussing some of the crap I went through and how I hid it might be good."

"Amber, if it's really causing you anxiety that they aren't coming, I can call them and talk with them."

"Nic, I'm more scared that it's just going to be us, Zach, Mr. and Mrs. Phelps, and Jessie that show up."

"Well, now you're just being silly. You're an awesome artist, plus there are others in this show.

You're going to make them feel totally inadequate."

"And you aren't biased at all." Amber smirked as she put her paint palette and brush down and pulled Nicole into her arms.

"Of course not," Nicole said before she brought their lips together in a reassuring kiss.

"What do you say we order a pizza and just cuddle tonight instead of cooking?"

"That sounds like a fantastic idea."

The couple ordered pizza and sat on the floor pillows and listened to the rain. They were each lost in thought and silently enjoying the closeness.

❦ ❦ ❦ ❦

Nicole met Amber outside the gallery so they could go to the appointment with Dr. Dyer together.

"So, how are you two doing today?" Dr. Dyer asked when they arrived.

"Fine," Amber said softly.

"I'm okay," Nicole said.

"Did Amber explain why she invited you here?"

"Um, she said she was having a hard time dealing with the fact that the gang has decided not to come to the showing."

"True, but there's more than that. It stems back to what happened to her as a child and how she had to hide from you and the others in your group."

"What do you mean it has to deal with stuff as a kid?" Nicole turned to Amber. "Baby, I know you hid a lot from us, but nobody blames you."

"It isn't that you blame me. It's more of what I had to do to hide my pain or hide my feelings, and I can't do that now. It's causing me to feel like I'm going to show too much, and you're going to want to leave…

or more importantly, you're going to realize how truly messed up I am."

"Nicole, yesterday, Amber and I talked about triggers and how there are going to be triggers that the two of you have and will have for the remainder of your life. Yes, you will overcome some of them and learn how to deal with them, but it will always be a possibility that they could bring up fears and other issues. I wanted you here so Amber could explain one that she's having right now and so you'll know it in the future and be able to be there for her and to help support her."

"Of course I want to be able to do that for her. Amber, I love you, and I want to do whatever I can to help you."

"I get that, I do." Amber took Nicole's hand in her own. "I just don't want to be a burden or for you to feel like you *have* to be here to take care of me."

"Baby, you are never a burden."

"Okay, I can see this is going to go 'round and 'round. Let me just stop it here," Dr. Dyer interjected. "Amber, why is it that you feel like you would be a burden to Nicole?"

"Because that's what I was told my whole life. My issues and problems were to be solely mine, and I was not to burden others with them because I wasn't worth the attention and care that would result from telling someone what my problems were."

"Amber, that was your stupid dad or brother talking. That wasn't someone who truly cared about you," Nicole said softly.

"But it's all I know, sweetie. When I was growing up, I had to be really creative in hiding the bruises and marks that they left or to hide the fear when I was around you and the others."

"What did you do?"

"There was the obvious wearing long pants or long-sleeved shirts when they were bad. Sometimes covering the bruises with makeup. There were times I would tell you and the others that I was grounded or not feeling well, and I would go and hide out at Old Miller's Pond or the back field of one of the nearby farms. Even the forest of trees at the edge of town became a survival place. When I was really scared, there was an old tree I would hide in. It was mostly hollowed out, so I would sleep in there and then stay up all night standing guard so to speak when I finally returned home to do my chores."

"I wish you would have come to my house. You know my parents were gone a lot of the time, so we could have kept you safe there."

"I know, but then you would have known what was going on, and I was so ashamed of the person they said I was. I spent years wondering what it was that made you guys want to be my friend, let alone why you would love me."

"You have no idea the amazing woman you are, do you?" Nicole asked, receiving a head shake from Amber. "Amber, after everything you went through, you still always had the most incredible heart of any of us. You used to make us all feel so inadequate with the care and compassion you showed people. Like that semester we had to work at the senior living facility. You realize you were the only one who got above a C in the class, right?"

"I was?"

"Yeah. You were the only one that was asked to come back after the semester. It had nothing to do with extra credit or a damn special project. You made those old farts feel loved and special. Then there were the times you stuck up for Heather when her mouth got her in trouble."

"She was just like Jill when it came to that." Amber laughed.

"Now, think about all you lived through, Amber," Dr. Dyer said. "You went through your own personal hell, and you still accomplished this level of care? You're a freaking saint."

"Um, she can't be because I know other stuff she has done." Nicole blushed.

"Oh, really?" Dr. Dyer raised an eyebrow.

"Do you remember the first time we made love when my parents were home?" Nicole asked.

"Oh, god." Amber blushed. "Yes…"

"Nicole, you're cheating," Amber said as Nicole unplugged the controller she was using from the console.

"Nuh-uh. I'm just trying to get a fair advantage here. How are you so good at Tetris anyway?"

"I'm good at looking at shapes," Amber said coyly.

Nicole paused the game and set their controllers down before pushing Amber onto her back on the pile of pillows they were sitting on.

"I'll give you a shape to play with," Nicole said lustfully.

Amber pulled Nicole on top of her and kissed her soundly while her hips ground into Nicole's hips and her hands ran down her backside. They stayed like this for several minutes before Amber started to remove Nicole's clothes.

"Oh, god, Amber. I want you."

"Mmm, I want you, too. We have to be quiet, though. I don't want your parents coming down here,"

Amber said as she removed the last of Nicole's clothing and quickly removed her own.

The two were lying naked on the pillows, their bodies pressed together, moving with need, desire, and raw lust. They hadn't been together many times, but they had learned each other's body in their marathon sessions.

"Nicole?" Sharon Brooks called from the top of the stairs.

"Oh, fuck," Nicole whispered before Amber stilled her hips, allowing Nicole to answer her mother. "Um, yeah, Mom."

"Are you two girls playing nice down there? Do I need to come down and talk to you both about fair play?"

Nicole and Amber's eyes went wide at the idea of Mrs. Brooks coming down at that moment. They were naked, and Nicole wasn't sure how she would explain it to her prude of a mother.

"We were just goofing around. Amber was showing me a couple of new moves, and I decided to try them in the game we're playing."

"Well, keep it down. Your father and I are trying to watch a movie directly above you."

Amber let out a low frustrated groan. Talk about being clit-blocked. Hearing Sharon say they were right above them was both arousing and mood killing.

"We promise," Nicole called back, then they heard the door to the basement close and Sharon's footsteps move from the door to the sofa.

"Oh, Nicole..." Amber moaned as their hips moved together again. Their lips pressed together to swallow the other's cries of need and desire as they came together.

After, they lay there holding each other for several minutes before getting dressed and cuddling on the *pillows again.*

"Your mother almost has Jill timing." Amber giggled. "Another couple of minutes, and I would have had you screaming your responses."

"I know. I can't believe we just made love with my parents directly above us."

"Keep talking like that, and it won't ever happen again," Amber said with an arched eyebrow.

"That looked like a good memory you two just shared. You're both beet red," Dr. Dyer said. "I'm certain it's best that I don't hear about it."

"Yeah, like that's the worst dalliance we ever had and the one that should have you the most shocked," Amber said before she could stop herself.

"Amber," Nicole exclaimed, before covering Amber's mouth with her hand. "Shush you."

"Oh, look at the time, I believe our session is over," Amber said sheepishly.

"Yeah, that's my line, horndog," Dr. Dyer teased.

"Oh, you have no clue, but Nicole is the horndog, I'm the prude," Amber laughed as Nicole just opened and closed her mouth several times, unable to respond.

"And…that crushed a lot of images I have of you."

"She's not nearly as innocent as she comes across. Trust me, Doc," Nicole said jokingly.

Nicole and Amber made another appointment for the next week before the art show and then headed home. Dr. Dyer sat there going over the revelations that had come out that night and shook her head. The more she learned about Nicole and Amber, the more complex she realized they both were.

Chapter Twenty-six

Learning New Things

"Amber?"

"Yeah?" Amber smiled at Nicole, who was working at her desk as Amber was making dinner.

"Why didn't you ever come over to my house when you were scared?"

"I wondered if you were going to bring that up."

"I just…you knew my parents were rarely around. I'd have given you your space," Nicole said, leaning back in her chair as Amber came over and sat on her lap.

"I've already explained that my father and brother threatened you guys. If I would have come over, you would have known. I had a hard time going through that stuff with Dr. Dyer when I first started seeing her. I used to get great nightmares on what would have happened. Then she started to help me get past them. I actually even stopped seeing her for a while, but when I started having nightmares and dreams more frequently again, I went back to see her, and I've continued to see her professionally ever since."

"How long did you go between professionally seeing her?" Nicole asked, concerned to learn that Amber had stopped seeing Dr. Dyer at one point but had to go back.

"There were only like three months between the

professional sessions."

"Do you know what brought on the need to go back?"

"I was almost mugged," Amber said so softly that she could barely be heard.

"I'm sorry? Can you repeat that?" Nicole lifted Amber's head so they were staring into each other's eyes.

"I was almost mugged one day leaving work. It scared me enough to bring the horrors of my past back. I know what you're thinking. New York City is no more dangerous than being back in Eagle Peak or any other town in the U.S. People get mugged and robbed everywhere. I wasn't going to let it scare me out of here. I really love it here."

"That wasn't what I was thinking at all. I was thinking, 'what the hell did you do?'"

"Oh."

"My second thought was the danger one." Nicole smiled at Amber, easing her fears.

"What did I do? Well, I may have taken a few self-defense classes at Dr. Dyer's urging to help with my self-confidence, and it helped me protect myself."

"What type of self-defense classes?"

"Krav Maga and kickboxing," Amber said sheepishly.

"Amber! You're telling me that you're this badass self-defense person now?"

"No, but it really helped with my confidence. Or I thought it had until the whole Jeffrey thing happened. I was so scared that I couldn't remember any of my training."

"It's okay, he traumatized you as a kid. I bet that would cause anyone's fight or flight response to be skewed. Enough about him, back to you being all badass and stuff."

"I loved the kickboxing. Zach thought I had a little too much fun with it."

"Do you still do it? Kickboxing, that is?"

"I haven't since I got back from Eagle Peak, but before then, I did it almost daily."

"Did you stop because of me? I don't want to be the reason you stop something you enjoy. Baby, please don't let me be the reason. You need to do things that make you happy. If it's because I'm here, I'll leave or whatever you need. I would—" Nicole babbled before Amber pressed their lips together to stop it.

"You are, but you aren't," Amber said as Nicole's face fell. "Nic, I did it to stay in shape. Since you've been here…I've had other ways to get my blood pumping and to work up a sweat."

"You have? What do you…oh." Nicole blushed, realizing what Amber meant.

"Yeah. See, prior to you coming here, I didn't have a sex life, so I needed to find a way to release some pent-up energy. I, however, prefer *our* way." Amber kissed Nicole. "I would like to take you to the gym with me some time. That is, if you're willing to go with me."

"Baby, I'd love to. I think I'll probably watch you, though. You know me and coordination, not so good friends and all."

"Kickboxing could help with that. What do you say tomorrow night after work we go to the gym and I show you some of what I've learned? I also think it may help with the nervous energy I have for the art show."

"You're getting nervous? Why?"

"What if people don't like my work? What if I let you, Zach, and Lucinda down? Plus, I'm rather let down that Heather, Jill, and Erik won't be here. I guess I wanted to show them what my life is like here…that I'm not the same person I was when we were kids."

"Amber, first of all, your work is amazing. I can only speak for myself, but I'm certain Lucinda and Zach would agree with me that you could never let us down. You doing this show is incredible. And as far as the gang goes…fuck 'em. I love them all dearly, but if they aren't willing to come here, then fuck 'em. We could all tell you weren't the same person when you came to town. Being here the past five weeks, I've seen the amazing person you've become and the life you've built for yourself. I'm honored that you've let me be a part of it. For the first couple of weeks, I'll admit that I thought you were going to get sick of me and send me home."

"Nic, I never want you to leave. I want you to move in here with me. I know that's basically what you've done, but I've tried to think of a way to tell you that I don't want you to go back. I want you to stay here with me. I just don't know the words or when to tell you or even if you'd want to…"

"You goof." Nicole laughed. "You just told me, and I'd love to live here with you. I have stuff I need to take care of with my house and work back home, but yeah, I could see staying here with you."

Amber ran a finger along Nicole's jawline and then leaned forward and kissed her.

"I love you," Amber said into Nicole's lips.

"I love you, too." Nicole smiled into the kisses she was receiving.

The next night, Nicole and Amber headed to the gym near Amber's place. They chose to walk the two blocks since it was a nice night. Amber signed them in, and they made their way into the locker room and changed.

"Ready?" Amber asked as she and Nicole headed toward the gym doors.

"If I said no, could I stay in here and hide?" Nicole laughed nervously.

"No." Amber laughed along, taking Nicole's hand in her own, bringing it up to her lips and kissing her knuckles.

The two women exited the locker room, and Amber still held Nicole's hand as she led her to a set of punching bags. There were a few women working out. One muscular woman with sandy-blond hair appeared to be instructing the other women.

"Hey, Amber," one of the women said. Nicole didn't see who spoke.

"Hey, Trina!"

"It's been a while. How are you doing?"

"I'm great, fantastic, and awesome all rolled into one."

"Uh-huh. I'm going to guess that your great, fantastic, awesome state has something to do with the attractive woman whose hand you're holding," Trina said with a smile as she walked over to stand near the two women.

"Yes, smartass. Trina, this is my girlfriend, Nicole. Nic, this is Trina. She's the one that taught me kickboxing and Krav Maga."

"It's nice to meet you." Nicole shook her hand.

"It's nice to meet you, too. So, I have to pry. How long have you been together? I've never seen you smile so serenely before," Trina said, looking at Amber.

"Well, we've been back together about six or seven weeks," Amber said proudly.

"Be honest. Technically, we've been together for twelve years." Nicole smirked. She knew it was quirky, but she loved the idea that she and Amber had only dated each other. It allowed her in her own mind to say they had still been together, even though Amber was in New York. It also meant she had never lost the love of her life for all those years.

"Six or seven weeks compared to twelve years?" Trina said. "I'm lost."

"Nicole was my girlfriend before I moved here. We never officially broke up because I left in the middle of the night. And neither of us dated anyone else in the ten years we were apart," Amber explained. "So, technically, we've been faithfully together for twelve years…but reacquainted with each other for about six or seven weeks."

"Okay, that is just too damn sweet. That also explains why I haven't seen you in several weeks." Trina smirked, raising a knowing eyebrow. Trina had noticed while they were talking that Amber was favoring one arm. "What'd you do to your left arm?"

Amber had gotten the all-clear from the doctor earlier that day to stop wearing the sling and to gradually start working her way up to doing fine art and full-time painting at work. She had also been told to take it easy with regards to working out but to make sure she did the exercises she was given by the physical therapist.

"I…um…injured my shoulder," Amber said hesitantly, sensing Nicole's disapproval in her explanation.

"Try again." Trina looked sternly. "Either that or I'll ask Nicole, and from the look she's giving you, I'll get the real answer. You suck at lying."

"Fine, I broke my collarbone and fractured my shoulder," Amber admitted.

"*And*," Nicole added.

"And I had surgery on my left side to remove a bullet and therefore cannot work out much. I just received the all-clear today to start doing more exercises, though," Amber finished.

"Wow, now there's a story that you're going to tell me," Trina said as she led Nicole and Amber away from the punching bags and to a small office.

Amber told Trina about what had happened with Jeffrey and her rehabilitation. Trina grabbed two books off a shelf behind the desk. After paging through and reading a couple of sections, she looked up and said she had just the exercises in mind that would help Amber regain her full range of motion and strength without the risk of injuring herself again.

"I'm a physical therapist, too," Trina told Nicole as she looked unsure about why Trina had medical-grade books.

"More accurately, she's a licensed and registered pain and torture therapist. I tweaked my knee when I started kickboxing, and she helped me with the rehab."

"Have you had issues with that knee since?" Trina received a laugh and shake of the head from Amber.

"Will you help me, oh, great one?" Amber teased.

"You know I will. And I still owe you. Amber helped me deal with things when my parents and brother were injured in a boating accident," Trina explained to Nicole. "Are you interested in learning to kickbox?"

"Me? Well, me and coordination aren't on speaking terms. I don't think I would be very good at it," Nicole said.

"Amber had the same issue. She turned out to be one of my best students. Please, let me work with you both. I owe her so much."

"We'd love it, Trina," Amber said before hugging her.

"Great! I look forward to working with you two. Nicole, we'll start easy, I promise. Amber will also be able to do a lot of what we're going to be starting with, so you should hopefully feel less overwhelmed."

"Thank you," Nicole said.

The three exited the office, and Amber showed Nicole around the gym and let her try a few pieces of equipment Amber preferred for her workouts. Trina went back to training the women she had been working with when they arrived.

After doing their rounds in the gym, Nicole and Amber changed out of their workout attire and walked home.

"That place is really nice," Nicole said as they walked up the stairs to the flat.

"Yeah, I really enjoy it. Trina is a great trainer."

"Does she own the gym?"

"No, she just works there. I know she'd love to have her own gym someday, but until then, she'll work there. The owners pretty much let her run it as her own anyway."

"That sounds like a great deal. Care to shower with me?" Nicole asked seductively.

"Mmm, that sounds like an offer I can't refuse." Amber started to remove her clothes and head into the bathroom. Nicole followed closely behind, removing her clothing, as well.

※ ※ ※ ※

Amber and Nicole met with Lucinda regarding the artist dinner. Lucinda helped them with what to wear both nights and what to expect. Amber was more than grateful for Lucinda taking the time to go over everything with them. Nicole had confided in Lucinda that she and Zach were going to surprise Amber with their friends from back home. Lucinda was glad Nicole had told her what they had planned. She had seen that Amber was really upset about being told that her friends couldn't make it.

"So, tomorrow night, I'll have a car pick you two up and take you to the restaurant," Lucinda started.

"That's too much," Amber interrupted. "You really don't have to do that."

"It's standard for all the artists we put into the shows. Now the car will pick you up and take you to the restaurant and then take you home. I'll have the same driver pick you up the following night and take you to and from the gallery. You'll have to be here about two hours early. I'm sorry, Nicole, that may be a very boring time for you. In the past, the dates of the artists have brought books to read or even handheld video games. I recommend bringing something to keep yourself entertained," Lucinda said.

"Thank you for the heads-up. I have a book on my phone I've wanted to read, so I'll be sure to have my phone charged and everything ready to entertain myself."

"What will I be doing?" Amber asked.

"Well, for the first hour, you and I will be going

over the art you have in the show and what you're planning to or should say about each piece. Then you and I will go over what you want the art priced at."

"Priced?"

"Yes, the art will be for sale," Lucinda said.

"I forgot that part," Amber said sheepishly.

"Amber, I've been a curator for a long time, and you need to trust and believe me when I tell you that you're an amazing artist, and you're going to sell several pieces. I've seen the other art that will be in the show, and you are one of the most talented."

"Shouldn't you have already gone over the prices and what Amber is going to say? How did you see the other art?" Nicole asked.

"Amber and I have gone over it, but I want to make sure we're all set on what she's going to say. As for the prices, I have my ideas, and I've found the artists are too nervous about the show to argue with the pricing structure if we go over it just before. And one of the perks to being the hosting gallery is I get to see the art so we can put the pieces up in a cohesive order. We don't want to set someone with an abstract art exhibit next to someone with early Renaissance-era art. It wouldn't flow properly and would be a disservice to both artists. That's also the reason I love hosting these things."

"Sneaky, Ms. Baer, very sneaky." Amber laughed.

They continued to go over what to expect. Lucinda had given Amber the day before, the day of, and the two days after the show off with pay. She knew the physical and emotional toll the show took on an artist, not to mention the added circumstances that played into Amber's anxiety and stress. Lucinda had gotten to know Nicole since she had arrived, and she was pleased with the happiness she brought Amber and the calming way she had with her.

After meeting with Lucinda, Nicole and Amber found dresses, shoes, and jewelry to wear both nights. Amber and Nicole each bought the other a necklace to go with their dresses. They laughed when they got home and opened the other's gift. They had chosen the same necklace.

"Well, we know we both have good taste." Amber laughed.

"That we do. I have one other thing for you, baby." Nicole pulled an item out of the nightstand.

"Nicole, the necklace was enough," Amber started before Nicole put a single finger over her mouth.

"This isn't from me, per se. Your mom wanted me to give this to you when we were together again. I was trying to come up with an appropriate time to give it to you, but, well, she wanted you to have this."

Nicole opened the box to reveal a Claddagh ring. Amber recognized the ring instantly.

"Nic?"

"Your Mom said this has been in your family since the mid-eighteen hundreds. It's something passed down from mother to daughter, she said. I can't wait to see how well it will look on you and with the dresses you're wearing."

"Is this why you insisted on that one dress for tomorrow night?" Amber asked.

"No, it isn't. I suggested the dress because it hugs in the right spots, and you look absolutely amazing in it. The ring is going to highlight your eyes. Did you notice how the blue of the stone matches the blue of your eyes? I told your mom that when she first showed me the ring. She said blue eyes were a trait of the women of your family. Well, the women on her side, that is. It wasn't until then that I noticed that you and your mom have the same color eyes. She said all the women of your family have that shade of eye color."

"I never thought about the fact that Mom and Grandma had the same color eyes." Amber got up and grabbed a picture of them. She noticed then that they did indeed have the same shade of blue eyes as she had. She felt a sense of pride in it. She had something to hold on to with her family heritage.

The two women made dinner together and decided to turn in early. Once they were in bed, Amber had some extra nervous energy, and Nicole offered to help her burn some of that energy off.

❧ ❧ ☙ ☙

With two hours before the car was supposed to arrive to take them to dinner, Nicole and Amber started to get ready. They had spent the day pampering themselves. They started with sleeping in, then they bathed in calming lavender bath salts, then washed each other's hair. Amber decided that they needed to have mani-pedis, so she asked Zach to go out on his lunch break to get the supplies they needed. Amber had the hardest time giving Nicole her pedicure since her feet were exceptionally ticklish. Once they finished, Mrs. Phelps came up and did their hair. She had insisted as she had been a hairstylist for many years, and she loved Amber as a daughter. Once they finished their hair, they had just enough time to get dressed without feeling rushed. Nicole was in the living room waiting for Amber when she heard a knock at the door.

"Mr. and Mrs. Phelps?" Nicole said as she opened

the door.

"Nicole, dear, you look incredible. We know you're leaving soon, but we wanted to get pictures of you two before you leave," Mrs. Phelps said. "Is Amber ready?"

"Not yet," Nicole said. "She should be out soon, though."

"Let me help you with that." Mr. Phelps took the necklace from her and helped her put it on. "You are stunning. You and Amber are so special to us. Thank you for making her so happy."

"She's my life," Nicole said, hugging him before they turned to see Mrs. Phelps coming out with Amber following.

❧❧❧❧

"Amber, I'm coming in," Mrs. Phelps said as she knocked on the door.

Mrs. Phelps entered to see Amber standing there in a blue knee-length dress that matched her eyes. The dress fit as Nicole had said. It hugged her in all the right spots, accentuating her curves. She could see that in the mirror, but she was unsure if it was the right thing to wear.

"Do I look okay?"

"You are stunning, my dear." Mrs. Phelps made her way over to Amber and zipped the dress the last inch. "This dress matches your eyes. I thought Nicole said earlier that you were wearing a black dress tonight."

"That's what I led her to believe. I had the store swap the black dress out for this one to surprise her," Amber said, smiling into the mirror.

"You're going to take her breath away."

"That's the plan." Amber handed her necklace to Mrs. Phelps, who helped her put it on. Amber then grabbed the ring her mother had given her and slipped it on her right hand. She looked at herself in the mirror one last time before turning to face Mrs. Phelps.

"I'm so proud of you. Let's go show you off."

The two women exited the bedroom. Mrs. Phelps led them into the living room where she saw her husband and Nicole turning to face them. She heard the two gasp when Amber came around the corner. It was the reaction she had expected. She knew Amber was a beautiful woman, but the outfit she was wearing showed off her true beauty.

"Amber," Nicole said breathlessly as her gaze roamed the gorgeous woman standing before her from head to toe.

"You are ravishing," Mr. Phelps said as he wrapped an arm around his wife.

Amber felt very much on display and started to blush and move uncomfortably. Nicole quickly closed the distance between them and cupped Amber's face in her hands.

"You are beyond beautiful. Where did this dress come from?" Nicole said.

"I had the store swap it out when I saw how much you liked the color. Are you sure it looks okay?"

"It's perfect." Nicole kissed Amber's lips. "You're going to make a lot of people stare and jealous tonight. I'm the luckiest woman in the world having you as my arm candy."

"Picture time," Mr. Phelps said, sensing that if he didn't change the mood one or all three women in the room were going to cry.

Nicole and Amber held each other as Mr. Phelps took several pictures with his camera, and then he used Nicole's phone to take a few more for the girls. Just as he was handing the phone back to Nicole, they heard the horn from the car that Lucinda had sent for them.

"Sounds like your ride is here," Mrs. Phelps said. "You two have an amazing evening, and we'll see you tomorrow night."

The couple left, and Nicole and Amber gathered their clutches and carefully headed down the stairs to the awaiting car. Once inside, Nicole texted a picture of her and Amber to Zach, Jill, Erik, Heather, and Jessie.

Gorgeous, both of you. I can't wait for tomorrow night, Zach replied.

You two are the most beautiful women on the planet, Erik replied.

Hot, hot, sexy, hot...DAMN... Heather said, causing the two women to laugh.

Stunning, both of you, replied Jessie. *Enjoy the night.*

You both clean up well. Have a fantastic night - we are with you in spirit, Jill said.

The car pulled up outside the five-star restaurant, and the driver opened the door and helped Nicole and Amber out of the car.

"Amber, you look incredible," said Lucinda, who had waited for them to arrive to greet them.

"Thank you," Amber said softly.

"You look beautiful as well, Nicole."

"Thank you, Lucinda. I'm just honored to have such a gorgeous date," Nicole replied, her gaze tracing the chain of the necklace she had given Amber down to just above her exposed cleavage. Nicole had to will herself not to stare or drool.

Lucinda escorted them in, and they greeted the other artists. Amber could feel several eyes on her, and although it made her feel uncomfortable, Nicole explained that they were staring because of how beautiful she was. Amber did her best not to let it bother her.

After dinner, the group had drinks in the restaurant's private lounge. Nicole and Amber ordered coffee while most of the others had mixed drinks or beer. Once the night was over, the car took the couple home, and once inside, they got ready for bed and held each other close.

"One night down, one night to go," Amber said stoically.

"I'm so proud of you. You handled tonight beautifully." Nicole kissed her forehead.

"I wouldn't have been able to handle it at all without you. Thank you for being here and loving me."

"That you never have to thank me for. It's a pleasure and honor to love you and be a part of your life."

They drifted off to sleep both knowing that night was easy compared to what the next night would have in store for them.

Chapter Twenty-seven

Showtime

Morning arrived, and the nerves hit Nicole and Amber. Nicole was nervous for Amber. She knew Amber's work was incredible, she knew the art would stand on its own. But she wondered how Amber would handle the crowds and the compliments. Amber's fear, like Nicole's, had to deal with the crowds, but also with her lack of self-confidence in her work. Part of her still didn't believe she was good enough to be in the show. She wasn't the type of person to enjoy the spotlight.

"Morning," Nicole said after they had lain awake for about an hour thinking and listening to the rain.

"Morning." Amber leaned over and kissed Nicole.

"So, do you have butterflies in your stomach?"

"More like bats." Amber laughed.

"I think you transferred a couple in that kiss. I have bats in my tummy, too," Nicole teased, trying to ease the stress and tension.

"I have a couple more if you would like them."

"No, but I would like another kiss."

Amber leaned in and pressed her lips to Nicole's. The kiss started slow and sensual before passion took over and their kisses became heated and driven by desire. Their hands roamed each other's body. Both women were turned on, but neither wanted to take it further. They were enjoying the feelings of need and desire.

After an hour of making out, Nicole's stomach growled, causing them to part and laugh.

"Breakfast." Amber raised an eyebrow and gave her a lopsided smile.

"I was thinking about having you," Nicole said in a sultry tone just before her stomach growled again.

"Maybe we should get up and have some real breakfast. I believe the bats in your stomach are hungry."

"Fine," Nicole said as they got out of bed. Nicole wrapped her arms around Amber's waist and pulled her close. "I'm so proud of you. I love you, baby."

Amber blushed and then did the only thing she could think of at that moment. She cupped Nicole's face in her hands and slowly brought their lips together. Barely touching but still together, feeling the love surge through their bodies.

"I love you, too," Amber said, pulling back.

The couple went to the kitchen and made breakfast. After they ate, Amber went to her favorite spot in the apartment to gather her thoughts. Amber sat on the pillows by the window. It was her Zen spot. Today, with the rain, Amber hoped it would help to calm her nerves.

Nicole allowed Amber her space and went back to the bedroom.

※※※※

"Hey, Nicole," Jill said, answering the phone.
"Hey, Jill. How are you this morning?"

"I'm good. Anxious to see Amber tonight and to see her show. Does she still believe we aren't going to be there?"

"Yeah, she does. I know it's hard on her, but I think the surprise of seeing you guys will be worth it. How long are you guys staying?"

"Well, we're here for a few days. Erik couldn't get more time off, and Heather doesn't like to be away from the hotel. I haven't decided how long I'll stay yet. I want to see this place that Amber has called home for so long."

"That's great. I know she's going to be so happy that you're all at least staying for a few days."

"I'm going to put you on speaker," Jill said. "Heather and Erik are here now, too."

"Hey," Nicole said.

"Nicster!" Erik said.

"Hey, Nic," Heather said. "How's Amber doing? How was last night?"

"Amber is doing as well as can be expected. She's nervous about tonight. I've seen the show, and Amber is definitely one of the best. And no, I'm not biased."

"Sure, you aren't." Erik laughed.

"Okay, maybe a little bit. Last night was a good night. There were a couple of people who were really nice. There were a couple who were just mean because they were jealous."

"How'd Amber handle them?" Heather asked, concerned for her.

"She did really well. I saw Lucinda, her boss, glare at the ones being mean."

"I like her boss," Erik interjected.

"Me too. She's a really nice woman and very supportive of Amber and her work. I don't think

Amber could have gotten a better boss."

"I'm glad. Amber definitely earned a whole lot of good in her life after what we learned about her past."

"I agree, Heather," Nicole said. "So, are you guys going to be there at the start of the show?"

"Actually, the plan is for us to show up after it starts. We'll be there within the first thirty minutes, though. We intend on supporting Amber throughout as much as possible, but we still want the element of surprise," Jill said.

"You're pretty quiet, Erik. What's up?" Nicole said.

"Are you ever coming home, Nic?" he asked sheepishly.

"I'm not going to get into this discussion today. We'll discuss it tomorrow, okay?"

"Okay."

Nicole could tell that Erik was upset that she had been gone for so long. She also knew he wasn't going to take it well when she told him that Amber had asked her to move in with her and that she had agreed. That wasn't something Nicole was going to dwell on today. Today was Amber's day.

※※※※

Amber cracked the window open about two inches, just enough to get some air flowing in and to be able to hear the rain on the street and trees. She sat on the pillows and stared at the raindrops as they dripped down the window and fell. This was one of the reasons she loved her place so much. She loved sitting here. She could hear the rain hitting the buildings, traffic splashing from a couple of blocks away. She could hear the rain hitting the leaves of the tree-lined street. The sound was relaxing and allowed her to clear her mind. It was shortly after Amber moved into this apartment that she found out how calming this spot was. It was after a particularly frightening nightmare.

"Bitch, you will listen to me and you will do as I say, or I'll tell Dad and you'll regret it," Jeffrey screamed as Amber cowered in the corner of the kitchen. "Do the dishes and do them now before I take what Dad has taught me and punish you myself."

Amber quickly stood and started to wash the dishes. She knew this was Jeffrey's chore for the day because he had gotten in trouble at school, but she knew that taking the punishment from him would result in her having to be more creative in hiding the bruises and pain from Nicole and the others.

"Get moving faster before Dad gets home. I swear if you even give a hint to him that you did my chore for me, I will make you regret it."

"I-I won't tell." Amber flinched away from Jeffrey as he clenched his fist.

Amber finished the dishes and rinsed out the sink. After she was done, she dried and put the dishes away. Jeffrey watched her the whole time, making it worse because she feared at any moment, he would lunge at her.

Jeffrey stood and took the towel from her. He told her to go to her room. As Amber started to walk away, Jeffrey snapped her with the towel on the back of her arm, leaving a giant welt. It was as the pain flashed through her mind that Amber awoke that night. She knew that going back to sleep would send her back into her dream if she couldn't clear her mind and calm her emotions.

She wandered around her new apartment and heard the rain hitting the window. She grabbed a pillow off the couch and sat near the corner window. She opened it wide, so she could feel the rain splashing in and hear it falling outside on the trees and street. Amber sat next to the window and felt the nightmare dissipate. She felt herself calming and enjoying the peace and solitude.

Since that night, Amber would sit here when she needed the peace it brought to her mind. She had bought a sound simulator to create the sounds of rain and several pillows to make the spot more comfortable over the years. She could never imagine giving up this spot. Her spot. She told herself that as long as the Phelpses would allow her to, she would live here. This single spot made her horrors seem like a thing of the past.

Amber had told Dr. Dyer about this spot and how she felt when she was in it. Dr. Dyer told her it was the rearview mirror effect.

"You're just making that up," Amber said.
"Not really. Okay, it's what I personally call it, but it doesn't diminish the meaning."
"So, what is the rearview mirror effect?"
"It's simple. Memories of our past may appear closer and more powerful than they are. You know they're behind you. You know you're the only one who can let them catch you and overtake you. But once you truly put them behind you, they can no longer do that. They're simply memories. I'm not saying they won't hurt like hell or scare the shit out of you, but you can stop the effect they have on you. Amber, that spot you found in your apartment, it's the catalyst that will keep

your memories at bay and allow them to never catch and overtake you."

"Wow, I never thought of things like that," Amber said.

"Well, if you had, then you wouldn't need to see me." Dr. Dyer laughed.

⁂

Now, sitting in this spot listening to the rain, Amber could feel the anxiety of the show drifting away. She was sad that her friends weren't going to be there, but Nicole was. Nicole was her silver lining. Having Nicole back in her life had for the first time ever made Amber truly hopeful for the future and for happiness in life. She almost felt like she was worthy or deserved to have good in her life. She also knew in time that she would get to the spot where she did deserve to have good in her life, it was just going to take some time. Now that Nicole had agreed to move in with her, she knew she had the time.

Tonight, I'm putting myself out there. Tonight, I'm showing off my heart and soul, Amber thought, chuckling to herself. *I'll be showing off Nicole, my heart, my true love, and my soul in my paintings. I suppose I should be more afraid, but Nicole makes it all seem possible.*

Amber sat there for a long time. She saw Nicole come back into the room and stretched her arm out. Nicole accepted the invitation and joined Amber on the pillows cuddling and listening to the rain. As time passed, the two moved closer to each other and desire flared, and they found themselves passionately kissing while hands roamed, causing them to moan.

"Bed?" Amber panted. Nicole could only nod. Amber picked Nicole up and carried her to the bedroom. They undressed each other before spending the rest of the morning and part of the afternoon making love.

≈≈≈≈

Nicole and Amber showered together before getting ready separately. They had agreed that the element of surprise the night before had been so much fun that they would wait to see each other again. Mrs. Phelps did their hair and helped them into their necklaces. Nicole was pacing the living room when Mr. Phelps arrived with his camera.

"Oh, Nicole, you look stunning tonight," Mr. Phelps said. Nicole was wearing a simple emerald green silk dress.

"Thank you." Nicole blushed.

"Have you seen what Amber's wearing?"

"I don't know. After she swapped out the dress yesterday, I'm not sure what she'll be in."

The two were laughing when Mrs. Phelps entered the room.

"What's so funny?" she asked, and Nicole explained. Mrs. Phelps joined in the laughter and said Amber was ready to join them.

Amber made her way down the hall and around the corner. She heard Mr. Phelps and Nicole gasp. She felt self-conscious about the dress, but she refused to let it stop her. Amber stood before them wearing an elegant black knee-length silk dress with three-quarter-length sleeves, a V-neck, and sequins. The light made the sequins shimmer as she walked.

"Wow," Nicole whispered in awe.

"Amber, you look amazing." Mr. Phelps wiped a tear from his eye. "You have always been such a beautiful woman, now the world is going to see it."

"He's right, Amber. You look incredible," Mrs. Phelps said. "I thought you were beautiful last night. Tonight, you are stunning, my dear."

"Nic? Does it look okay? Do you like it?" Amber asked shyly.

Nicole was speechless. Her gaze roamed Amber's body. The dress hugged her curves and showed off her body. Instead of trying to find the words, Nicole took both of Amber's hands in her own and looked deep into her eyes.

"Breathtaking!"

Nicole and Amber entered the gallery and made their way over to Lucinda.

"Amber, you look amazing," Lucinda said. "You too, Nicole."

"Thank you," they said in unison.

After talking with Lucinda for several minutes, they made their way over to the other artists. They joined in the small talk, but everyone was just trying to contain the nervous energy.

"You'll do great, baby," Nicole whispered into Amber's ear as she entwined their fingers together.

"All right, may I have everyone's attention please?" Lucinda said as everyone turned to face her and the conversations died down. "Thank you all for agreeing to show your work and be a part of this showing. I know I speak for all your sponsors when I tell you how incredible your work is and how proud we are to have you here."

With that, the artists made their way to their work, and Lucinda opened the doors. Amber had requested that Lucinda put her at the back of the exhibit, so it was a few minutes before she saw Zach make his way to her and Nicole.

"Wow, Amber, you look amazing." Zach hugged her. "You look pretty good too, Nicole."

"Thank you for coming," Amber said.

"I wouldn't miss this for the world. Your work is incredible. I must say, the picture of you, Nicole, looks pretty damn good blown up like that."

"Yeah, I'm a bit self-conscious standing here with it hovering over me." Nicole laughed.

"Where is Jessie? I thought you two were coming together," Amber said.

"She was so excited she had to pee," Zach blurted out just as Jessie walked up.

"Thank you, Captain Subtle," Jessie said. "Wow, you two look gorgeous. I had no idea you cleaned up that well."

"She does clean up well, doesn't she?" Amber teased before kissing the back of Nicole's hand.

"Aww, that's so sweet," Jessie said.

"Okay, we're going to go check on the other art pieces quickly. I see you have some people coming your way."

Zach and Jessie left as the crowd made their way to Amber's exhibit. Amber spoke with several patrons as Nicole stood back and let her shine. Nicole had never seen Amber glow the way she did when she talked about artwork. Several people asked if Amber was still doing photography and if she would consider doing some pieces on commission. Lucinda overheard this and advised them that if they were truly interested, they could leave their cards with her and Amber would be in contact.

"Thanks," Amber said, relieved that Lucinda had come back to check on her.

"How are you doing?" Lucinda asked.

"I'm not as bad as I thought I would be."

"It's because she's talking with them about stuff she's passionate about." Nicole joined the two women. "She absolutely glows when she's discussing art with the guests."

"That's fantastic to hear. Now I have to tell you that you were the first to sell a piece tonight."

"What?" Amber said, shocked.

"The painting in the lower left, it sold after ten minutes." Lucinda grinned.

"It wasn't to Zach or Jessie, was it? Or you, Nic?" Amber said.

"Nope. It was bought by Mr. Gunderson." Lucinda motioned toward an older man wearing a black tuxedo and carrying a flute of champagne. "He said he wanted to display it in the lobby of his law office."

"Amber, that's fantastic!" Nicole said.

After talking for a few more minutes, Lucinda left to continue her rounds in the gallery. Nicole watched Amber answer questions with the guests but noticed a dark spot in Amber's glow.

"Baby, what's wrong?"

"I just wish the others could have made it. This is me, the person I am now. I was looking forward to showing them and not having them know me by the description I gave them before..."

"I didn't know it was weighing on you so much,"

Nicole said.

"I'm trying not to let it, but it's still there," Amber said.

"Hey, you two," Jessie said. "Look who we found at the entrance."

Amber saw Jill, Heather, and Erik standing before her.

"Wow, Amber, you are smoking hot," Erik said as he hugged her close.

"Amber, you look amazing. The exhibit looks amazing." Jill then hugged her, too.

"And to think I was almost over my lustful crush on you. Wow, you look breathtaking tonight," Heather whispered.

"Don't let Nicole hear you say that," Amber said, pulling back and winking at Heather. "What are you guys doing here? I thought you said you couldn't get away."

"Oh, yeah, about that…" Jill said. "We lied. Nicole and Zach thought it would be fun to surprise you."

Amber turned to see Nicole and Zach blushing and looking sheepishly at her.

"Oh, they did, huh? I'll deal with you two later," Amber said.

The group chatted casually and strolled around checking out the exhibits while Amber entertained the art community and answered their questions about her art. Nicole stayed close to Amber and made sure she always had a glass of water or champagne handy. Amber was grateful, her throat was hurting from talking so much.

As the show came to an end, Lucinda informed Amber that she had sold all her work. Amber was a bit surprised that someone bought the photograph of Nicole. Not because it wasn't good, but because it was of someone. Nicole was the center subject of the piece. Lucinda told Amber that she bought it. She loved the aesthetics and symmetry of the photograph. She also advised Amber that she had received several cards for people wanting to commission her for art or photography projects.

"I would say tonight was a success." Nicole wrapped her arm around Amber's waist.

"Yes, it was." Amber kissed the side of Nicole's head. "Thank you for surprising me with the gang."

"You honestly believed we wouldn't be here for this?" Jill asked.

"I was gone for ten years. You guys only saw me for a little bit when I was back there. I…"

"You didn't think you were deserving or that we loved you as much as we ever did?" Heather asked, receiving a slight nod from Amber. "That's where you're wrong."

"You're family, Amber. We love you, and we'll always be here and support you." Erik kissed her forehead.

"How long are you guys staying in New York?"

"A few days," Heather said, smiling.

"Great, so why don't you come by my apartment tomorrow morning and I'll make breakfast? Wait, where are you staying?"

"With me," Zach piped in. "I'll bring them by in the morning."

"Great, and, Jessie, you and Zach are expected to be at this breakfast," Nicole said, reading Amber's mind.

"Sweet, I love Amber for breakfast! Er, I mean

Amber's breakfasts." The slightly buzzed woman blushed.

"That better be what you mean, or you and I are going to have a little chat," Nicole said, offering Jessie a mock glare.

The night ended as Nicole and Amber made their way back to their apartment. For the first time in a while, Amber felt like she was a part of a family and her life was turning around.

Chapter Twenty-eight

Life in NYC

Amber was in the kitchen getting ready to make breakfast when she heard the knock at her door. Nicole was in the living room and answered the door. She smiled and escorted her friends into the apartment.

"Wow, this place is awesome," Erik said, looking around at the spacious room.

"I thought apartments in New York were small and expensive," Heather said as Amber joined them in the living room.

"They usually are. Mr. and Mrs. Phelps are fantastic landlords, and they aren't in it for the money. This brownstone has been in their family since it was built." Amber hugged her friends and wrapped an arm around Nicole's waist.

"How are you feeling after last night?" Jill asked.

"Good actually. I still can't believe that all my work sold."

"Of course it sold, baby. You're an amazing artist," Nicole said, before kissing Amber on the side of the head.

"You, my love, are biased," Amber said, smiling at her.

"No, you are an amazing artist," Jessie agreed as she let herself into the apartment.

"Nice of you to join us," Nicole said. "You do know that Amber is *making* breakfast and she is *not* breakfast?"

"Ugh." Jessie groaned. "I cannot be held responsible for the things I say when I'm under the influence of alcohol."

"Sweetie, don't tease Jessie, she knows how to hypnotize people."

"She wouldn't…would she?"

"I would. I'm evil that way," Jessie said, giving Nicole an evil grin.

"Jessie, be nice," Amber warned. "Now who wants coffee? Breakfast is cooking and should be ready in about twenty minutes."

"I do," Amber heard in a chorus as everyone made his or her way to the kitchen area.

After everyone had coffee, Amber gave Heather and Jill a tour of the apartment.

༄༅༄༅

"So, Nic, are you ever coming home?" Erik asked after Amber took Jill and Heather to see the rest of the apartment.

"Yes and no. Amber asked me to move in with her, and I told her I would. So, I'll be coming back to get some stuff. We haven't talked about selling the house yet or not."

"Are you serious? You've barely been together for two months."

"Erik, it's Amber. I've never loved anyone else. I've never wanted anyone else in my life."

"So, you'll give up everything to come here? She won't come back home?"

"This is her home. You saw her at the show last night. This is where she belongs. And I belong with her. Plus, I can't ask her to come back to that place. Not with all the memories of her father and brother. That would do more damage than good."

"Wow, I know I should have assumed this was going to happen, but I'm in shock."

❧ ❧ ❧ ❧

"This is my room," Amber said as they entered the master bedroom with the large attached bath.

"Wow, that is a nice tub. I bet you and Nicole could have some fun in there," Heather teased.

"We have," Amber said nonchalantly before turning and heading out the bedroom door as Jill and Heather stood there with their mouths agape.

Amber then showed them her studio.

"Amber, these paintings are amazing." Jill looked at the various canvases in the room.

"Thanks."

"Is this Old Miller's Pond?" Heather held up a painting of a dock with the setting sun reflecting off the water and a tree in the background.

"Yeah. I have a series of paintings from back home."

The group went back into the living room.

"Hey, Nic," Heather said. "Have you seen her paintings of back home?"

"You have paintings of back home?" Nicole asked.

"When I got homesick, I painted the things I remembered...the happy times."

"Why haven't I seen them? I thought you showed

me all your paintings."

"Um, I was scared to show them to you," Amber said. "Most of them are places that made me remember times with you."

"Baby, you never have to be scared to show or tell me anything."

Nicole and Amber stared into each other's eyes for a long minute before they were drawn together. They kissed softly, and the others averted their eyes, allowing them as much privacy as they could get with five other people in the room.

~ ~ ~ ~

After breakfast, Jessie and Zach excused themselves, leaving Amber and Nicole with their other friends.

"So, what do you guys want to do?" Amber said.

"Show us your life. We want to get to know the New York Amber," Jill said.

"Before we go out and do that, guys, I think you should know that Amber asked me to move in with her and I said yes. I'm going to be moving to New York soon," Nicole announced as she cuddled closer to Amber.

"Excuse me?" Jill looked between the two women and then at Erik. She was sure he'd be freaking out at this.

"She told me earlier." Erik shrugged, but his face revealed his true feelings.

"That's so cool. You two seem so happy," Heather said encouragingly.

"We are, Heather," Nicole said before kissing Amber's cheek.

"Why don't we go to the gallery, maybe Central Park, and then get something to eat," Amber suggested, trying to avoid any more of the awkward silence.

"Maybe we can go to the club tonight, too," Nicole added.

"That sounds like fun," Heather said.

"I suppose," Erik said.

"I'm game," Jill said.

"If you have better things to do, Erik, please don't let me keep you from them," Amber said coldly.

"No, going out sounds fine."

"Can you guys excuse us for a minute?" Nicole motioned that she wanted to talk to Erik alone.

"Sure." Heather pulled Jill and Amber toward the door. "We'll meet you both downstairs."

"What the hell is your problem, Erik?" Nicole said in an angry and hurt tone.

"Simple, it's dangerous here. I don't want my best friend moving someplace that she can get hurt and I can't be there to protect her."

"And back home is much better?"

"Yes, it is."

"Think about what Amber went through for years. We weren't able to help her."

"Had she told us, we could have helped her."

"Look at what happened to me at home."

"That was a rarity. That only happened—"

"That only happened because some deranged lunatic came after me," Nicole cut Erik off. "New York is no more dangerous than being home."

"You don't know each other like you did before.

You're different people. Don't throw away all that you've worked so hard to accomplish."

"I'm not throwing it away. I will still have my business, I'll just be based out of New York instead. I'm hoping to still have my friends, but only if they're going to be supportive of Amber and me. If you aren't going to try to get to know who she is now and see what life she has built for herself here, just go home. I don't want you here if you're going to make her feel bad or if you aren't going to realize this is my life to make my way in, and that includes me making my own mistakes."

"So, if I asked you to choose between Amber and me, you're going to choose her?"

"Yes. I love her and want to build a future with her. I've always wanted that. We lost ten years of our lives together, I'm not willing to lose any more time. It's your choice. Either you stay and get to see Amber's life and what my life will contain or you go home. I'm not saying our friendship is over, but if you aren't supportive, I don't want you here."

"I guess I'll see you when you come back home," Erik said, and he turned and walked out, leaving Nicole stunned.

⚜⚜⚜⚜

"I don't want to come between them," Amber said as she sat in front of the brownstone with Heather and Jill.

"You can only come between them if they let it." Heather sat next to her.

"Squirt's right. If Erik chooses to not support Nicole staying here, that's his choice. The last time

Nicole was this happy was before you left ten years ago." Jill put a hand on Amber's shoulder.

"Amber?" came a woman's voice behind her.

"Mrs. Phelps, good morning."

"Is everything okay, dear?"

"Yes, ma'am. I'd like you to meet two of my good friends from back home. This is Heather and Jill Woods. Guys, this is Mrs. Phelps. She and her husband have looked after me for so many years."

"It's so nice to meet you," Jill said, shaking Mrs. Phelps's hand.

"Thank you for taking care of Amber." Heather hugged the older woman.

"It's nice to meet you both. And taking care of Amber is easy. She's such a sweet and amazing woman. Nicole has truly brought her out of her shell and opened her up."

"They've always been like that together," Jill said as Amber blushed.

"Erik?" Amber said as he exited the brownstone and made his way toward a cab that was stopped at the end of the block.

"Well, it was nice to meet you both. Amber, I know something is up, you know where to find me when you're ready to talk."

"Thank you," Amber said, nodding absently.

Mrs. Phelps went inside, and Amber watched as Erik got in a cab and the cab drove away. Nicole came out of the front door and joined the three standing out front.

"What happened?" Jill asked

"I told him if he couldn't be supportive of my choices, I didn't want him here. He chose to leave. I'm not going to let Erik Harrison ruin today. He made his choice, and he can live with it. Now, where are we starting?"

"Sweetie." Amber ran her hand through Nicole's hair. "Are you sure about this?"

"I am. I love you, and I want us to build the life we were meant to have together but were robbed of."

"Okay, then let's get this tour started," Heather said.

Amber hailed a cab, and the four women made their way to the art gallery where she worked. After giving Jill and Heather a tour, the group went out for lunch, then headed to Central Park. Amber showed them the fountains she liked to sit by, the bridges she found especially inspiring, and then they walked through the zoo. Nicole tried to hide how much it bothered her that Erik had left, but everyone knew.

"Sweetie, I think I know what will help you feel better." Amber wrapped her arms around Nicole's waist.

"What's that?" Nicole asked skeptically.

"Let's go show Heather and Jill the gym." Amber smirked.

"Really? You think Trina can help with this?"

"I know she can. She has some very good techniques."

"Plus, you need to check in with her," Nicole said.

"That too."

"So, who is this Trina and what is this gym thing?" Jill asked as the four of them got into a cab and Amber gave the driver the address.

"Trina is my—well, our—personal trainer," Amber said.

"Wait, what does she train you in?" Heather asked as the cab stopped outside the gym.

The women got out and headed inside. They saw Trina standing outside her office.

"Amber, are you here for your session? You missed the last rehab session," Trina said as she made her way to the group.

"I'm not, but Nicole could use some workout time."

"Amber, really?" Nicole said.

"It helps, sweetie."

"Nicole is going to work out? Isn't that dangerous for anyone in the area?" Jill teased, trying to lighten the mood.

"When she first started a couple of weeks ago, I would agree with you, but now, she's pretty good," Trina said.

"Trina, this is Jill and Heather, friends of ours from home. Jill, Heather, this is Trina, our personal trainer."

The three shook hands. Trina turned and Nicole told her she would go get changed. When Nicole returned, she and Trina went to work on some kickboxing as Amber, Heather, and Jill watched. After an hour of working out, Nicole showered and got dressed and joined the others.

"Thank you, Trina," Nicole said.

"You're welcome. Remind your girlfriend that the only way her shoulder is going to get better is if she comes in and works out with me."

"I will," Nicole said. "She is rather stubborn and hard-headed at times."

"Hello, I'm standing right here," Amber said.

"Yes, but you appear to listen to Nicole more than me." Trina stuck her tongue out.

"Fine, I'll be in this week," Amber conceded.

"Happy?"

"Thank you." Trina hugged Nicole and Amber before heading over to a group of women who were preparing for a training session.

"So, you both do kickboxing?" Heather asked.

"Kickboxing and Krav Maga," Nicole said.

"Seriously?" Jill said, surprised. "Wow. Erik better watch what he says around you two."

The group left the gym and went back to Nicole and Amber's.

※※※※

"Hey, Zach, it's Erik," Erik said as he rounded the corner after leaving the brownstone.

"Hey, what's up? I didn't think you'd be calling me so soon."

"Nicole and I sort of had a falling out, and she told me if I couldn't support her, she didn't want me here. So, I need to get my stuff, so I can head home."

"Dude, are you sure you want to do that? I know Nicole means a lot to you."

"She does, but I can't support her being here. New York is too dangerous."

"There's so much that you don't understand about Nicole and Amber's life here. Let's talk before you head home. There are some things you should know before you jump to too many conclusions and ruin your friendship with Nicole and Amber."

"Fine," Erik said.

Zach gave Erik directions on how to get to Central Park and where he was having coffee.

When Erik arrived, Zach explained to him that yes, it seemed as though there was a lot of crime in

New York, but that needed to be taking in perspective; this was a very large city, and if he looked at the full picture, there really was no more crime here than any other city. The two walked around Central Park. As they were walking around, they spotted Nicole, Amber, Heather, and Jill. Zach kept his distance, but he and Erik followed the women. Erik was amazed at how comfortable Amber seemed navigating the park. They followed the women to the gym and while staying out of sight watched as Nicole worked out her frustration kickboxing.

"She could have kicked my ass into next week earlier," Erik said.

"Oh, kickboxing isn't all they do." Zach pointed toward a Krav Maga class that was just starting. He heard Erik audibly gulp when he saw the women attacking the man in the protective suit. "As I said, kickboxing isn't all they do."

"You're trying to show me that they can defend themselves, aren't you?"

"Yep. I'm also going to show you that they aren't alone and that they have people who care a lot about them. They're going to the club soon. We need to go get changed and get there before they do."

They made their way back to Zach's apartment and got changed and headed to the club to wait for the girls.

≈≈≈≈

"Amber, are you sure I look okay?" Heather asked for what felt like the hundredth time.

"You look gorgeous. Stop worrying."

The four women entered the club, and after

getting drinks, they found an out-of-the-way table.

"Wow, this place is awesome. Do you come here often?"

"No, she doesn't, and I'm starting to think she's cheating on me," a male voice said from behind them.

"I would never cheat on you," Amber said as she stood and hugged the man. "Trevor, this is Heather and her sister, Jill. Guys, this is Trevor, he owns the club."

"It's very nice to meet you ladies. Nicole? No hug?"

Nicole jumped up and hugged Trevor tight.

"Girl, you better get off my man," Tony said in his best girly voice as he joined the group.

"Honey, I'm leaving you for the redhead," Trevor teased.

"Then I'm taking the blonde," Tony said, picking Amber up.

"Put me down," Amber said. Once Tony had set her down, she introduced Jill and Heather to him.

"Beware, Beth is roaming around here," Trevor warned.

"Thanks, Trev," Nicole said.

"Who's Beth?" Jill asked.

"Someone who doesn't understand how repulsive she is and who won't leave Amber alone," Nicole answered.

"Well, well, if it isn't Blondie and Red." Beth walked up to the table. "Who are these lovely women you brought with you?"

"Leave, Beth." Amber growled.

"Nope, I don't want to. You see, I'm thinking there are four of you, and even if you say you only want the redhead, that leaves two for me."

"No, they're family and therefore off-limits to you," Nicole snapped.

Beth moved over to stand between Jill and Heather. She asked if either would like to dance. They both declined and asked her to leave. When Beth made no move to leave, Amber motioned for Tony, and he came over and escorted Beth to the door.

"Thanks, Tony," Amber said when he returned.

"My pleasure, love. You enjoy your evening."

"Amber has her own bodyguards, interesting," Jill said.

"Time to dance." Amber grabbed Nicole and Heather's hands.

The four made their way to the dance floor and started to dance, laugh, open up, and shine. They never noticed Zach and Erik sitting off to the side.

"Wow, that isn't the Amber I know." Erik watched the group dance.

"Nope, and you're throwing that friendship away over your own stupid pride. Tony and Trevor adore Nicole and Amber. They keep a close eye on them. There are rumors that Trevor is in the mob, but nothing confirmed, and nobody is going to mess with them."

"Why didn't they ever tell me about the gym and this place?"

"Would you have listened if they had?"

"No, I guess not. I was a jackass earlier. It's what you've been proving to me, correct?"

"Yep! Now do you want to go apologize, or do you still want to go home?"

"I think I should apologize," Erik said, and they made their way toward Nicole and Amber.

"Freeze," the burly man said.

"Hey, Trevor. We're just going to talk to Nicole and Amber," Zach said.

"I see, well, next time say hi when you get here." Trevor shook Zach's hand, and Erik flinched seeing Trevor's one hand engulf Zach's.

"I promise."

Zach and Erik made their way over to the table holding the four women.

"Hi," Erik said sheepishly.

"Erik," Amber said coldly as she saw Nicole lower her head and stare at the table.

"I'm a big old jackass. I'm sorry for earlier, Nic. I was being selfish and childish. I love you, and I love how happy you are with Amber. I just don't want you to move here and forget about me."

"Yeah, like that could happen." Nicole glanced up to see the sincerity in his eyes.

"Will you all forgive me? Zach helped me see the error of my ways."

"I just showed you how to stalk four women, I did nothing more," Zach joked.

Erik bought the next two rounds of drinks before they called it a night. They agreed that Erik, Jill, and Heather would stay with Nicole and Amber. They stopped by Zach's apartment and got their stuff before making themselves comfortable in the brownstone.

Chapter Twenty-nine

Rearview Mirror

Amber spent the next several days showing everyone around New York and her favorite places to visit. Erik and Jill had to admit that Amber had changed and that she was nothing like the girl they knew back in school. Heather enjoyed her time with Amber. She knew she had missed Amber in her life, but this proved it. She knew that no matter what, she was not going to let her out of her life again.

"I wish we didn't have to go back," Jill said on their last night. "I think I'm finally starting to understand the appeal of this place."

"It's a great city to live in," Amber said, cuddling closer to Nicole.

"So, I hate to be a downer, but—" Erik started.

"Then don't be," Heather interrupted, receiving a glare from him.

"Someone has to. So, Nic, what are your plans?"

"I'm staying here with Amber. We've been through that. I'll be coming home at some point, but Amber and I have to talk about what to do with the house and everything."

"Are you sure?" Erik pressed.

"Yes," Nicole said, her tone telling everyone that she was done with this subject.

"We'll be right back," Amber said, standing and

pulling Nicole up and behind her as they made their way to their bedroom.

"Amber?" Nicole asked, confused by Amber's move.

"Don't let him get to you," Amber said once they were in the bedroom, and she had pulled Nicole into her arms.

"I'm tired of him second-guessing everything I say and do," Nicole said through gritted teeth as she held Amber close.

"I know, but this is their last night here. Don't let it bother you. I know you love me and that we're in this forever," Amber said before cupping Nicole's face and kissing her gently.

"How is it, even at my most frustrated point, you can make me relax?"

"My lips cast a spell on you." Amber gave Nicole a sultry smile.

"Mmm, and what kind of spell can they cast on me later?" Nicole pressed her body tightly against Amber's.

"We'll have to see," Amber said before kissing Nicole again. "Now let's go spend some time with our friends."

The two left the bedroom and joined the others. It was obvious from the tension hanging in the room that something had transpired while they were gone.

☙☙☙☙

Jill, Heather, and Erik watched as Nicole and Amber left the living room.

"What the hell is wrong with you?" Heather snapped. "Are you a fucking moron?"

"Hey, I was going to ask that," Jill said.

"I just want to make sure that Nicole is doing this because she wants to, not because she feels obligated or because it's Amber."

"Of course she's doing it because it's Amber. Nicole has been in love with Amber since we were kids," Jill said. "They're both in love and want to be together."

"Why can't Amber come back home?"

"Erik, have you not seen the life she's built here? Were you not at the gallery with us for her art show?" Heather asked. "Amber is strong, confident, self-assured, and most of all, happy."

"She could be happy back home, too."

"No, she couldn't," Jill said. "Amber has become the person she is now *because* she got away. She has more things to haunt her there than she has for reasons to be there."

"She has us."

"Yeah, and she also has the memories of the mental and physical abuse she suffered for all those years. She doesn't need to be reminded daily about what she went through."

"You and Heather don't get it. We could make it better for her. Make new memories for her. We'd have her and Nicole."

"It's her choice. I think it'll be good for Nicole to get away and heal, as well," Jill said, looking down the hall to where Nicole and Amber had disappeared. "Plus, look at this place."

"Yeah, and did you hear the rain last night?" Heather asked. "I sat by the window like Amber says she does and listened. It was amazing."

"I'm glad you like the rain," Erik said sarcastically.

"I'm worried about Nicole. I don't think it's fair that she gives up her life because of Amber."

"I guess that's good you don't make her decisions for her," Jill said angrily. "Nicole is an adult and can make her own decisions."

"I know that," Erik said. "I just don't know that she's making them for the right reasons."

"Again, not your decision," Jill said.

"I thought you learned your lesson on doubting them when you were out with Zach. What changed?" Heather asked.

"We're leaving, and Nicole isn't coming with us. I'm worried about her and will always worry about her. I'm supposed to protect her. I failed once, now how am I supposed to do it when she's here?" Erik said.

"You do it by being a friend and not an asshole. That would be a good start," Jill said as they heard the door down the hall open.

※※※※※

Nicole and Amber rejoined the group. The tension was intense, but nobody was sure where to start.

"Erik, I know you don't want me to move here," Nicole started, looking at him. "But this is where Amber and her life are. I want to be with her."

"I get that, Nic, I do," Erik said. "I just don't understand why you're giving up everything you have. You and Amber haven't been together for that long. You've both changed a lot over the years."

"Erik!" Jill and Heather exclaimed.

"I don't mean to sound like an ass. I love you, Nicole. I love you, too, Amber. I just think it's a huge step."

"You're right, it is a huge step, but it's our decision to make," Amber said calmly.

"Yes, we haven't been back together long, but we were truly only apart physically. The love and devotion we've felt for each other, that hasn't changed. If anything, it has grown," Nicole said.

"So, no matter what, you're staying?"

"Exactly. We'll be back once we decide what to do with the house there. We'll be back to visit, as well. I like it here, I love Amber. What more is there?"

The tension in the room started to subside and allowed them to enjoy their last day together.

Over the next few months, Nicole and Amber made several trips back to Eagle Peak to visit their friends and to prep Nicole's house for Erik to rent. He had been living at the fire station so much prior to Nicole moving that he had let his lease lapse.

"Nic," Erik said as he entered the house.

"Hey, I was just finishing up packing the last of my things. Are you sure you don't mind me keeping things in one of the spare rooms?"

"It's still your house. You keep stuff wherever you want. I'm just going to mooch off your kindness and cheap rent." Erik laughed.

After returning to Eagle Peak, Erik started to see a lot of their past, the good and the bad. It was then that he was able to understand why Amber could never live there again and why it would be good for Nicole to move, as well. Once he realized that, he embraced their decision.

"Hello?" Amber called from the front door.

"Back here, baby," Nicole called from the lanai.

Amber smiled when she saw Nicole and Erik standing together. She was happy that the tension was gone and that it was no longer awkward to be back here or at least in the same room as Erik. Amber made her way over to Nicole and kissed her.

"I missed you," Amber said softly. Erik heard her and rolled his eyes, causing both women to laugh.

"How are things going with you two lovebirds?"

"Amazing," the two women said in unison, earning them another eye roll.

"We've had our moments of tension, but after everything we've been through, they're trivial," Nicole said as Amber wrapped her arms around Nicole from behind.

"Dr. Dyer has helped us a lot, as well."

"How so?" Jill asked as she and Heather entered with a pizza and beer.

"I don't want that greasy, stainy stuff in here." Nicole pushed Jill toward the door.

The five made their way to the living room before finishing their conversation.

"Dr. Dyer has helped us to see that the past is behind us and only we can allow it to get closer and overtake us. Trina has been helping with the physical frustration," Amber said.

"Some of it," Nicole said before she and Amber blushed.

"Details?" Heather asked hopefully.

"Still no." Nicole and Amber laughed.

"You can't blame a girl for trying." Heather laughed along.

"Yes, we can," Nicole mumbled playfully.

Nicole and Amber explained how they had rearranged the house and how they were making things work.

※ ※ ※ ※

Once they returned from Eagle Peak, Amber and Nicole were unpacking when they heard a knock at the door. Amber opened the door to find Mrs. Phelps standing there.

"Good evening, Mrs. Phelps," Amber said, opening the door wider for her to enter.

"I'm sorry to interrupt. I know you two just got home."

"You never interrupt," Nicole said as she entered the room and escorted Mrs. Phelps and Amber to the couch. "What can we do for you tonight?"

"Well, I was hoping we could do dinner tomorrow night."

"Of course," Amber said, taking Nicole's hand. "What can we bring?"

"Oh, just yourselves," Mrs. Phelps said.

"Are you certain?"

"Positive. Max and I have something we'd like to talk to you two about tomorrow night."

"Any hints?" Nicole asked.

"None," Mrs. Phelps with a laugh. She then left the two women to themselves.

"I wonder what that was about," Amber said.

"I guess we'll find out tomorrow night."

"What do you say to us showering together, and then some naked snuggles in bed?"

"I think that sounds perfect, my love."

The couple made their way to the shower, and

then to bed. It wasn't long before they were sound asleep.

※※※※

Nicole and Amber made their way down to the Phelps's apartment for dinner the next night. They had opted to bring a bottle of wine.

"Oh, you two didn't have to do this," Mr. Phelps said as he took the bottle from Nicole.

"It's just a little token of our appreciation and love for you both," Amber said.

"Well, it'll go great with tonight's dinner."

Amber and Nicole took a seat in the living room while Mr. Phelps put the wine in the kitchen and Mrs. Phelps was finishing up dinner. Over dinner, Nicole and Amber talked about their latest trip to Eagle Peak and how they had finally gotten Erik settled into Nicole's house. After dinner, they retired to the living room again, and Mr. and Mrs. Phelps sat together on the loveseat and Nicole and Amber sat on the couch.

"We wanted to talk to you both about something," Mrs. Phelps started.

"You have our undivided attention." Amber took Nicole's hand in her own.

"Well, since we're both getting older, we met with our attorney over the past week, and we've decided we'd like to leave you girls the brownstone. You're like daughters to us. And since we didn't have kids, well, we just wanted to make sure you two were okay with this," Mr. Phelps said.

"Wow, I don't know what to say," Amber said.

"Wow, that's huge," Nicole added.

"Will you accept the brownstone when we pass?"

Mrs. Phelps asked.

"Of course, but that isn't going to be for a very long time," Amber said.

"Be that as it may. We needed to make sure that our girls are looked after and taken care of."

"Thank you, and we love you both, as well." Nicole got up and hugged them. Amber followed behind, hugging them and feeling truly blessed to have found such amazing people to integrate into her life after all she had been through.

❧❧❦❦

Amber Knight had been dealt a rough hand in life, but she had overcome every challenge. Now, she had the woman she had loved since they were little in her arms nightly, friends who truly cared and looked out for her, and a career she loved. The rearview mirror now contained the past, a past that no longer hindered her future.

About the Author

BL Clark lives in Southern Wisconsin. As a child, BL dreamed of becoming an author, she is now living her dream. In her free time, you can find BL working on various story ideas, or playing with some form of technology.

You can follow BL Clark at:
Twitter: bl_clarks
Facebook: blclark.author
Website: blc.bkclark.net

Check out BL's other books.

To Love Again - ISBN - 978-1-939062-99-4

Jade Donovan felt like she had everything in life, a great marriage, a beautiful daughter, and then fate intervened. Now she needs to learn how to move forward, not only for herself, but her four-year-old daughter. Jade's best friend Kristel hopes to help her get back on track by attending a grief counseling group run by Rachel Cassidy, a widow herself. With time, Jade is able to take the steps forward to heal and finds herself falling for Rachel. Not everybody is happy with the path that Jade has started on.

Will Jade be able to overcome the loss of her wife and the other obstacles life has in store for her, to be able To Love Again?

Haunted by Darkness - ISBN - 978-1-943353-21-7

Kristine Holt is haunted by the darkness of her past. She has spent years dealing with frequent nightmares and night terrors stemming from years of mental and physical abuse inflicted by her parents while she was growing up. With the help of her best friend Grace Barnes, she is able to escape her parents' clutches, but not the darkness within.

Will Kristine find the light or will she be consumed by the darkness of her past?

Other books by Sapphire Authors

Highland Dew – ISBN – 978-1-948232-11-1

Bryce Andrews, west coast sales director for Global Distillers and Distribution, is tired of the corporate hamster wheel. She needs a change.

A craft whisky trade show offers her inspiration and a chance to revisit Scotland and the majestic scenery of the Speyside region—best known for the "Whisky Trail." Bryce and her coworker, Reggie Ballard, need to find a wholly original whisky for their international distribution division by visiting a number of small distillers.

A blind curve, a dangling sign, and weed-choked driveway draw Bryce directly into a truly unique opportunity. She discovers a struggling family, a shuttered distillery, and a spitfire of a daughter called home to care for her confused father.

Fiona McDougall—the only child and heir to the MacDougall & Son legacy, had her career teaching in Edinburgh curtailed by fate…or serendipity.

When the stars finally align, the two women work together to resurrect a dream for themselves and the family business—if they can weather the storms of unscrupulous business practices in the competitive whisky market.

McCall - ISBN - 978-1-948232-32-6

Sara Brighton is a quickly rising culinary star in Savannah after Food & Wine magazine named her restaurant Best New Restaurant of the South, until it burns to the ground in an accident and she impulsively packs her truck and heads for McCall, Idaho, the last place she remembers being truly happy.

Sam Draper, head of the Lake Patrol division of the McCall PD, knows the last thing she needs is another entitled tourist making her life difficult on the water. However, after Sara surprises her by helping her avoid a near professional disaster, Sam teaches her to drive a boat. The chemistry between them is hot and instant, and as the summer heats up, Sam finds herself fall-ing in love until Sara buys her late father's iconic diner and turns it into the newest hotspot for pretentious culinary tourists.

Can the love Sam and Sara found on the water survive the lingering ghosts waiting for them back on dry land?

Silver Love – ISBN – 978-1-948232-51-7

Jill, Dory, Robby, and Charlene are a fantastic foursome that embodies the varying experiences that come with being Lesbians of a Certain Age. They are vibrant and vulnerable, wise and foolish, introspective and outgoing. The close-knit friends fight aging at every turn—or just ignore it altogether. These four will never go quietly into the night, redefining life after fifty. They are the new mature woman.

But along with twenty-first-century attitudes come twenty-first-century problems. Public office candidate and retired judge Charlene is confronted by a wannabe blackmailer, Jill's passions threaten to swamp her common sense, Dory's best-selling book could turn out to be a national disaster, and Robby must confront the hard reality of learning that her wife may not be the woman she thought she was. Steadfast in their faith in themselves and each other, and bolstered by the rich history of their friendship, the four women struggle with twists and turns as they try to navigate a landscape generated by the actions of others as well as their own choices, proving that experience does not always pave a smooth road.

In a world where everything increasingly seems relative, these women remind us that some things don't change—like the bedrock of relationships. Silver Love is all about love; love among friends, love between lovers, and the unexpected role of love with acquaintances who may not always be what they seem.

If you can keep up, join the ride and follow these ageless heroines as they pursue their adventures in the modern world.

www.ingramcontent.com/pod-product-compliance
Lightning Source LLC
Chambersburg PA
CBHW030105100526
44591CB00009B/287